CORPORATE SOCIAL PERFORMANCE:
A STAKEHOLDER APPROACH

Corporate Social Responsibility Series

Series Editor:
Professor David Crowther, London Metropolitan University, UK

This series aims to provide high quality research books on all aspects of corporate social responsibility including: business ethics, corporate governance and accountability, globalization, civil protests, regulation, responsible marketing and social reporting.

The series is interdisciplinary in scope and global in application and is an essential forum for everyone with an interest in this area.

Also in the series

Perspectives on Corporate Social Responsibility
Edited by David Crowther and Lez Rayman-Bacchus
ISBN 0 7546 3886 3

Nonprofit Trusteeship in Different Contexts
Rikki Abzug and Jeffrey S. Simonoff
ISBN 0 7546 3016 1

Human Values in Management
Ananda Das Gupta
ISBN 0 7546 4275 5

Corporate Social Performance:
A Stakeholder Approach

STUART COOPER
Aston Business School, UK

ASHGATE

Published by
Ashgate Publishing Limited
Gower House
Croft Road
Aldershot
Hants GU11 3HR
England

Ashgate Publishing Company
Suite 420
101 Cherry Street
Burlington, VT 05401-4405
USA

Ashgate website: http://www.ashgate.com

British Library Cataloguing in Publication Data
Cooper, Stuart
   Corporate social performance : a stakeholder approach. -
   (Corporate social responsibility series)
   1. Social responsibility of business
   I. Title
   658.4'08

Library of Congress Cataloging-in-Publication Data
Cooper, Stuart, 1970-
   Corporate social performance : a stakeholder approach / Stuart Cooper.
        p. cm. -- (Corporate social responsibility series)
   Includes bibliographical references and index.
   ISBN 0-7546-4174-0
   1. Social responsibility of business. I. Title. II. Series.

   HD60.C635 2004
   658.4'08--dc22

2004010330

ISBN 0 7546 4174 0

Printed in Great Britain by Antony Rowe Ltd, Chippenham, Wiltshire

Contents

List of Figures

List of Tables

Chapter 1

Corporate Social Performance and Accountability

Introduction

This book is concerned with the social performance of corporations. Traditionally, from accounting, corporate performance has been measured in financial terms, such that the annual report and accounts provide three primary financial statements. These are the profit and loss account, the balance sheet and the cash flow statement.[1] These three statements are argued to enable a user of the accounts to understand the profitability, efficiency, liquidity and financial strength of the corporation. Therefore students of financial accounting are told how to calculate numerous ratios in order to understand a corporation's performance. These ratios include profit margins, returns on capital, current ratios and gearing ratios. When considered together these ratios are argued to enable the user of the accounts to build up a picture of the organization's historical performance and starting position for the future. In fact probably the most vociferous criticism of these measures has been that it usually considers historical performance, is too concerned with past activities and hence fails to adequately consider the future of the organization. Certainly the profit and loss account reports on performance in a period that has already finished. The annual report and accounts are principally provided for shareholders and potential investors, although these are by no means the only users. The information provided is supposed to assist the (potential) shareholders in deciding whether to buy, hold or sell shares in the organization. Throughout modern finance and accounting literature and texts it is widely suggested that shareholders invest their money purely to make returns and therefore the management of an organization must run that business in order to maximize shareholder wealth. This is certainly the message that many finance and accounting students receive, as is evidenced by the following quotes:

> Of course, ethical issues do arise in business as in other walks of life, and therefore when we say that the objective of the firm is to maximise shareholder wealth we do not mean that anything goes. (Brealey and Myers, 1996, p.25)

> The company should make investment and financing decisions with the aim of maximising long-term shareholder wealth. (Arnold, 2002, p.7)

> Nevertheless, the view adopted in this book is that, broadly, firms seek to maximize the value of future net cash inflows (that is future receipts less cash

payments) or to be more precise the present value of future net cash inflows. This
is equivalent to maximizing shareholder value. (Drury, 2003, p.7)

Within management accounting the emphasis has similarly been on
financial measures and it is only more recently that non-financial measures and
multi-dimensional performance measurement frameworks have increased in
popularity. Perhaps the best known and most commonly used of these frameworks
is the balanced scorecard, as created by Kaplan and Norton (1992, 1996).[2] The
Balanced Scorecard operates in four perspectives the financial, customer, internal
business and learning and growth perspectives. Originally these four perspectives
were considered to be balanced, but more recently Kaplan and Norton's (2000)
strategy mapping draws a causal relationship between the different perspective
with the ultimate aim being to improve financial performance and hence
shareholder wealth. As such this multi-dimensional performance measurement
framework is competing with the more explicitly shareholder value models that
have also become popular over the last decade. These shareholder value
approaches vary, but each explicitly recognizes the shareholder as the primary
stakeholder and hence target shareholder value creation. Perhaps the most well
known of these is economic value added (EVA®) as proposed and sold by Stern
Stewart, which is a residual income type approach to performance measurement.[3]

Each of the approaches above are aimed at one specific stakeholder group,
namely the shareholder. This has consistently been the emphasis of accounting and
corporate reporting. This book, however, is interested in a wider conception of
performance. It is interested in corporate performance not purely to or for the
shareholder, nor purely in financial terms, but is interested in corporate
performance to the society within which an organization operates. For the purposes
of this book this has been called corporate social performance. The remainder of
this chapter provides an introduction to this area of research and positions this
work in the wider field of corporate social responsibility. At the same time it
explains the structure of the remainder of the book and introduces some of the key
concepts and debates that are discussed in more detail later.

Business in Society and Corporate Social Performance

As we have just seen, the most commonly accepted objective, within the finance
and accounting fields, for a company is to maximize shareholder wealth. The
justifications for the appropriateness of this as an objective are manifold, but most
importantly it is argued that through the workings of efficient markets this
objective will not only benefit shareholders, but society as well. In chapter 2, we
explore the arguments that have been used to support this conjecture and
furthermore we consider if there is any evidence to support that this actually works
in the real world. The most commonly proposed alternatives within the business
ethics literature are stakeholder theory and social contract theory. Therefore
chapter 2 contrasts the arguments that support these alternative theories. The
stakeholder concept is an important one for this book. The term has increased in

popularity[4] since Freeman's (1984) seminal text 'Strategic Management: A Stakeholder Approach'. Freeman defines stakeholders in numerous ways, but the most commonly quoted definition is:

> any group or individual who can affect or is affected by the achievement of the organization's objectives.

It is interesting to note that Freeman explicitly regarded the stakeholder approach to be a strategic management tool, as opposed to an ethical theory. In fact, according to Stoney and Winstanley (2002) this is one of the key confusions within the stakeholder literature. In the words of Stoney and Winstanley there are 'intrinsic' and 'instrumental' reasons for adopting a stakeholder approach. Goodpaster (1991) actually uses the terminology strategic stakeholder management model and the multi-fiduciary stakeholder approach. The terms are different, but the underlying distinction is the same. There are some that see the stakeholder concept as a way to improve the strategic management of an organization, and hence to improve performance, usually measured in terms of financial performance. Then there are those that see stakeholder theory, as an ethical approach to management. This is to say that stakeholder theory is a normative approach that some argue is more ethically and morally acceptable than a shareholder value approach. This confusion has resulted in a lot of criticism of stakeholder theory and this is considered in chapter 2.

The supporters of both the shareholder and stakeholder approaches suggest that they should be preferred because they provide benefits to a society as a whole. This would be consistent with the social contract theory that can trace its roots back to the work of Rousseau and Hobbes. Social contract theorists argue that a society would only allow a business to operate within it if the benefits of the business outweigh its detriments to society. Both shareholder and stakeholder theories are therefore subsumed within social contract theory. In fact both claim to be the best way to ensure that an organization satisfies its obligations to society. If we accept that businesses should provide a contribution to society then the question is how can this be achieved?

It seems a great leap of faith to simply accept that by operating a shareholder approach society will benefit. Clearly it will benefit in some ways in terms of employment, revenue from taxes and an injection of money into an economy. There are, however, potentially scarce resources that the organization will use not least in terms of natural resources. There are also externalities created by the operation of businesses, for example emissions and pollution, that can detract from the quality of life of some of the members of that society. There are many, many ways in which an organization can affect a society and it is here that the stakeholder approach is helpful. As noted above the stakeholders are those groups from within a society that are affected by an organization's activities. Therefore a stakeholder framework can be used to consider corporate social performance.

Stakeholders and Corporate Social Performance

In this book the stakeholder concept is used as a framework for considering corporate social performance. It draws upon many different strands of literature including strategic management, business ethics, social accounting and performance measurement to do so. The social accounting literature is especially important and in many ways chapters 5, 7 and 8 of this book are an attempt to produce a social account. Just as financial accounting can be considered to be an account to shareholders so social accounting can be considered to be an account to society. Gray *et al.* (1997) suggest that social accounting includes all possible accountings and as such financial accounting is only one, relatively small, part of social accounting. This is in exact opposition to the majority of financial accounting texts, which if they include or mention social accounting at all, is considered to be a smaller part of financial accounting. These textbooks see social accounting as something that can be added on to the traditional financial accounting, but the traditional financial accounting remains dominant. Within these texts, therefore, the shareholder remains primary and other stakeholders very much secondary.

The social accounting literature clearly places a different emphasis upon the non-shareholder stakeholder groups. Social accounting attempts to make transparent the workings of an organization (Owen *et al.*, 1997). Through this process it is hoped that society will become better informed about the operations of an organization such that where an organization is not benefiting society some corrective action can be taken. Therefore it is hoped that this process will result in a 'more benign' form of business activity (Gray *et al.*, 1997). Effectively the line of reasoning is that a better informed society will be empowered to ensure that the organizations operate to the benefit of that society. By ensuring that organizations are accountable to society for their actions so those actions can be changed to the benefit of that society. Within the social accounting literature the relevance of the stakeholder concept is recognized. Gray (1998) suggests that a stakeholder approach could be used to produce a social account. In fact it is stakeholder accountability that Gray (2000) argues is at the very heart of social accounting.

> The social account may serve a number of purposes but discharge of the organisation's accountability to its stakeholders must be clearly dominant of those reasons and the basis upon which the social account is judged. (p.250)

This book draws upon the stakeholder concept in this vein. It sees corporate social performance as something that is important as it can be used to inform society. The more we know about corporate social performance the more society can attempt to reform those organizations so that they operate in socially beneficial ways. It may be that organizations are already benefiting society, but until the corporate social performance is measured we can not say whether this is the case. Furthermore there are significant social and environmental problems in the world, Europe and within the UK. One of the causes of these problems could well be the way that modern business is organized. This is reflected in the following quote:

> Our world is one of immense inequality, poverty and violence, with "catastrophic global and local environmental degradation; poverty and conflict in the Third World; unemployment, poverty and inequality (in Britain); widespread disaffection with the political system and political parties; (and) a loss of community" (Real World Coalition 1996, p vii). (Adams and Harte, 2000, p.56)

It is these real world problems that many social accountants want to see redressed. The level of reform required to do so is a source of debate. Those from the critical accounting school argue that much, if not all, of the social and environmental accounting is flawed as it does not address the problem of the capitalist system. They argue that it is the capitalist system that leads to the problems noted above rather than the actions of individual organizations. Therefore social and environmental accounting will fail to bring about the desired changes because the system will remain. Unless the capitalist system can be changed then the systemic conflicts within society will remain and therefore the social benefits will not follow. Gray *et al.* (1995) acknowledge that this argument is persuasive, but suggest that if social accounting recognizes and highlights the conflicts then it can still achieve its purpose. As such the vast majority of social accountants do not necessarily require the end of capitalism. Gray *et al.* (1995) do, however, suggest that a 'neo-pluralist' approach to society is required if these conflicts are to be identified and accounted for. Again this leads us back to the stakeholder concept, which is indeed a pluralist conception of society. Multiple factions are identified and their needs and relative welfare are considered.

In fact the relative importance of different stakeholders, from completely unimportant and therefore one which receives no consideration, to the most important, or primary, which have certain rights, is a source of much debate within the stakeholder literature. It is the strategic management aspect of the stakeholder literature that has the most to say about this. It is actually one of the key purposes of this part of the literature to rank the different stakeholders and hence manage the stakeholder relationship. Perhaps the best known example of such strategic stakeholder management models is that proposed by Mitchell *et al.* (1997). They propose that organizations should measure each stakeholder's salience and then based on this should decide how to prioritize the needs of that stakeholder group. Stakeholder salience consists of the power, urgency and legitimacy of the stakeholder group. If all three are present then the stakeholder requires a great deal of attention and must be prioritized within the strategic management of that organization. This strategic stakeholder management model is not consistent with the stakeholder accountability discussed above. It is concerned with the instrumental rather than intrinsic value of stakeholders and will therefore not address the problems discussed above.

Chapter 3 concludes with a consideration of a number of different attempts to identify stakeholder groups and in fact there is a great deal of consistency between these different models. Therefore as this book continues to consider corporate social performance it does so through using a stakeholder framework that concentrates upon a number of key stakeholder groups, and these are:

- Shareholders;
- Employees;
- Consumers;
- Suppliers;
- The Environment.

It must be stressed here, and it is again later in the book, that this does not intend to demean or down play the importance of other stakeholder groups. This book does, however, concentrate on this relatively small number of stakeholder groups. There is a further requirement for further research into the needs of other stakeholder groups. The more stakeholder groups incorporated into a consideration of an organization's performance the more completely, it can be argued, that we reflect the corporate social performance. Also it could be argued that included here are some of the more powerful stakeholder groups that require little or no protection. Further, some of the very weakest, or least salient, stakeholder groups are not included in this list and it could be argued that it is these groups that require the most protection of all. Nevertheless this research has concentrated upon the above primary stakeholder groups.

A Model of Corporate Social Performance

As noted above there are many different strands of literature that are concerned with performance measurement. Clearly, as discussed in the introduction to this chapter, finance and accounting is concerned with performance, but in a very narrow way. This is to say that it is primarily concerned with financial performance for the benefit of shareholders. A conflicting view of the purpose of accounting was provided by *The Corporate Report* (ASSC, 1975)[5] that recognized a wide range of 'constituents' (stakeholders) that would use and require detailed information from corporate reports. One of the key recommendations was that a value-added statement should be produced. The benefit of such a statement is that it provides a breakdown of how the value-added by an organization is distributed between the different stakeholders that have created the value. It is this ability to represent distribution of benefits that differentiates value-added statements from profit and loss accounts. It is also for this reason that value-added analysis has been used in academic research to identify redistribution of wealth between stakeholder groups. Value-added statements and analysis are considered in more detail in chapter 4, but suffice it to say here that it proves to be an extremely useful and powerful analytical tool used in this research.

In addition there are specific stakeholder measures that can be used to provide a greater detail of analysis than that enabled by a value-added analysis alone. The model developed here is based is based upon a stakeholder framework. It considers each stakeholder group and starts by considering relevant performance measures from the available academic literature. For the stakeholder groups identified here there is a significant amount of such literature and this is reviewed in chapter 4. This chapter demonstrates that throughout different academic disciplines a considerable amount of time has been used contemplating appropriate ways to measure performance. The model developed in chapter 4 is purely from academic and practitioner literature, but, in chapter 6, this model is reconsidered through a number of interviews held with stakeholders and organizations. These interviews firstly sought to identify the information needs of the different stakeholder groups. This interview process was used to analyze the findings from the literature, therefore these interviews identified gaps in the literature or in some cases prioritized issues for the stakeholder groups. These interviews were undertaken with stakeholder groups with a specific interest in the electricity industry in England and Wales. This industry provides an interesting case study, as is discussed in the following section. By incorporating specific stakeholder measures the model proposed goes beyond the value added analysis previously undertaken.

Privatization, Regulation and the Electricity Industry in England and Wales

In order to present the corporate social performance model this book considers the case of the electricity industry in England and Wales for the period from privatization to March 1997. Privatization, where state owned organizations were sold in to private ownership, has been one of the most controversial economic policies of recent times. It is a policy that has been adopted in many countries throughout the world, from New Zealand to Chile to Eastern European countries, and was vigorously employed by successive Conservative governments in the UK from 1979 to 1997. The most controversial aspect of this policy was the privatization of the utility industries (Ogden and Anderson, 1995) that contain a network, or grid, which suggests a natural monopoly. This is to say that due to the nature of the industry it is most efficient for the network element to be operated by a single organization, as it would be inefficient to duplicate it. In the UK each of the network industries, namely telecommunications, gas, water, electricity and rail, were privatized in the 1980s or early 1990s. Each of these privatizations was different, but in each instance it was recognized that the industry would require regulation. In each case price-cap regulation was used, as it was believed that this provided the best efficiency incentives and would therefore benefit the consumers more than other forms of regulation.[6] The reasons for this are returned to at the start of chapter 6.

　　By selecting a single industry to examine the researcher can provide both depth and context to the research. The electricity industry in England and Wales is unique even within the utility industries privatized in the UK, as it was the first to be both horizontally and vertically separated at the time of privatization.[7] The structure of the industry at the time of privatization was as follows:

- Generation, a potentially competitive industry and therefore not requiring formal regulation. Two privatized generating companies, Powergen and National Power, provided the majority of the generating capacity in England and Wales.
- The National Grid, the transmission company, that owned and operated the network of wires that transported electricity from generators to the distribution networks. These wires are an example of a natural monopoly as discussed above.
- Twelve supply and distribution companies, which immediately subsequent to privatization held regional monopolies. This is horizontal separation and enabled the regulator to use yardstick competition until introducing true competition later.[8]

Therefore the industry was vertically separated into three different sections, as this was seen to provide the opportunity to minimize regulation. Effectively it is only the wires, the transmission and distribution elements of the industry that require regulation. Therefore the supply and generation industries should be able to be competitive and hence not require regulation. It is now the case that the supply and distribution companies have been separated and opened up to competition. This separation of the industry was different to what had happened in the earlier privatizations of telecommunications, gas and water. It can be argued that the more separated industry structures are the most theoretically advanced, with the revised structure being based upon the experience gained from earlier privatizations.

The electricity industry in England and Wales was the first of the advanced privatizations and therefore provides a unique case, which has been selected to demonstrate the value of the stakeholder model developed in this book. The selected industry can be regarded as a single case as a single regulator regulates it. Both the context of the research and the nature of the research questions justify this methodology.

> In brief, the case study allows an investigation to retain the holistic and meaningful characteristics of real-life events-such as... the maturation of industries. (Yin, 1994, p.3)

> A second rationale for a single case is one in which the case represents an *extreme or unique case*. (Yin, 1994, p.39)

The validity of the case study approach has been questioned as it can be biased and further that it lacks scientific rationale. Ryan *et al.* (1992) suggest that there 'can be no such thing as an 'objective' case study' (p.126) and the question of bias is indeed a difficult one to refute, as the area of research is indeed one that the researcher held some views on before embarking upon the research. Prior knowledge of the research area can raise questions as to the bias of the researcher, but surely this is not restricted to case studies alone. In most pieces of research the researcher must have had some knowledge of the research area otherwise they would not have been interested in the research question. This view is supported by McSweeney and Duncan (1998) (as well as others, for example Samuels, 1981; and Carr, 1981) who suggest that their:

> paper draws on the argument that an understanding of something is profoundly shaped by the prior images of the analyst. There cannot be a "view from nowhere" (Nagel, 1986). "An interpretation", Heidegger states, "is never a presuppositionless apprehending" (1967). (p.332)

In order to combat concerns of bias multiple data sources have been used to try and triangulate (as per Smith, 1975) the findings of the research. The different methods include academic literature reviews, interviews and data collection from publicly available sources. The use of publicly available data (from company reports, press comment and research bodies) to analyze the case hopefully increases the objectivity of the research. This is data triangulation as the data is collected from different sources.

The interviews undertaken had two key objectives. Firstly, to consider the validity, in the eyes of stakeholders of the industry, of the stakeholder model proposed. The findings from these interviews are discussed in chapter 6. This chapter also reports on the responses to the model from representatives from four of the privatized companies. Further, the interviews were designed to explore how different stakeholder groups perceived the performance of the industry over the post-privatization period.

It is recognized that the interviewees themselves may be biased. In fact Easterby-Smith, Thorpe and Lowe (1991) state the following:

> The possibility that the client [interviewee] will have preferred outcomes from the study returns us to the issue of whether research will automatically become "contaminated" by such political considerations. If this happens some people argue, the results will be valueless, and therefore this kind of research [interviewing management] should be avoided. Our view, however, and that of Buchanan *et al.* (1988), is that this kind of contamination is unavoidable in social research, especially when it is conducted within the management levels of an organisation. (p.57)

The use of a single case is criticized for lacking scientific rationale and generalizations to a wider population will not be possible. Despite this the quotes from Yin above certainly suggest that this approach is an acceptable research method. In this instance the primary purpose of the case study is to explain the performance of the electricity industry for the period of time under consideration. Further, single cases can be used to generate hypotheses, or frameworks, that can be further researched in other areas to consider their general applicability. In this case the issues of corporate social responsibility, accountability and corporate social reporting are considered in the light of the findings of the case and these are areas where some generalization may be possible. Any generalization will not be statistical generalization, but more theoretical in nature as advocated by Ryan *et al.* (1992). Further, a case study approach can be criticized for a lack of objectivity. This is acknowledged and steps have been taken, in terms of triangulation of data, to restrict this problem. The final word on this subject I leave to Ryan *et al.* (1992), as this appears to adequately recognize the problems facing all social science researchers:

> it has to be accepted that case study research provides an interpretation of the social system being studied, not an objective representation. But can any social science research method claim to do more? (p.126)

The electricity industry in England and Wales provides an interesting and revealing case within which to consider corporate social performance. The corporate social performance model developed is tested for validity through stakeholder interviews and the model shows it can provide evidence, see chapters 5, 7 and 8, on how wealth is distributed between the different stakeholder groups. It does not adequately explain why such redistribution occurs and it is to this that we now turn.

Stakeholder Theory, Institutional Theory and Resource Dependence

Chapter 2 notes that some have questioned whether or not stakeholder theory is actually a theory. It is suggested that Freeman (1984) himself considered the stakeholder concept more as a framework than a theory and it is in this way that it has been used in much of this book. It is unable to explain why the corporate social performance is as it is. Therefore chapter 9 draws upon Oliver's (1991) framework of strategic responses to provide this explanation. This framework is developed from both institutional theory and resource dependency theory. It predicts that organizations will respond in certain ways depending upon a number of predictive factors. In this case Oliver's framework when applied to the stakeholder groups identified here appears to provide a valuable lens through which to understand corporate social performance.

Within the electricity industry in England and Wales the institutional and resource pressures make this an interesting case. Certainly from privatization it is apparent that shareholders were given a great deal of legitimacy and that the privatized companies were required to be efficient. Legitimacy and efficiency are predictive factors within Oliver's framework and when these are considered to be high then it is expected that the organization will acquiesce to the demands of that stakeholder group. In contrast, in the UK, throughout the 1980s and early 1990s the legitimacy and efficiency of the employee group was questioned and undermined. In which case the appropriate strategic response of an organization is very different, but, according to this framework, can range from compromise to manipulation.

Overall, though, the insights from Oliver's framework and more generally from institutional theory emphasize the importance of the government and the professions. These are 'the great rationalizers of the twentieth century' (DiMaggio and Powell, 1983, p.147). It certainly is apparent in the case considered here that the state, both directly through government departments and indirectly through the regulator, is extremely important in considering the performance and responses of these privatized companies. Therefore despite privatization the influence of the state remains of paramount importance to the industry. This was a clear message from the interviews undertaken and the Oliver's model confirms this.

The Internet and Social Accounting Standards

The final chapter of this book considers the developments made in internet reporting and social accounting standards. Some argue that the internet has the power to increase accountability, as it can provide information more cheaply and to a greater number of people. Clearly this is only true for people with access to the internet who have the ability to use it. Whilst the number of people this applies to is increasing, at present it remains in the hands of the minority. This book considers the use of the internet by companies that were operating within the UK electricity industry in the year 2000. It certainly provides evidence that the vast majority of these companies are making use of the internet to provide information to a number of stakeholder groups. The information provided, however, is selective and is effectively being used as another channel for organizational propaganda, as opposed to enhancing accountability.

Three social accounting standards have been developed relatively recently that can be used by organizations that want to improve their stakeholder accountability. Each of these standards recognize stakeholders other than shareholders. By far the most detailed of these is the Global Reporting Initiative (GRI, 2000, 2002), which separates corporate performance into economic, social and environmental indicators. The GRI guidelines provide a framework that does identify, and require organizations to report on, many of the issues that were identified as important to stakeholder groups in this book. Certainly organizations adopting these guidelines would provide significantly more stakeholder information than those that simply follow financial reporting standards. The GRI guidelines are clearly voluntary and therefore there is, at present, a need for further research into discovering how widely and comprehensively they are used. Further, these guidelines could not be called standards, as is the case for financial reporting standards. The level of detail provided is insufficient to deal with the complexities of measurement issues and this will need to be addressed if these guidelines are to be made mandatory in the future.

Notes

[1] The primary financial statements are by no means the only items reported in the financial statements. We also see notes to the accounts and reports from the directors and officers of the organization. In fact purely in terms of space the primary financial statements make up a very small component part of the annual report and accounts. Certainly Crowther (2002) argues that the purpose of corporate reporting has changed.

[2] This is certainly not the only such framework. See for example the Result and Determinants framework (Fitzgerald *et al.*, 1991), the Service Profit Chain (Heskett *et al.*, 1994), and the Performance Pyramid (Lynch and Cross, 1991).

[3] There are a great number of different approaches. There are those based on cash flow such as cash flow return on investment (CFROI, see Madden, 1991). There is also Rappaport (1986) shareholder value analysis approach, which identifies seven key drivers of shareholder value. These approaches are discussed again in chapter 4.

[4] The stakeholder concept has also enjoyed political popularity. Prior to the 1997 UK election Tony Blair campaigned using the concept of stakeholder capitalism as a new and alternative approach to business and the economy. Since his election in 1997 the government appears to have forgotten this. Although the term has been used, for example in 'stakeholder pensions', a more pluralist stakeholder approach has been rejected by the company law review. Instead it preferred to advocate an enlightened shareholder value approach. See DTI (2000a).

[5] What makes this contribution more remarkable is that it was instigated and proposed by the accounting profession itself.

[6] Rate of return and sliding scale regulation have also been proposed, but have not been adopted in the UK.

[7] The rail industry was subsequently vertically and horizontally separated and the gas industry has been restructured after privatization.

[8] Yardstick competition is where there are a number of similar organizations whose performance can be compared. This enables the regulator to compare the performance of the organizations and hence decide upon whether any efficiency gains made are comparable.

Chapter 2

Business in Society – Ethics and Stakeholders

Introduction

Business organizations are social institutions in that they cannot exist except in relation to the society within which they operate (Bucholz and Rosenthal, 1997). Further Bucholz and Rosenthal argue that as this is the case the field of study commonly referred to as 'Business and Society', which they suggest implies that business and society are separable 'roughly co-equal' entities, is misleading and should be replaced by the name Business In Society. The ethical justifications for competing theories of business in society are considered here. The most common distinction made is between shareholder (or agency) theories and stakeholder theories. In fact Shankman (1999) suggests that the conflict between these two theories of the firm 'has long been entrenched in organizational and management literature' and that they have been construed as 'polar opposites'. He continues that this conflict is due to the different import given to moral and ethical implications of business within the economics and business ethics fields (Bowie and Freeman, 1992). Hasnas (1998) actually broadens this dichotomy of theories and suggests that there are in actual fact three leading normative theories of business ethics and that these are 'the stockholder theory [the agency or shareholder theories], the stakeholder theory, and the social contract theory.' Each of these theories has been proposed, and subsequently criticized, as being the most appropriate foundation for business activity and these arguments will be reviewed. This chapter considers the ethical justifications for each of the theories and concludes that social contract theory is an all-encompassing concept in that both shareholder theory and stakeholder theory can be justified on the grounds of benefits to society. In addition it is suggested that the stakeholder concept is a useful one in that it provides a research framework from which societal benefit can be considered.

Shareholder Theories of the Firm

The efficacy of shareholder theories of the firm has been argued from many different standpoints. The justifications emerge from both moral and legal arguments but an overarching justification is that the adoption and application of this theory will result in increased wealth for the whole of society. It has been likened to a win-win situation; when businesses correctly implement this strategy everybody benefits, not only shareholders. Irrespective of the justification, there is a widely held belief that shareholders should be considered first and foremost, and their wealth maximized, by the management of business (Rappaport, 1986). Shareholder primacy was earlier defended by Friedman (1962) who wrote that:

> there is one and only one social responsibility of business- to use its resources and engage in activities designed to increase profits so long as it stays in the rules of the game, which is to say, engages in open and free competition, without deception or fraud.

The premise that shareholder wealth maximization results in benefits for the whole of society is often supported by theoretical arguments based on conditions of efficient markets (see for example Drucker, 1984 and Jensen, 1991). In these instances the efficiency of the market has been defined as the best allocation of social resources (Quinn and Jones, 1995). The actual efficiency of markets in the real world has often been questioned and when this assumption is relaxed then the conclusion that all will benefit does not necessarily follow. Quinn and Jones (1995) argue that there are four principles for markets to work efficiently. Honouring agreements and avoiding lying, are the first two principles. These are consistent with Friedman's (1962) limitation on an organization's pursuit of profit and are crucial to agency theory. The other two principles are argued to be a respect for the autonomy of others and a requirement to avoid harming others. Shankman (1999), in considering the work of Quinn and Jones (1995), suggests that these final two principles are fundamental for the condition of liberty, which is itself a prerequisite for the functioning of efficient markets. Therefore the effect on others of an organization's actions must, for moral reasons, be a constraint on shareholder wealth maximization. Caeldries (1993) points out that there is a consensus, running through the works of Adam Smith, Schumpeter and Hayek, that a relatively high level of morality is a requirement of healthy and efficient capitalism.

Historical Roots of Shareholder Theory

The idea that self-interested behaviour, similar to that recommended for businesses by shareholder theory, can be beneficial to society is not new. Libertarian views are such that individuals' rights to maximize their own self-interest are fundamental and virtually all intervention by, say, the state, in the realms of economics and politics, should be minimized as they infringe upon these individual rights. Utilitarian views as expressed by Bentham (1789) also advocate the pursuance of individual self-interest in terms of maximizing utility or happiness. John Stuart Mill (1863), whilst still often categorized as a utilitarian, was one of the earliest critics of this conception of self-interested behaviour when he attempted to refine the theory through a consideration of other effecting actions and the distinction between higher and lower interests. The first of these criticisms recognized the possibility of certain self interested actions having a detrimental effect on others, which would therefore not necessarily result in an overall improvement of welfare.

Secondly he argued that certain actions are more worthwhile, 'higher', and should therefore be given a certain degree of precedence. Sen (1987) also suggests that in addition to a person's utility (or happiness) his or her freedom is also valuable and that the omission of this is a distinct limitation of the utilitarian concept.

The utilitarianist thoughts were very much based on the actions of individuals and it was the economic theory of Adam Smith (1776) which, it is claimed, championed a similar strategy for businesses. It is argued that Smith suggested that businesses should behave in a self-interested manner, as the market place would regulate their behaviour. The 'invisible hand' of the free market would ensure that businesses' actions would benefit society. Brennan (1994) actually argues that economics has been guilty of oversimplifying Smith's writings and this has resulted in a mistaken tendency to identify self-interest with rationality. To illustrate Smith's wider moral philosophy, a subject in which Smith was a Professor, Brennan provides the following two quotes:

> to restrain our selfish, and to indulge our benevolent affections, constitutes the perfection of human nature. (quoted from *The Theory of Moral Sentiments*)

> a man ought to regard himself, not as something separated and detached, but as a citizen of the world, a member of the vast commonwealth of nations...and to the interest of this great community, he ought at all times to be willing that his own little interest be sacrificed. (quoted from *Wealth of Nations*)

Sen (1987) also argues that Smith's work has been defined in far too narrow terms in modern positive economics and that his work is concerned with ethical questions. Certainly Smith was not blind to the potential problems that might arise from allowing businesses to pursue profits unchecked. In fact he predicted that if this were allowed profits would be achieved not through gaining a competitive advantage but rather by eliminating competition (Monks and Minow, 1991). This was exemplified by the contention that when two 'businessmen' met they would spend their time colluding to the detriment of the operations of the market in order to improve profits.

Another important consideration is that the present capitalist societies differ from those envisaged by Smith and Mill in a fundamental respect. When promoting the 'self-interest' theories it is posited that both Smith and Mill took for granted a supporting social principle (Hirsch, 1978). This implies that the following of self-interest is beneficial but would only be so within a society that shares certain moral and ethical standards. Hirsch argues that this construct within which self-interest is beneficial has been 'curiously neglected' (p.128) and is no longer reflected in the Western capitalist societies where the model is most used. The extent of this neglect is a moot point as we can see that even Milton Friedman (1962) recognized the need for a business to stay within the rules of the game. The fundamental disagreement concerns the question: what constitutes appropriate ethical standards? For Friedman this simply entails operating in competition, without deception or fraud, whereas I believe Hirsch had a very different, and a more far reaching, conception of moral and ethical standards. Hirsch also suggests that Keynes, a more recent but no less influential economic thinker, had a similar view to those of Smith and Mill. Hirsch argues that the economic system, as proposed by Keynes, was separated into two distinct parts: micro managers, those responsible for managing a business unit, and macro managers who are responsible for overseeing the system. An implicit assumption within this view was that the macro manager would be 'cleverer' and that they would be following a more moral and ethical code of conduct through which society would benefit. Again this basic element of the present economic system appears to have been awarded limited attention by academics. As a discipline, Sen (1987) suggests that modern, or positive, economics has placed too little importance on relevant ethical issues such as these.

Shareholder Theory or Agency Theory

The shareholder theory of the firm is often also referred to as agency theory, as the role of the management of a firm is to act as the agents of the shareholders (the principals). The separation of ownership and control that is apparent in most large modern-day (joint stock) organizations is another significant change since the days of Smith and Mill. It is this separation that leads to what is known as the principal – agent relationship. It is also argued that within this role it is only appropriate for managers (the agents) to use the funds at their disposal for purposes authorized by shareholders (the principals) (Hasnas, 1998; Smith and Hasnas, 1999). Further, as shareholders normally invest in shares in order to maximize their own returns, then managers, as their agents, are obliged to target this end. In fact this is arguing that, as an owner, a shareholder has the right to expect his or her property to be used to his or her own benefit. Donaldson (1982, 1989) disagrees and suggests that it can only be morally acceptable to use the shareholder's money in this way if it is to further public interest. The ethical and moral acceptability of this suggestion is questionable and Smith and Hasnas (1999) point out that such an act would contravene Kant's (1804/1981, p.37) principle. This principle states that a person should be treated as an end in his or her own right rather than as a means to an end. By using shareholders' money for the benefit of others it is argued that the shareholders are being used as a means to further others ends. This defence of shareholder theory is as ironic as it is compelling given that the exact same principle is often cited to defend stakeholder theory (see later).

Assumed within agency theory is a lack of goal congruence, and that there is information asymmetry, between the principal and agent that makes it costly or difficult to confirm the agent's actions (Eisenhardt, 1989). In saying this it is suggested that, left to their own devices, the agents will prefer different options to those that would be chosen by the principals. The agents would make decisions and follow courses that further their own self-interest as opposed to that of the principal. This assumption, that agents' behaviour will be driven by their own self interest and nothing else, has been criticized as being an overly simplistic conception of human behaviour (Williamson, 1985). It is argued that in addition to self-interested motives, altruism, irrationality, generosity, a genuine concern for others etc. also characterize multi-faceted human behaviour. Sen (1987) agrees and actually states that 'to argue that anything other than maximising self-interest must be irrational seems altogether extraordinary'.

It is also argued that shareholders should have rights to determine how their property is used, as should an owner of any asset under private property rights. Etzioni (1998) suggests that this view of shareholders' property rights, which are both moral and legal, is 'widely embedded in the American political culture' and therefore needs no further introduction. Etzioni observes, however, that such property rights are a social construct, as opposed to natural or inalienable rights, and as such society has the opportunity and the ability to change them if it is considered necessary. A closer consideration of what is meant by private property, as it has been socially constructed in present day Western societies, has been undertaken. Donaldson and Preston (1995) argue that the philosophy of property 'runs strongly counter to the conception that private property exclusively enshrines the interests of owners'. They specifically note the work of Pejovich (1990) as recognizing that ownership does not entail unrestricted rights as they cannot be separated from human rights. Further, Honore (1961) suggests that the rights are restricted where their use would be harmful to others. Donaldson and Preston (1995) suggest that as property rights are restricted then they need to be founded on distributive justice. Interestingly, Sternberg (1998), a proponent of shareholder theory, because 'it alone respects the property rights that are so essential for protecting individual liberty', also suggests that ethical business must also be based on 'distributive justice' along with 'ordinary decency' (Sternberg 1994, 1998). Donaldson and Preston (1995) follow Becker's (1992) suggestion that the 'three main contending theories of distributive justice include Utilitarianism, Libertarianism and social contract theory'. Utilitarianism and Libertarianism have already been commented upon above and Social contract theory is considered separately later in the chapter as it was identified as a competing theory of the firm.

Within the legal system in the UK, and the US, the managers of a business have a fiduciary duty to the owners of that business. This duty to shareholders is 'more general and proactive' than the regulatory or contractual responsibilities to other groups (Marens and Wicks, 1999; Goodpaster, 1991). These more general duties have also been used as a justification of the appropriateness of shareholder theories of the firm. Marens and Wicks (1999) considered the purpose and meaning of fiduciary duty and they suggest that in actual fact this duty does not limit managers to a very narrow shareholder approach. They argue that the purpose of the fiduciary duty was originally designed to prevent managers undertaking expenditures that benefited themselves (Berle and Means, 1933). Further, Marens and Wicks (1999) suggest that fiduciary duties simply require that the fiduciary has an honest and open relationship with the shareholder and does not gain illegitimately from their office. Therefore the tension between fiduciary responsibility and the responsibility to other stakeholder groups, the so-called stakeholder paradox (Goodpaster, 1991), is not as apparent as is often assumed. This argument has also received some support from the US courts. When shareholders have challenged management's actions as being too generous to other stakeholder groups then the court has 'almost always' upheld the right of management to manage. Management's justification or defence has often been on rational business performance grounds, such as efficiency or productivity, and the accuracy of such claims is difficult to prove. As such Marens and Wicks (1999) suggest 'virtually any act that does not financially threaten the survival of the business could be construed as in the long-term best interest of shareholders'.

The Practice of Shareholder Theory – Is it Successful?

Shareholder theories of the firm have been practised for many years in the UK and US. Brignall and Ballantine (1996) suggest that the Fisher-Hirshleifer model (Fisher, 1930; Hirshleifer, 1958) has shown that shareholder wealth is maximized 'by investing in all projects offering a positive Net Present Value (NPV)'. The NPV maximizing criteria is therefore not new, although there has more recently been increased interest in a more explicit shareholder value oriented approach to managing a business; such an approach has become more generally known as Value-Based Management (VBM) or Shareholder Value Management. This increased interest has arisen not only within the academic discourse but also among practitioners and business managers. In particular these specific shareholder value techniques have been adopted, primarily in certain large US and UK companies, since the middle of the 1980s. The adoption of such techniques in these countries, as opposed to other advanced capitalist countries, is not too surprising as the UK and US have long been associated with shareholder theory. In fact, when we consider the evidence that has been provided to support the shareholder theory of the firm, a dichotomy is made between the shareholder value focused countries, the UK and US, as opposed to the more stakeholder oriented countries of Japan, Germany and France.

To provide some evidence of wealth creation by shareholder value approaches, two studies are discussed below. These studies analyze differences in levels of GDP per capita in certain countries. In these studies GDP per capita is taken to be a proxy for societal wealth. The analysis below is based on the assumption, in these studies, that it is the level of shareholder focus within these countries which is responsible for differences in GDP per capita, and thus societal wealth. It must be acknowledged here, however, that there are many other differences between these economies that may influence the performance reported; not least is the possible long-term effects of World War II. Copeland, Koller and Murrin (1996) analyze GDP per capita in the US, UK, Germany, France and Japan over the period from 1950 to 1990.[1] They show that the 'US, with shareholder value focus remains the GDP leader' (p.10), despite acknowledging that the other, less shareholder value focused countries were actually closing the gap in the period from 1950-1980. In fact the country which has closed the gap least of all is the UK, arguably the second most shareholder value focused country. Similarly, The Economist (1996) reported that annual growth in GDP per capita has, over the last 40 years, been at 5.5 per cent in Japan, 3.0 per cent in Germany, 2.0 per cent in Britain, and 1.7 per cent in America. Again this work suggests that the shareholder focused countries, Britain and America, are creating less wealth over this period than the more stakeholder orientated economies of Japan and Germany. Both studies place great emphasis on the fact that the improvements in Germany and

Japan do not appear to have continued in the last 10 years. This does not change the fact that over the last 40 years Germany and Japan have outperformed, in terms of increasing GDP per capita, the US and UK

In addition to consideration of the average level of GDP per capita it is also interesting to consider the distribution of this wealth. We can see that the more shareholder value focused economies are shown to have a larger inequality of distribution. One of the most commonly used indices of distribution inequality is the Gini coefficient (Atkinson, 1996), where a coefficient of 0 per cent is when each unit has the same income and 100 per cent is when a single unit has all of the income and the rest none. Atkinson collates, from various studies, the Gini coefficients for different countries over the period from 1970 to 1992 and this indicates that firstly the inequality of distribution of income in the UK has increased from a low point of 23.4 per cent in 1977 to 33.7 per cent in 1991. Over the period from 1970 the US has also seen an increase from 39.4 per cent to 43.3 per cent, Japan an increase from 27.3 per cent in 1980 to 29.6 per cent in 1991 and in Germany it has been very consistent at 25-26 per cent. Of the economies discussed the US shows the highest GDP per capita, although by a reducing margin, and the highest level of inequality, therefore it could be argued that the higher inequality can be justified by a higher overall level of wealth. However, the second shareholder focused economy, the UK, shows the lowest GDP per capita and the second most unequal income distribution. Proving the superiority of a shareholder focus through GDP per capita studies is problematic as there are many differences between the economies considered other than their degree of shareholder focus. In addition this average figure does not accommodate the separate, but no less important, issue of wealth, or welfare, distribution. In conclusion, it is certainly not proven that a shareholder focus results in a higher overall social welfare.

Concluding Thoughts on Shareholder Theory

Justifications for shareholder theories of the firm have been both ethical and legal in nature. An overriding justification is that following a shareholder approach will actually benefit society as a whole. The theoretical accuracy of this claim has been considered, as has the limited supporting empirical evidence. In addition it is apparent that a common feature of the critiques of this theory is its failure to recognize how certain actions affect others in a society. A further feature of the critiques of shareholder theory is as to whether it results in distributive justice. Both of these critiques also form important components of stakeholder theory that we consider next. In my opinion the most convincing and appropriate defence of shareholder theory is that to not use a shareholder's investment for his or her own benefit would fail to meet Kantian ethical standards. As mentioned earlier, this is ironic, as the same argument is often used by advocates of stakeholder theory.

Stakeholder Theory

Stakeholder theory is often considered to be a relatively recent development and many cite Freeman (1984) as the landmark work in this area. Freeman himself actually refers to an internal memorandum at the Stanford Research Institute in 1963 as an earlier use of the term, and Preston and Sapienza (1990) traced the approach, as opposed to the term, back a further 30 years. Donaldson and Preston (1995) examine stakeholder theory and suggest that the theory can be justified on the basis of three aspects. These three aspects are its 'descriptive accuracy, instrumental power, and normative validity'. Taking each of these three aspects in turn, it has been argued that stakeholder theory is important as it correctly reflects, and predicts (Brenner and Cochran, 1991) how businesses operate - not by simply considering shareholders, but other stakeholders as well. The second aspect, instrumental power, argues that adopting a stakeholder approach will improve the organization's performance, either in terms of economic performance or some other criteria, and that in this case the theory would be classified as having instrumental power. This is to say that stakeholder theory is a tool that can be used to improve results. The normative validity justifications, however, refer to the moral rights of individuals and therefore may require a complete reconsideration of the bases of modern Western capitalist societies. It is not sufficient to say that shareholder wealth should be maximized, or that stakeholder theory should be used to achieve this end, without first considering its ethical appropriateness. Each of these justifications will be returned to later.

A fundamental feature of stakeholder theory, in any of its aspects, is that it attempts to identify numerous different factions within a society to whom an organization may have some responsibility. It has been criticized for failing to identify these factions (Argenti, 1993), although some attempts have been made.[2] In a similar vein the stakeholder concept has also been likened to that of a democratic right in the sense of de Tocqueville (in Democracy in America, 1835), where any group can question any other group on the grounds of interest or value (Hummels, 1998; Kuhn and Shriver, 1991). A further step is taken by some stakeholder theorists in suggesting that an 'essential premise' (Jones and Wicks, 1999) of stakeholder theory is that the 'interest of all (legitimate) stakeholders' have intrinsic value, and no set of interests is assumed to dominate the others (Donaldson and Preston, 1995). The premise that the stakeholder groups are considered equal, in that they do not dominate the others, does not receive universal support within stakeholder theory and Gioia (1999) suggests that this 'portrayal to be not only misleading but hopelessly idealistic'. In fact when stakeholder theory is used as a managerial tool it is specifically concerned with identifying which stakeholders are more important and as a result should receive a greater proportion of management's time. Therefore the consensus is only that there are multiple stakeholders who have a stake in an organization. This still leaves us with the question as to what is a stakeholder, and even this is contentious within the field. Numerous definitions of what constitutes a stakeholder have been used within the literature. Sternberg (1997) demonstrates that Freeman himself has used multiple definitions of stakeholders and cites the following two:

those groups without whose support the organization would cease to exist.(p.31)

any group or individual who can affect or is affected by the achievement of the organization's objectives. (p.46)

Sternberg states that the second of these definitions, which is now the more commonly used, has increased the number of stakeholders to be considered by management adopting a stakeholder approach. Therefore a group can be affected by an organization without necessarily being able to bring about its cessation by withdrawing its support. In fact the difference in these two definitions has resulted in a distinction between primary and secondary stakeholders (Clarkson, 1995); where a primary stakeholder is one whose continued support is necessary if the firm is not to be seriously damaged. Again, this appears to be another modification of the definition, where instead of an organization ceasing to exist it is 'seriously damaged' by the withdrawal of support.

Descriptive Accuracy

Stakeholder identification is especially important when considering stakeholder theory from a managerial perspective and when attempting to develop an accurate, descriptive stakeholder theory that accurately describes how managers act. This is suggesting that managers, when managing, actually take into account the different stakeholder groups affected by their actions. If this is the case the managers will need to be able to identify relevant stakeholders and have some system of reaching a decision where there is stakeholder conflict. The approach taken to identifying stakeholders and resolving stakeholder conflict will very much depend on whether a manager's motivation for stakeholder management is instrumental or normative and is to these two aspects we now turn.

Instrumental Power

At first glance the two ideas of shareholder wealth maximization and stakeholder management would appear to be diametrically opposed; a firm can not serve both its shareholders and stakeholders at the same time. The instrumental power of stakeholder theory, however, suggests that stakeholder management can be used to achieve shareholder value. Shankman (1999) suggests that a balance between the different stakeholder groups' interests is essential in ensuring that the organization continues to be viable and achieves other performance goals. Jones (1995) suggests that this should be expected, as if contracts between organizations and stakeholders are on the basis of trust and co-operation, a competitive advantage will follow. This will be because less expense will be required in monitoring and enforcing such contracts. Numerous empirical studies have been performed that attempt to verify the instrumental power of stakeholder theory through attempting to link improved stakeholder management with improved economic performance and hence shareholder wealth maximization (Aupperle *et al.*, 1985; Waddock and Graves, 1997a and b; Greenley and Foxall, 1997). An underlying assumption which is not always explicitly recognized in these studies is that the firm should be operating for shareholders, i.e. they should be shareholder wealth maximizing. Therefore stakeholder management is not an end in itself but is simply seen as a means for improving economic performance. These studies appear to legitimate stakeholder management through its usefulness in achieving a firm's primary objective, namely maximizing shareholder wealth. This assumption is often implicit, although it is clearly stated by Atkinson *et al.* (1997) and is actually inconsistent with the ethical reasons for adopting stakeholder theory. Therefore instead of stakeholder management improving economic, or financial, performance it is argued that a broader aim of corporate social performance should be used (Jones and Wicks, 1999). Further, Jones and Wicks note that certain ethicists need no instrumental justification as moral behaviour 'is, and must be, its own reward'.

Another illustration of how stakeholder management has been argued to result in shareholder wealth maximization is the 'balanced scorecard' performance measurement system (Kaplan and Norton 1992, 1993, 1996a, 1996b). This system, it is claimed, actually balances the competing needs of an organization. In its original form (1992) the balanced scorecard was credited with the ability to 'allow managers to look at the business from four important perspectives'. These four perspectives were the:

- customer perspective;
- internal perspective;
- innovation and learning perspective; and
- financial perspective.

Shareholders, as denoted by the financial perspective, and customers are two specific stakeholders that are clearly identified within the balanced scorecard. Continuous improvement and innovation would also indicate the need for employee development and supplier relations should be incorporated within the internal-business-process perspective (as it was referred to in 1996a). In fact each business is expected to design and adopt its own scorecard to meet its own needs. Kaplan and Norton (1996a) explicitly state that they:

> don't think that all stakeholders are entitled to a position on a business unit's scorecard. The scorecard outcomes and performance drivers should measure those factors that create competitive advantage and breakthroughs for an organization.

Having said this it is likely that the perspective of each primary stakeholder would be incorporated at some point within the balanced scorecard and as such it could be considered to be a stakeholder based performance measurement system. The overarching objective of the balanced scorecard, however, is to achieve both short-term and long-term financial success and it is actually competing with other more explicitly shareholder value based approaches as a method to enable businesses to achieve this. This is most clearly demonstrated in the most recent development of strategy mapping (Kaplan and Norton, 2000).

The appropriateness of stakeholder theory, as a mechanism for corporate governance, has been criticized as containing four fundamental errors by Sternberg (1994). The first criticism relates to the premise, noted above, that as stakeholders are intrinsically valuable then the needs of one group should not dominate the needs of the other, so suggesting equal rights for all stakeholder groups. Sternberg argues that the participants in a business are not equal and by considering them as such 'stakeholder theory confounds business with government' where citizens are equal under law. Secondly she argues that simply because a business affects or is affected by its stakeholders this does not require them to be accountable to those stakeholders. This is in the same way that businesses are affected 'by gravity' but are not accountable to it. The third criticism is that stakeholder theory 'effectively destroys accountability' in that a business 'accountable to all, is actually accountable to none'. The final criticism is that stakeholder theory does not provide a suitable criterion by which the interests of stakeholders can be balanced. These criticisms are addressed by certain stakeholder theorists, see for example Mitchell *et al.* (1987) and Clarkson (1994) discussed in Chapter 3, in that they provide methods by which stakeholder theory is used to restrict the number of relevant stakeholders and to identify the more 'salient' stakeholders. Therefore these techniques do not balance but prioritize certain stakeholder groups. In addition it is also noted above that it is often the case that shareholders are still, either implicitly or explicitly, given primacy. The managerial and descriptive accuracy aspects of stakeholder theory have been discussed so far, but possibly the most far-reaching aspect of the theory is its normative justification and we consider this next.

Normative Validity

This approach to stakeholder theory raises a critical issue with regard to what is ethical or moral behaviour. The actual moral and ethical models used in conjunction with stakeholder theory have been manifold and include Kantian ethics, social contract, the common good (Argandona, 1998), Rawlsian theories of distributive justice and Aristotlean ethics. The works of Kant and Rawls are the most commonly referred to in the stakeholder literature and these will be discussed below. Social contract theory is also discussed in a separate section.

The work of Kant has been considered in the fields of corporate social responsibility (L'Etang, 1995) and stakeholder management (Evan and Freeman, 1988). Firstly, it is argued that it is 'wrong to use people as a means for one's own needs'. Therefore, consideration of stakeholders, and the use of individuals within a stakeholder group, merely to improve shareholder wealth would be considered wrong under this criterion. Both Donaldson and Preston (1995) and Smith and Hasnas (1999) have questioned the sufficiency of this argument. Even if it is accepted that there is a requirement to treat all stakeholders as ends in their own rights, 'this claim appears to imply only that no stakeholder may be forced to deal with the corporation without his or her consent' (Smith and Hasnas, 1999). They continue that this is a fundamental gap in the reasoning of stakeholder theory and this gap actually questions its adequacy as an ethical theory for business. The level of choice for stakeholders, or individuals dealing with large businesses, is interesting. It is certainly difficult to avoid dealing with large businesses as a whole, because they are so pervasive in modern societies. Individuals' lives are affected in many ways by the actions of these organizations. They provide the majority of work, the majority of products, and the most widely accepted investment opportunities. Therefore it would be a difficult, and some would say extreme, action to choose not to deal with large businesses at all. Obviously this is not suggesting that there is not a choice between large organizations.

Rawls (1973) developed a framework for considering ethical concepts specifically with regard to distribution and justice. He derived two principles from his 'original position' of a 'veil of ignorance' which were, firstly, that individuals have certain equal rights to basic liberties; and secondly, that social and economic inequalities are 'just only if they result in compensating benefits for everyone, and in particular for the least advantaged'. Thus Rawls is not a utilitarian, although certain individual rights are protected there is a need for some distributive justice (Moore, 1999). If we follow Rawls' argument, then if society as a whole is to benefit, the distribution of welfare within that society must at least be considered. Wood (1994) suggests that a 'normative stakeholder theory is much more compatible with a Rawlsian view of just distribution than with an egocentric or firm-centric view of wants.' Freeman and Evan (1990) apply the concept of a veil of ignorance to stakeholders where the stakeholder does not know 'which particular stakes he or she actually holds in the corporation'. They suggest that from this initial position it would be 'rational' for stakeholders to choose to have a 'voice' in terms of board representation. Freeman and Evan's application of a Rawlsian 'veil of ignorance' has been criticized by Child and Marcoux (1999). They suggest that it is not appropriate 'in form, nor purpose, nor the level of knowledge' as the stakeholder would still require an incredible amount of knowledge about economic activity and the corporate world. This being said, Husted (1998) does not use a Rawlsian 'veil of ignorance' but rather justice theory as taken from the 'social psychological literature' to reach a similar conclusion: that for issues of distributive justice the relevant stakeholder requires a 'voice' in the decision making process. Child and Marcoux (1999) also criticize this conclusion, as they argue it fails to show that giving stakeholders a voice, or board membership, is necessary for their protection. They conclude that it is not necessarily rational for all stakeholders to have board membership when they are protected by 'the market, the law of corporations, contracts, and torts, and perhaps some judicious government regulation'. Similarly, Hasnas (1998) suggests that this argument simply concludes that businesses must deal honestly with stakeholders and that stakeholders should be free to choose whether to deal with a business or not. This is not the same as requiring an involvement in the decision making process.

Stakeholder Theory?

Trevino and Weaver (1999) argue that, as stakeholder theorists have attempted to develop a more precise stakeholder theory, the tendency has been to rely more on concepts from other theories already existing in the organizational literature. This makes stakeholder theory appear, to them, a 'special case application, of these existing organizational science theories of resource dependence, power, conflict and negotiation, legitimacy'. They further note that the work of Rowley (1997) utilizes 'network analysis, resource dependence theory and institutional theory' when considering stakeholder influences. In fact they suggest that stakeholder theory is not actually a theory, but this is possibly not that surprising considering the fact that Freeman (1984) himself described his work as more a 'framework' than a 'theory'. This use of a multitude of theories leads Trevino and Weaver (1999) to conclude that stakeholder theory is in actual fact not a theory but a research tradition. Stakeholder theory is better described as a research tradition because

> research traditions incorporate multiple, varied theories that are focused on the same domain of observed or postulated phenomena or related sets of questions or problems. (p.224)

Therefore a stakeholder perspective may be an appropriate research approach for addressing a research question, but it is not a theory in which to ground the research.

Concluding Thoughts on Stakeholder Theory

In terms of our considerations here it is the normative justifications for stakeholder theory that are of most interest. The theory has been criticized in that it fails to provide stakeholders with any rights other than the need to consent to the activity. In the case of most stakeholders, the voluntary stakeholders, this is not a problem as they can withdraw their consent and therefore no longer transact with the organization. If this is the case then it is the involuntary stakeholders, who do not actively choose to transact with the organization, that need some form of voice or protection. A further criticism is that stakeholder theory does not suggest the need for stakeholder management as the rights of the different groups can be upheld through other means, for example law and regulation, rather than through specific management practice.

Social Contract Theory

Social Contract Theory is most often associated with the work of Hobbes (1651) and Rousseau (1762) where a contract, usually considered to be implied or hypothetical, is made between citizens for the organization of the society and as a basis for legal and political power within that society. The idea is that for the legal and political system to be legitimate it must be one that the members of society would have rationally contracted into. Social contract theory has been applied to the question of business in society in a similar fashion by considering 'what conditions would have to be met for the members of such a society to agree to allow corporations to be formed' (Smith and Hasnas, 1999). The conclusions reached by the theorists include that the members of society would demand that the benefits outweigh the detriments, implying a greater welfare for the society while remaining 'within the bounds of the general canons of justice' (Donaldson, 1982). This can be summarized into two basic requirements that relate to social welfare and justice. Hasnas (1998) suggests that

> when fully specified, the social welfare term of the social contract requires that businesses act so as to 1) benefit consumers by increasing economic efficiency, stabilizing levels of output and channels of distribution, and increasing liability resources; 2) benefit employees by increasing their income potential, diffusing their personal liability, and facilitating their income allocation; while 3) minimizing pollution and depletion of natural resources, the destruction of personal accountability, the misuse of political power, as well as worker alienation, lack of control over working conditions, and dehumanization. (p. 32)

The justice term is less agreed upon but Hasnas suggests that one thing it should require as a minimum is that businesses do not 'systematically worsen the situation of a given group in society.' This obviously has a strong resonance with stakeholder ideas. Social contract theory has been criticized most usually because, as mentioned earlier, the contract is either argued to be implied or hypothetical. Therefore there is no actual contract (Kultgen, 1987), that members of society have not given any formal consent to such a contract, and that they would be surprised to learn of its existence. Donaldson (1989) freely admits that the contract is a 'fiction' but continues that this does not undermine its underlying moral theory.

Conclusion

Business ethicists have argued in considerable detail about what ethical theory should underpin business and what implications this has for the way businesses operate. The argument is specifically concerned with whether the fiduciary duty to shareholders, that is presently upheld, inappropriately privileges this group within society. In terms of the ethical justification of business activities it appears that the social contract theory is an all-encompassing concept, as both shareholder and stakeholder proponents have argued, in terms of benefits to society. The competing shareholder and stakeholder theories are actually conflicting in terms of how this is achieved. If the true objective of the firm is accepted to be to benefit society, then the question remains, how can this best be achieved? Shareholder theory would suggest that this is through shareholder wealth maximization, although this must not prevent the ethical treatment of other stakeholders (Sternberg, 1998). Stakeholder theory has been argued to be not a theory but more a framework and in addition it has been claimed (Jones, 1995) that it provides an integrative theme for the corporate social responsibility field. This would appear to be supported in the use of the stakeholder concept in considering corporate social performance and responsibilities (Litz, 1996; Roberts, 1992).

The social impact of organizations is very much influenced by the legal constraints on their activity. Incorporated organizations actually depend upon law for their very existence and all their dealings must take into account the 'laws and regulations of the jurisdictions in which they are constituted' (Sternberg, 1998). These laws and regulations are socially constructed and therefore an important argument in the business and society field is to consider what role public policy or government regulation has to play. Free market economists argue that business should be allowed to operate with far lower levels of government intervention (Miller, 1998). One area of specific interest in this book is whether it could or should be used to 'recalibrate the balance' of power between shareholders and other stakeholder groups (Marens and Wicks, 1999). This can be achieved through considering the corporate social performance of organizations to different stakeholder groups. As a first step to achieving this the next chapter looks at how to identify the relevant stakeholder groups and further how an organization's stakeholder performance can be measured.

Notes

[1] The use of GDP here can be criticized for its failure to measure value or profit, but is the preferred measure by the authors of these studies.
[2] See chapter 3 for more on stakeholder identification.

Chapter 3

Social Accounting and Stakeholder Identification

Introduction

In chapter 2 we saw that advocates of both stakeholder theory and shareholder theory argued that the benefits of both theories were in terms of society as a whole. This is to say that both shareholder theory and stakeholder theory claim that when organizations operate in a specific way they lead to the maximization of societal welfare. As such there appears some justification for a form of social contract between society and business, whereby the existence of business within society is justified by the benefits to society. At present, however, these organizations are only required to produce financial accounts to shareholders rather than a wider account to society. This is because shareholder theory is presently accepted and it is therefore believed that if the organization is operating efficiently in maximizing shareholder wealth then society is benefiting. This does not, however, recognize the criticisms of the shareholder approach discussed in chapter 2. Further, it does not consider the effect on others that such behaviour has and we can not therefore be clear whether societal welfare is being improved or maximized.

In response to the failings of financial accounts to deal with the issues of societal welfare and distributive justice social accounting has developed. Social accounting can take an infinite number of different guises and have a number of different purposes, as the following section of this chapter will consider. At the heart of much of social accounting, however, is the desire for organizations to be held accountable to the broader range of stakeholders that make up society. As such it is not restricted to reporting only financial results aimed at delivering accountability to shareholders. In fact much of social accounting is concerned with providing an account to stakeholders in non-financial terms. This is not to say that a social account is only narrative in nature, as there are a great deal of non-financial, but numerical, measures that have been developed to account for the social performance of organizations. This chapter considers how social accounting can be used to maintain the accountability of the organization to the society within which it operates. It begins by considering the social accounting literature and argues that the stakeholder concept provides a helpful framework. It then continues to consider how the relevant stakeholders can be identified before chapter 4 considers specific measures for each of the different stakeholder groups identified.

The Theoretical Contexts of Social Accounting

Gray, Kouhy and Lavers (1995) suggest that there are three theoretical contexts for social accounting (or corporate social reporting) research. The first of these has been subject to many empirical studies and relates to the 'decision-usefulness' of the information provided by such accounting. Much of the academic research in this area has been an attempt to provide evidence of the relevance, primarily to financial investors, of social and environmental information (see for example Belkaoui, 1984; and Aupperle, 1984). This is considering the instrumental value of social and environmental performance. Here the social and environmental performance is not important in its own right, but is rather seen as a way in which shareholder value can be increased. Therefore this form of social accounting fits very firmly within the shareholder theory model discussed in chapter 2. The results of these studies are not conclusive, although Mintzberg (1983) suggests that there is enough evidence to tentatively suggest that it 'pays to be good, but not too good'.

The second area is in the area of positive accounting theory and agency theory and Gray, Kouhy and Lavers (1995) suggest that this has little to offer social accounting research. In fact they state that:

> Apart from the intellectual doubts that one must have concerning the approach, its principal tenets of, first, (allegedly) avoiding any concern with what "should be" and, second, deferring all wisdom to (allegedly free) "markets" runs entirely counter to principal concerns of CSR which is motivated primarily by the market failures (especially injustices, anti-democratic tendencies, information assymetries and "externalities") and desire to change current practice. In addition, its central assumption that all actions are motivated by a morally degenerate form of short-term self-interest (see for example Gray *et al.*, 1994) seems not only empirically implausible but also highly offensive. (pp.51-52)

The final category is social and political theory in which they identify 'stakeholder', 'legitimacy' and 'political economy' theories. In addition to these three areas social contract theory, accountability, and a polyvocal citizenship perspective can be added from other literature and we can now consider each of these.

Mathews (1993, 1995) calls our attention to social contract theory and suggests that this is the most 'persuasive moral argument in favour of increased social and environmental disclosures'. He supports this contention with the following passage from Shocker and Sethi (1974, p.67):

> Any social institution - and business is no exception - operates in society via a social contract, expressed or implied, whereby its survival and growth are based on:
> 1. the delivery of some socially desirable ends to society in general; and
> 2. the distribution of economic, social or political benefits to groups from which it derives its power.

This argument that social accounting can be justified on the grounds of social contract theory is in line with the conclusions to chapter 2.[1] Therefore social accounting can be a means to consider the societal benefit of an organization's activities. One way that this can be achieved is through a stakeholder framework and such a view is supported in the accounting literature. Roberts (1992) argues that stakeholder theory provides the basis to:

> analyze the impact of prior economic performance, strategic posture towards social responsibility activities, and the intensity of stakeholder power on levels of corporate social disclosure. (p. 610)

Similarly Gray (1998, p.210) suggests that a 'stakeholder analysis ... would be enough to show a social account.' Further, Gray (1998) suggests that in actual fact 'the standpoint of accountability and transparency' are the most frequently used. In his earlier work, Gray (1992), defines accountability as concerned with 'the right to receive information and the duty to supply it' (p. 413). Within a wider literature different types of accountability are identified. Laughlin (1990) distinguishes between 'contractual accountability', which is dominated by primarily formal (often accounting type) information flows, as opposed to 'communal accountability', which is dominated by less structured 'talk'. Stewart (1984) identified a ladder of accountability including a legal accountability, process accountability, performance accountability and policy accountability. Laughlin's communal accountability can be likened to Stewart's policy accountability, where the goals and processes 'are undefined and uncertain'. A similar distinction can be drawn from Corbett's (1992) work where there is a political, legal and constitutional accountability and a separate personal and ethical accountability. These distinctions between the more and less formal accountabilities has an interesting resonance with the ideas of voluntary and involuntary stakeholders, which we will return to later in this chapter. Suffice it to say here that voluntary stakeholders, who choose to, or not to, transact with the organization can be likened to those with a contractual accountability and the involuntary stakeholders, who have no such choice, may be more dependent upon communal (or policy or ethical) accountability.

Gray *et al.* (1997, p.335) suggest that a stakeholder and accountability approach may fail to provide for all stakeholder needs. Their concern is that these approaches would be 'too inert and only slowly responsive to changing stakeholder needs.' In order to address this concern they see the need for a 'polyvocal citizenship perspective' (PCP), which they claim offers an 'alternative conception of social accounting' because the social account would, on the whole, but not entirely, report 'the voices of stakeholders'. The emphasis here is very much on a 'dialogue' with stakeholders, such that their concerns with issues are efficiently and quickly incorporated into the management of the business. This has identified the need for developing a model:

> focused on deepening stakeholder relationships around core non-financial as well as financial values and interests. (Zadek, 1998, p.1421)

This gives stakeholders a much more proactive role in an organization than either stakeholder theory or accountability necessarily suggests. In opposition to the theoretical contexts for social accounting discussed so far, which could be argued to be from an ethical standpoint, there are also more managerialist perspectives. The first of these is legitimacy theory, which argues that organizations must be seen to be legitimate. There is a degree to which this can be seen to be part of the social contract, as one way to gain legitimacy is to act within the cultural values of the society within which the organization operates. Woodward, Edwards and Birkin (1996) in fact suggest that this is the most typical form of legitimacy for organizations, although legitimacy can also stem from 'the accepted social structure' and can be designated by a 'powerful' individual or group. Lindblom (1994) suggests that social accounting, when considered in light of legitimacy theory, can take one of four forms:

- To educate the stakeholders about how the organization will improve performance;
- To seek to change stakeholders' perceptions of an event;
- To distract attention away from an issue; and
- To seek to change expectations about organizational performance.

In fact of these strategies it is only the first that entails the organization changing. The remaining three motivations do not actually involve any change to the organization's social and environmental performance. From this perspective social and environmental reporting can be seen to be about managers within an organization attempting to manipulate external perceptions with no, or very little, ethical concern being shown.

Finally, social accounting can be seen to fall within political economy. The following quotation from Jackson (1982) is a useful definition:

> Political economy is the study of the interplay of power, the goals of power wielders and the productive exchange system (Zald, 1970, 233). As a framework, political economy does not concentrate exclusively on market exchanges. Rather it first of all analyses in whatever institutional framework they occur and, second, analyses the relationships between social institutions such as government, law and property rights, each fortified by power and the economy. (p.74)

Gray, Kouhy and Lavers (1995) distinguish between 'Bourgeois' political economy, as associated with the likes of John Stuart Mill, and 'Classical' political economy more in keeping with the works of Marx. It has been argued that much of the social and environmental literature fails to take into account the conflicts between different interests within society. Possibly the strongest critique of the mainstream social and environmental literature came from Tinker, Lehman and Neimark (1991). This work argues that the majority of social and environmental literature does not recognize the structural inequalities and conflicts present in modern societies. It is argued that due to its 'pragmatic' approach the social and environmental literature fails to consider the important issues of social justice and the systemic social ills (for example 'waste, exploitation, extravagance, disadvantage or coercion'). They further argue that such an approach 'denigrates the importance of accounting in shaping social struggles.' The preference of Tinker *et al.* is for a 'conflict-based perspective' that places power asymmetries at the 'foreground in the analysis' and acknowledges that it is the 'basic inequalities' that cause the problems faced by modern societies.[2] Gray, Kouhy and Lavers (1995) accept some of these criticisms of the earlier social accounting literature and suggest that they:

> are much persuaded by Held (1987) construction of neo-pluralism as a partial meeting place for Marxism and liberalism. The neo-pluralist conception recognizes that power will be distributed unevenly, that there will be conflict of interests (possibly structural) and that the focus of observation (e.g. observable corporation-society interactions like CSR) may, indeed, take place within a captured or controlled system.

A neo-pluralist conception is accepted within this book, as discussed in earlier chapters, this work is influenced and informed by stakeholder theory and the concept of accountability. In addition evidence of strategies of legitimation and attempts towards stakeholder dialogue are discussed in the analysis chapters to follow. However, the power asymmetries and resulting appropriation of different levels of returns by different stakeholder groups are considered of fundamental interest to this research. Therefore in chapter 9 the analysis is revisited to consider the issue of (institutional and resource) power within society and how this can provide a deeper and more meaningful explanation of events. Having discussed the theoretical contexts of social accounting it is also interesting to look at some practical attempts at social accounting, so some of these are considered in the following section.

Practical Attempts at Social Accounting

Interest in social accounting has been cyclical and has also varied in its form. In the UK in the early 1970s there was a form of social accounting undertaken by Social Audit Ltd that was very radical and at times extremely critical of the organizations being audited. In fact Gray (2002) suggests that:

> The motivations are those of outrage, engagement, passion, disruption and empowerment. The seminal text within which all these motivations are present and from which this version of the social accounting project depends is that of Medawar (1976). (p.700)

Medawar was the driving force behind Social Audit Ltd and therefore the work of this organisation was very much influenced by these motivations. At the same time *The Corporate Report* (Accounting Standards Steering Committee (ASSC), 1975), was published, which attempted to redesign the scope of corporate reporting for wider stakeholder groups. The next section considers *The Corporate Report* and the work of Social Audit Ltd in some more detail. The levels of interest in social accounting waned dramatically in the 1980s and this has been argued to be because of the changing politics of the time. With the election of Margaret Thatcher in 1979 economic policy in the UK shifted away from the social towards a *laissez-faire* attitude and a belief in the efficiency and efficacy of the free market. It is only more recently that there has been a renewed interest in social accounting and these are significantly different in both form and motivation from those introduced above. The new social audits, although still claiming an interest in accountability, are being justified in terms of the 'business case' (Owen, Swift, Humphrey and Bowerman, 2000). Therefore the benefits to organizations are made in terms strategic management, planning and decision-making. As part of this new social accounting movement a number of social accounting standards have been developed. These initiatives provide a framework for social accounting and this chapter introduces the Global Reporting Initiative (GRI), AccountAbility1000 (AA1000) and SA8000. They are very different in their scope and level of detail. By far the most comprehensive in terms of specific measures is the GRI, but few details are provided as to how to calculate the measures. As such this initiative could be considered more as a framework for social accounting as opposed to a standard. As has been witnessed from financial accounting standards, that often run to tens in not hundreds of pages in length, the devil is in the detail and this is not provided by the GRI.

The Corporate Report

The specific aim of *The Corporate Report* (ASSC, 1975) was to consider and 'seek to satisfy, as far as possible, the information needs of users'. With this aim in mind the following user groups were identified and their information needs considered:

- The equity investor group;
- The loan creditor group;
- The employee group;
- The analyst advisor group;
- The business contact group (including customers, suppliers, competitors...);
- The government; and
- The public (including taxpayers, consumers and special interest groups).

The user groups identified by the ASSC are in effect the stakeholder groups that they identified and stakeholder identification is an issue that is reconsidered at the end of this chapter. What purpose *The Corporate Report* could serve was also reviewed and a total of fifteen specific contributions to user information needs were identified. These included information that would enable the user groups to evaluate the performance, effectiveness, and efficiency of both the organization and the management. In terms of the overall performance of the organization it is suggested that a statement of value added puts profits into 'proper perspective'. The value added by an organization, as measured by turnover less purchased materials and services, is used to pay the contributing factors in terms of employee wages and benefits, dividends and interest, taxation, and amount retained for reinvestment. It was suggested that this statement provides a useful indicator of performance and activity.

Burchell, Clubb and Hopwood (1985) provide evidence that the value added statement grew in popularity in the late 1970s, but that this interest dwindled in the 1980s. They suggest that there are two strands to value added. Firstly it represents wealth created by the organization and this 'provides a basis for the improved calculation of certain important indices of enterprise performance, namely efficiency and productivity (e.g. Ball, 1968)'. The second strand suggests that value added can reveal 'something about the social character of production, something which is occluded by traditional profit and loss accounting.' This is to say that value is created by a combination of efforts from different stakeholders co-operating. Therefore an important part of the rationale for value added was that it would make for a 'harmonious', 'democratic', 'co-operative' and 'efficient' organization. A slightly different understanding of the role of value added was offered by Morley (1978), who suggested that there were three possible views of value added and these were:

- To increase the rate at which power was shifting from capital to labour and government.
- To warn business that there was a shift in power occurring so that they respond against it.
- To help the 'new masters to make sensible decisions'.

In addition to the value added statement *The Corporate Report* also suggested that corporations should publish further reports to other constituents such as employee reports and reports to government. These additional statements were again to move the emphasis away from purely the shareholder. Therefore these additional statements gave important reports to other stakeholder groups that have traditionally been excluded from financial accounts.

The interest in the value added statement, and the other recommendations of *The Corporate Report*, went into decline with the election of the Conservative government in 1979. Burchell *et al.* (1985) argue that this was due to a shift in economic and industrial relations policy. Therefore stress was placed on competition, training and 'shedding "surplus" labour', and the moves towards industrial democracy were, if anything, a hindrance to this as opposed to being consistent.

The ability of a value added analysis to reflect shifts in power and to provide insights into the social side of business is valuable and therefore a value added analysis is considered to be an important tool when considering the social performance of an organization. Other researchers have used value added analyses to critically consider organizational or industrial performance. This work demonstrates the power of value added analysis, as it provides clear evidence of a redistribution, as opposed to a creation, of wealth (see for example Shaoul, 1997; Froud, Haslam, Johal, Shaoul and Williams, 1998; Froud, Williams, Haslam, Johal, and Williams, 1998). In chapter 5 of this book an example of value added analysis is provided. In order to demonstrate the use of value added analysis the case of the electricity industry in England and Wales from privatization in 1990/1 to the election of the Labour government in 1997 is considered. Therefore in order to see further detailed workings of how to undertake such analysis please see chapter 5.

Social Audit Ltd

Social Audit Ltd was set up for the explicit purpose of 'undertaking social audits of different companies and different industries' (Social Audit Ltd, 1973a). The quarterly publication 'Social Audit' contained investigations into Tube Investments Ltd (Social Audit Ltd, 1973b), Cable and Wireless and Avon Rubber Company Ltd, as well as other more general issues such as the 'social costs of advertising'. This was seen as important as it would provide information, which although insufficient to correct all failings, would be an 'indispensable' part of the interaction between organizations and society. As such Social Audit Ltd identified certain groups 'most affected by what a company does'. These include shareholders who need additional information on a company's 'social policy' to inform shareholders' actions. It was argued that the correct ethical response is not to sell shares, but rather that this is an 'evasion of responsibility'. Therefore additional social information was necessary for shareholders to hold the management of the organization accountable for its actions. Employees were also identified specifically in the areas of redundancies, minority hiring, health and safety and 'working for Britain abroad', which was primarily concerned with employment practices in South Africa. It was also argued that consumer sovereignty was failing, as 'big business' has too much control over a market and therefore the consumer is left relatively powerless. Therefore it was argued that consumers need information with regard to products and price, innovation, disposability, inertia in business and consumer representation. The community was also discussed in light of the relationship between an organization and the community within which it operates. This discussion was similar in many ways to the social contract argument as to whether community benefits or profits should come first. In addition to these groups, the environment was also identified. Key areas of concern in the environmental agenda, such as the use of natural resources, restoration and recycling, waste and pollution, were identified.

Here again we see a list of stakeholders that were considered most relevant to the work of Social Audit. We immediately see that there is consistency with the stakeholder groups identified here and those identified by the ASSC. The difference being that the ASSC went further and identified more groups than Social Audit. As with the recommendations of the ASSC the Social Audit did not survive the test of time. In fact the wide-ranging and often critical nature of the Social Audits resulted in organizations refusing to agree to social audits.

The popularity of social accounting in both academia and practice was significantly reduced in the 1980s and in fact it is from this time and through the early 1990s that a greater emphasis was placed upon the environment and environmental accounting. It is only in the late 1990s and the increased concern with sustainability, which encompasses both environmental and social issues that a broader social and environmental accounting has re-emerged. One practical result has been the development of a number of social accounting initiatives and it is to these that we now turn.

Social Accounting Standards

This section considers the development of three accounting standards relating to social, ethical and environmental reporting. These are:

> The Global Reporting Initiative (GRI) is a long-term, multi-stakeholder, international process whose mission is to develop and disseminate globally applicable *Sustainability Reporting Guidelines* (*"Guidelines"*). These *Guidelines* are for voluntary use by organisations for reporting on the economic, environmental and social dimensions of their activities, products, and services. (GRI, 2002, p.1)

> AccountAbility 1000 (AA1000) is an *accountability* standard, focused on securing the quality of *social and ethical* accounting, auditing and reporting. It is a *foundation* standard, and as such can be used in two ways:

> a)   As a common currency to underpin the quality of specialised accountability standards existing and emergent.

> b)   As a stand-alone system and process for managing and communicating social and ethical accountability and performance.' (Institute of social and ethical accountability,)

> This standard [SA8000] specifies requirements for social accountability to enable a company to:

> a)   develop, maintain, and enforce policies and procedures in order to manage those issues which it can control or influence;

> b)   demonstrate to interested parties that policies, procedures and practices are in conformity with the requirements of this standard.

> The requirements of this standard shall apply universally with regard to geographic location, industry sector and company size. (SAI, 1997; p.4)

The GRI provides reporting guidelines for entities in the three areas of economic, social and environmental reporting. The guidelines hope to provide a consistent and clear format for corporate social reporting. It is recognized within the guidelines that of these the most advanced is the environmental, but that each area still requires further work. The guidelines include generally applicable measures under each category as well. The complete list of measures is available from the GRI website www.globalreporting.org. The GRI recognizes the importance of 'stakeholder engagement' within its 'Governance Structure and Management Systems' section. More specifically, in terms of 'Stakeholder Engagement' the GRI (2002, p.42) advocates that a report should include:

> 3.9 Basis for identification and selection of major stakeholders.
> This includes the processes for defining an organisation's stakeholders and for determining which groups to engage.
>
> 3.10 Approaches to stakeholder consultation reported in terms of frequency of consultations by type and by stakeholder group.
> This could include surveys, focus groups, community panels, corporate advisory panels, written communication, management/union structures, and other vehicles.
>
> 3.11 Type of information generated by stakeholder consultations.
> Include a list of key issues and concerns raised by stakeholders and identify indicators specifically developed as a result of stakeholder consultation.
>
> 3.12 Use of information resulting from stakeholder engagements.
> For example, this could include selecting performance benchmarks or influencing specific decisions on policy or operations.

The GRI provides a large number of specific measures under each of the economic social and environmental areas and many of these can be considered in terms of measures relevant to specific stakeholder groups. These specific measures will be considered in more detail in chapter 10. The GRI is certainly the most comprehensive initiative for corporate social reporting, but it remains very much voluntary and because of this it has been adopted by only a small number of organizations. Even where the GRI has been adopted the reports are often not complete and a further problem is the need for verification. On this point the GRI (p.9) says:

> Accordingly, the GRI supports in principle the independent verification of GRI reports, while recognising that organisations need time to assess their needs, readiness, and options for verification.

The AccountAbility 1000 (AA1000) standard considers the principles underpinning social and ethical accounting and also provides a set of 'process standards' by which it can be carried out. As such it differs from the GRI, as it does not provide a list of measures that need to be reported. Firstly, it is not only concerned with reporting, but the wider process which also includes planning, accounting, auditing, embedding and stakeholder engagement. Part of the aim of the standard is to provide a way for organizations to identify appropriate measures through 'stakeholder engagement'.

The principles and process model shows this standard to primarily relate to a process, very similar to a standard accounting process, that organizations can follow to help them become accountable to their stakeholders. As mentioned above, the standard does not provide specific measures, but in fact refers to GRI, SA8000 and ISO14001 as other standards that can be integrated with AA1000 to provide a more comprehensive social and ethical accounting system.

Social Accountability 8000 (SA8000) is primarily concerned with labour and is concerned with the need for organizations to comply to national and international labour law. The specific areas of concern are child labour, forced labour, health and safety, collective bargaining, discrimination, disciplinary practices, compensation, and management systems. This again is a different tack to that taken in the GRI as the reporting would be of adherence to legal requirements and conventions as opposed to specific measures. Owen, Swift and Hunt (2001) call for companies to report more generally on compliance, or non-compliance, with legal requirements as a first step towards a more substantive social reporting.

These three standards are very different in scope and design. In fact AA1000 suggests that they can be integrated into a more complete social and ethical accounting system. Specifically in the area of measuring performance, GRI is the most developed and if adopted more widely would, in my opinion, enhance the present level of social reporting. SA8000 suggests that organizations should be accountable for their actions with respect to adherence to laws, which would appear to be a minimum requirement for ethical organizations. Overall these standards do provide guidance for organizations who want to go further than is presently common, but this should be seen as a starting point for the future development of social accounting – an area that will continue to evolve, as the business context changes to societal and environmental pressures.

This section has shown that both academics and practitioners when thinking about social accounting think about stakeholders. The need for stakeholder dialogue, corporate social reporting and verification are all areas that many accounting academics and practitioners agree on. One form that a social account of an organization can take is as a report to stakeholders. This therefore leads to the next question, which stakeholders should be engaged with and reported to. Therefore the next section of this chapter considers a number of different stakeholder identification models that have been developed and discusses their relative benefits. It must be remembered that one of the criticisms of stakeholder theory, by Sternberg (1997) for example, is that stakeholder theory has failed to appropriately identify relevant stakeholders. It is argued therefore organizations are left with a potentially infinite number of stakeholders that makes it impossible for managers to manage their business and actually destroys accountability as accountability to all is effectively accountability to none.

Stakeholder Identification

We have seen in the preceding section that one way to consider the social performance of an organization is to analyze its performance from different stakeholders' perspectives. In order to be able to perform such analysis, however, it is first necessary to identify the relevant stakeholder groups. This is a difficult problem, not least because of the multiple definitions of what constitutes a stakeholder, as discussed in the previous chapter. Several attempts have been made to identify and distinguish stakeholder groups and three of these are now considered in detail. Mitchell, Agle and Wood (1997) developed what they call a stakeholder salience model, which suggest that the importance of a stakeholder group is dependent upon its salience. The salience of a stakeholder, they argue, is dependent upon the stakeholder's power, legitimacy and urgency and each of these three elements is now considered in more detail. Mitchell *et al.* (1997, p.865) quote Salancik and Pfeffer (1974) when suggesting that power is the 'ability of those who possess power to bring about the outcomes they desire', and further from Etzioni (1964) they suggest that the bases for power are resources, either physical, material or financial, or symbolic. To be legitimate actions must be 'desirable, proper, or appropriate within some socially constructed system of norms, values, beliefs, and definitions' (Suchman, 1995, p.574). For urgency Mitchell *et al.* argue that the relationship must be 'time-sensitive' and critical to the stakeholder. If all three elements are apparent in a stakeholder relationship then management have a 'clear and immediate mandate to attend to and give priority to that stakeholder's claim'. Mitchell *et al.* refer to these as the definitive stakeholders. Agle, Mitchell and Sonnenfeld (2001) attempted to test this model empirically to consider whether CEOs of large U.S. organizations considered these three aspects to be important when considering the salience of stakeholder groups. Their results suggest that from a managerial perspective the stakeholder salience model is valid. This is to say that when adopting stakeholder management practices organizations are influenced by the power, legitimacy and urgency of the different stakeholders. This, however, is a different use of stakeholder theory to the one in social accounting discussed above. The managerialist conception of stakeholder theory is very much instrumental in nature and has little in common with stakeholder accountability. This is exemplified by the case of a legitimate stakeholder who has little power and is not urgent is classified as 'discretionary'. This therefore suggests that legitimate stakeholders can be ignored, but such a conclusion is not in line with the normative aspect of stakeholder theory, which are far more consistent with the stakeholder accountability concerns of social accounting.

An earlier method for identifying stakeholders was suggested by Clarkson (1994) and he claims that this alternative method incorporates the normative concerns of stakeholder theory. He suggested that a stakeholder should be identified if they 'bear risk as a result of a firm's activities' where risk is defined as 'a hazard, a danger, or the possibility of suffering harm or loss' (p.5). This definition of a stakeholder also addressed the criticism that stakeholder theory was evolving to a position where 'every conceivable animate or inanimate object' would need to be considered as a stakeholder by management. Using this risk model of stakeholder identification, it is argued that the firm is only responsible to those who have invested in the firm. In this respect Etzioni (1998, p.683) defines investment 'as the outlay of money, time, or other resources, in something that offers (promises) a profitable return.' 'According to this framework, governments, competitors, terrorists, the media, and activists who bear no personal risk from a firm's activities fall outside the stakeholder designation and therefore require no reciprocal moral consideration' (Vidaver-Cohen, 1999). Clarkson (1994), however, also introduced another distinction, between voluntary and involuntary stakeholders. Certain stakeholders choose to invest some form of capital in the organization and the organization accepts and uses this investment. These are the voluntary stakeholders (these include shareholders, investors, employees, managers, customers and suppliers) who can withdraw their stake and as a result they should be provided with some value added. It is argued that involuntary stakeholders (such as individuals, communities, ecological environments, or future generations) do not choose to enter into, nor can they withdraw from, the relationship with the organization. If we refer back to the stakeholder salience model of Mitchell *et al.* (1997) we can foresee circumstances where these involuntary stakeholders could be ignored, or certainly given a low priority, as they have no power or urgency. In contrast the risk model, as developed through normative concerns, suggests that organizations have a moral obligation to minimize the risks and potential harms these involuntary stakeholders face, and to internalize any potential costs such risks may incur. This more normative approach to the problem of stakeholder identification appears more appropriate in the context of the social contract argued for in the previous chapter.

Wheeler and Sillanpaa (1997) have approached the issue of stakeholder identification from their practical experience and they 'define stakeholder in four ways' (p.167), as summarized in Table 3.1 below:

Table 3.1 Wheeler and Sillanpaa's (1997) stakeholder typology

Primary social stakeholders	Secondary social stakeholders	Primary non-social stakeholders	Secondary non-social stakeholders
Shareholders and investors	Government and regulators	The natural environment	Environmental pressure groups
Employees and managers	Social pressure groups	Future generations	Animal welfare organizations
Customers	Civic institutions	Nonhuman species	
Local communities	Trade bodies		
Suppliers and other business partners	Media and academic commentators		
	Competitors		

Source: Adapted from Wheeler and Sillanpaa (1997, pp.167-8)

The most significant difference between the two models is that Wheeler and Sillanpaa's secondary stakeholders do not feature in Clarkson's model. There is, however, a strong resonance between the primary social stakeholders and Clarkson's voluntary stakeholders and between the involuntary stakeholders with primary non-social stakeholders. If we summarize the stakeholder groups identified within the literature, including those already discussed in this chapter we can see, from Table 3.2 below, that there is a great deal of consistency.

Table 3.2 Relevant stakeholders

Stakeholders	Social Audit Ltd (1973a)	ASSC (1975)	Doyle (1994)	Clarkson (1995)	Woodward, Edwards and Birkin (1996)	Wheeler and Sillanpaa (1997)
Shareholders	✔	✔	✔	✔	✔	✔
Non-equity investors		✔	✔	✔	✔	✔
Customers	✔	✔	✔	✔	✔	✔
Suppliers		✔	✔	✔	✔	✔
Managers			✔	✔		✔
Employees	✔	✔	✔	✔	✔	✔
Competitors		✔				✔
Governments / regulators		✔	✔		✔	✔
General public / community	✔	✔	✔	✔	✔	✔
The physical environment	✔			✔	✔	✔
Special interest groups	✔	✔	✔			✔

Therefore from the literature and practice discussed in this chapter there are a clear number of key stakeholder groups that are widely recognized as being of importance. These are shareholders, other investors, managers, employees, customers, suppliers and the environment. Therefore the remainder of this book will concentrate on these groups. It is important, however, to recognize that this is far from complete list of potential stakeholders and further work needs to identify and consider other stakeholder groups. In fact the stakeholder groups identified here are likely to be more powerful than those excluded from this list. In fact the other stakeholder groups are likely to be involuntary stakeholders who may have an even greater need for protection as suggested by Clarkson (1994).

Conclusions

This chapter has considered the development of social accounting both within the academic literature and within practice. One clear message is that the stakeholder concept is very much at the heart of social accounting. Stakeholder engagement and accountability are crucial to the concept of social accounting. Throughout this chapter we have seen that both in the social accounting and the stakeholder identification literature there are instrumental and normative reasons provided. This chapter emphasizes the importance of the ethical reasons for social accounting. The fact that organizations impact upon different stakeholder groups such that the distribution of wealth between them is effected means that a social account needs to reflect corporate social performance.

This chapter has also considered some social accounting initiatives from the 1970s and more recently. The GRI, AA1000, and SA8000 have all been developed to assist organizations in producing social accounts. At present each of these three developments are completely voluntary and only a minority of organizations are adopting them. Further many of the organizations that have adopted them have not been able to do so completely. Therefore incomplete reports are produced that fail to fully reflect corporate social performance. It is also the case that these initiatives have been developed, most especially the GRI, very much in collaboration with business and this has resulted in criticism that they have been 'captured'. It is certainly true that there are still many that argue the 'business case', instrumental reasons, as the most convincing argument for the need to consider social performance. Under these arguments corporate social responsibility, and reporting as part of this, will benefit all stakeholder groups including shareholders. This ignores the inherent conflict between the different stakeholder groups that will be explored in the following chapters of this book.

Finally, this chapter has also considered the stakeholder identification literature. From Table 3.2 above we can see that there is a relative consensus that the shareholder, other investor, managers, employees, customers, suppliers and the environment are the most widely recognized stakeholders. In a study of large UK companies Cooper, Crowther, Davies and Davis (2001) discovered that in these companies the shareholders, employees and customers were the most widely recognized stakeholder groups. They also found that a large number of companies also considered the environment and suppliers to be important stakeholder groups. There therefore appears a good degree of consistency between the academic literature and practice. Chapter 4 looks in more detail at each of the stakeholder groups identified to consider how an organization's stakeholder performance can be measured.

Notes

[1] In Chapter 2 it was argued that the social contract theory is an all-encompassing concept, and that both shareholder and stakeholder proponents have argued, in terms of benefits to society.

[2] Tinker (1985) provides a more in depth 'social critique of accounting', which considers competing theories of value and some suggestions towards 'radical systems of accounting'.

Chapter 4

Stakeholder Performance
Measurement in Theory

Introduction

Performance measurement is effectively a comparative process (Churchman, 1967). Therefore an organization's performance is considered in relation to either its own performance in a different time period or the performance of another relevant organization. This still leaves the question as to what should be measured? According to Enderle and Tavis (1998), 'measurement grants importance' in that if a dimension of performance is not measured then it appears to be less significant. If we consider the implications of this for stakeholders we can argue that an organization's failure to measure its performance for a stakeholder group implies that this performance, and therefore this stakeholder group, are less important.

In chapter 3 competing models of stakeholder identification were considered and a broadly consistent categorization of key stakeholders was discovered. Therefore under Clarkson's (1994) model of stakeholder identification the following voluntary stakeholder groups were suggested:

- Shareholders;
- Investors;
- Managers;
- Employees;
- Customers; and
- Suppliers.

In addition to these voluntary stakeholder groups it is also intended to consider the effects on the environment, an involuntary stakeholder group. This chapter takes those stakeholder groups and reviews relevant literature to uncover appropriate measures of performance for each group.

Stakeholder Performance Measurement

Stakeholder performance measurement has been considered within the strategic management literature. Chakravarthy (1986) argues that traditional financial measures are inadequate to assess an organization's strategic performance and that in addition stakeholder satisfaction and the quality of an organization's transformation[1] are important. In terms of specific stakeholders, Chakravarthy considers shareholders, customers, employees and the community and the performance of these organizations is measured in terms of the organization's perceived reputation as reflected in the Fortune survey of corporate reputations within an industry. As such no objective stakeholder measures are developed. A somewhat similar approach to measuring stakeholder performance was adopted by Bendheim, Waddock and Graves (1998). In this paper the authors consider five primary stakeholder groups (community relations, employee relations, environment, customers and shareholders) where performance to the first four stakeholder groups is measured in terms of an organization's specific rating in that category by Kinder, Lydenberg, Domini (KLD).[2] Performance to the fifth group (shareholders) is measured by a 'moving average of 10-year financial return to shareholders'. In a similar but earlier paper Waddock and Graves (1997a) measure financial performance to shareholders through the use of three different measures, '10-year compounded total return to shareholders (a market measure), ROA (return on assets), and ROE (return on equity).'

From within the Business and Society field, Clarkson (1995) considered 'stakeholder management' as the most appropriate framework for considering corporate social responsibility. Over a period of ten years Clarkson developed a 'reasonably comprehensive, but not exhaustive' list of some fifty corporate and stakeholder issues. The stakeholder groups identified in this work are: employees, shareholders, customers, suppliers and public stakeholders. If we reconsider the stakeholders identified for the purpose of this study, we again find that there is a great deal of consistency. The specific differences are that in the earlier list investors are included in addition to shareholders and that management has been separated from employees although in reality they are employees of the organization. The public stakeholders, referred to in Clarkson (1995), include environmental, social, and community relations. It is argued that it is the management of these particular issues that defines how well an organization has performed. If these specific issues are appropriately managed then the stakeholders of the organization should be satisfied.

The remainder of this chapter intends to draw on the literature mentioned above in addition to other literature that more specifically pertains to the information needs of the various stakeholder groups identified.

Shareholders

The financial performance of an organization for its shareholders has been widely discussed within the finance and accounting literature as well as elsewhere. A distinction that can be made is whether this performance is measured in terms of accounting or market based information. In terms of accounting information the emphasis is on profitability and this is usually stated in relation to either sales or capital employed. The limitations of these measures are well known and have been for a quite considerable period of time. Chakravarthy (1986) suggests the following five problems in using measures based on financial accounts:

- Scope for accounting manipulation;
- Undervaluation of assets;
- Distortions due to depreciation policies, inventory valuation and treatment of certain revenue and expenditure items;
- Differences in methods of consolidating accounts; and
- Differences due to lack of standardization in international accounting conventions.

The manipulation of accounts, or in other words creative accounting, is widely acknowledged to adversely affect the comparability of different organizations' performance through the use of financial accounting data. Smith (1992) analyzes the financial accounts of UK companies that ran into financial distress but appeared to be operating profitably according to their financial accounts. His analysis identified that these companies had been making use of accounting policies that could be construed to be creative. The conclusion is that such practice could well make such financial accounting measures meaningless. Since this time there have been many developments in both UK and International Accounting Standards, which have attempted to address these problems both at generic and prescriptive levels. Despite these attempts areas of subjectivity, scope for accounting manipulation, and a lack of International standardization still exist and therefore still threaten the value of financial accounts.

Despite acknowledging criticisms of financial accounts similar to those mentioned above Woo and Willard (1983) surveyed the performance measures used in strategic management and found that profitability measures were by far the most commonly used. In fact they conclude, 'when properly complemented by other measures, this study shows that ROI [Return on Investment] is essential to the comprehensive representation of performance.' In terms of accounting profitability measures, Chakravarthy (1986) selected return on sales, return on total capital, and return on book equity to analyse the performance of 14 computer companies. He notes that these measures are consistent with those selected by Peters and Waterman (1982). Chakravarthy (1986) found that it was not possible to distinguish between excellent and 'non-excellent' firms using these profitability criteria. Further evidence of the popularity of profitability measures is provided by Waddock and Graves (1997b), who also considered return on assets, return on equity and return on sales. In addition to these profitability measures Chakravarthy (1986) made use of a market-based measure of performance, as did Waddock and Graves in a later paper with Bendheim (1998), and it is to these that we now turn.

As mentioned above, accounting measures of profitability have been heavily criticized. A further concern, especially in the strategic management field, is the historical nature of financial accounting. As Chakravarthy (1986) notes, 'accounting-measures-of performance record only the history of the firm'. The market capitalization of an organization reflects the value of the organization as perceived by the market. It is simply found by multiplying the current number of shares by the current share price on the market. According to Stewart (1991) this does not provide an appropriate measure of shareholder wealth creation because:

> Any company can maximise its total value simply by spending as much money as possible (both by retaining most of its earnings and raising new capital).[3] (p.190)

Stewart proposes that it is how investor's money is used that is important for measuring shareholder wealth creation and that this can be done by also taking into account the capital in the organization. Stewart's preferred measure is Market Value Added (MVA) and is calculated by:

MVA = Market Value − Capital

Both the market value and capital elements include both the debt and equity of the organization. Stewart suggests that the measurement of capital is based on an 'adjusted book value', i.e. an accounting valuation subject to some adjustment (Crowther, Davies and Cooper, 1998). MVA is an absolute measure and therefore does not compensate for the different sizes of organizations. A similar measure, but one that is stated in relative terms, is the market to book (M/B) ratio. This is calculated by dividing the market value of the organization by the organization's value as reflected by the balance sheet. Chakravarthy prefers this as a strategic performance measure. He cites Rappaport (1981), who states that this measure reflects the perceived ability of an organization to provide returns to shareholders in excess of their expectations. Similarly, Peters and Waterman (1982) suggest that this measure should reflect the future wealth creating potential of an organization. A problem with both of these measures is the use of accounting figures that, as mentioned above, can be manipulated. Also both measures ignore dividends as a source of wealth to the shareholders.

A measure that incorporates both the increase in market value and the level of dividends received is total shareholder returns (TSR). This is measured by the following formula:

$$TSR = \frac{(P1 - P0) + D}{P0}$$

Where: TSR = Total Shareholder Returns,
D = Dividends in period,
Pn = share price at time n

This provides us with a one-period percentage increase in wealth to the shareholder. Waddock and Graves (1997a) use a '10-year compounded total return to shareholders' and they defined this as the '10-year average compounded rate of return, assuming that dividends are reinvested in the company's stock when paid and brokerage costs are negligible.' Such a TSR measure effectively records the change in wealth of a shareholder over a period of time, but can be criticized as failing to take into account the risk of the investment. Finance theory suggests that shareholders are risk averse and as such require a higher return for riskier investments. Perhaps the most popular way to measure the risk of an investment is by using the Capital Asset Pricing Model (CAPM). The CAPM was first introduced by Sharpe (1964) and has become one of the most influential models in finance. It suggests that shareholders should be rewarded depending on the level of risk that they take and this can be measured by Beta. Beta is a measure of an organization's systematic (or market) risk only as it is argued that all other risks can and should be diversified by the shareholder. CAPM suggests that the cost of equity or the required return to shareholders can be measured by:

Cost of equity = Risk free rate + (Beta * Market risk premium)

A more detailed description of CAPM and its related problems can be found in most finance textbooks (see, for example, Arnold, 2002). A risk adjusted total shareholder return would appear to be the most appropriate market-based measure of financial performance. However, as with all market-based measures it is actually based on the perceptions of shareholders. One problem with this is that the actual market price of a share is affected by many factors, some of which will be related to the macro-economic situation as opposed to the specific performance of an organization. Therefore it is also important that economy or market wide influences are accounted for and this can be done by comparing an organization's performance with that of the market as a whole.

We have seen that measuring performance for shareholders can be separated into two categories: accounting-based measures; and market-based measures. Both types of measures have been criticized but at the same time widely used in a variety of guises and for a variety of purposes. In order to gain a well-rounded picture of the shareholder performance both types of measure have something to offer. In terms of accounting-based measures there appears to be some level of agreement that return on equity, return on capital employed, and return on sales are valuable. In terms of market-based measures it is argued that total shareholder returns as adjusted for risk and market-wide factors is most appropriate. Therefore it is proposed here that through an analysis of these measures an appreciation of an organization's shareholder performance can be gained.

Investors

This stakeholder group constitutes part of what is called the loan creditor group in The Corporate Report (ASSC, 1975). The investors' information needs are to enable the investor to assess the organization's ability to honour the future payments required of them, in both the short and long term. The actual information needs of this group were identified as including information on economic stability and vulnerability and working capital and liquidity (ASSC, 1975).

In terms of the economic stability and vulnerability of an organization the biggest concern is that of bankruptcy. Perhaps the best known measure of bankruptcy is the Z score as developed by Altman (1971). The Z score is calculated through using a weighted multi-variable formula and has been found to be able to predict, to some extent, future bankruptcy. The Z score is calculated as follows:

$$Z = 0.012a + 0.014b + 0.033c + 0.006d + 0.010e$$

Where: a = working capital / total assets;
b = retained earnings / total assets;
c = profit before interest and tax / total assets;
d = equity market value / total liabilities book value;
e = sales / total assets.

If Z is less than 1.8 you are almost certain to go bust, if it is more than 3.0 you almost certainly will not. (Argenti, 1976, p.57)

Chakravarthy (1986) notes that the actual success of Z scores in predicting bankruptcy has been mixed but acknowledges that it can be 'a valuable index of the company's overall well-being' (p.446). As such it should be useful in considering the economic stability and vulnerability of an organization.

In terms of working capital management and liquidity there are several well-established accounting measures. As overall measures of liquidity perhaps the two most commonly used are the current ratio and the quick ratio. Each of these measures attempts to consider the ability of the organization to pay its liabilities due in the near future. The difference between the two measures is that the current ratio includes stock as a source of funds from which the liabilities can be paid. Therefore the two ratios are:

Current ratio = Current Assets / Current Liabilities

Quick ratio = (Current Assets – Stock) / Current Liabilities

In actual fact both the Z scores and the liquidity measures are likely to be of interest to most, if not all, stakeholder groups including shareholders. However, they are included here, as they are consistent with the specific information needs of the loan creditor group as discussed in The Corporate Report. It should also be remembered that all of these measures are based on accounting numbers and will therefore be subject to the same criticisms as the other accounting-based measures mentioned when considering shareholder performance measurement.

Managers

The management of an organization is in a considerable position of power as they are the stakeholder group that is in day-to-day control of the organization. In effect they are the group that decides the strategic direction of the organization. The potential problems that this may cause were discussed in chapter 2 and would come under the auspices of agency theory. Despite this managers are employees of the organization and as such the information needs and measures discussed for the employee stakeholder group below should be of equal relevance to managers. Therefore attempts will be made where possible to apply the employee measures to the managerial stakeholder group.

Employees

Employees are a primary stakeholder group, without whom the organization can not operate, and it has been argued that they therefore have a legitimate right to accounting information (George, 1983). This 'legitimate right' has not always been reflected in British company law and *The Corporate Report* (ASSC, 1975) suggested that:

> Nothing illustrates more vividly the nineteenth century origin of British company law than the way in which employees are almost totally ignored in the present Companies Acts and in corporate reports. (p.51)

Despite this lack of a legal requirement to provide employees with information examples of employee reporting can be found prior to The Corporate Report. Parker, Ferris and Otley (1989) suggest that examples of financial reporting to employees can even be found in the late 1800s and Woodward (1970) reported their use in the 1950s. Interest in employee reporting increased rapidly from the time of The Corporate Report to the early 1980s and this was reflected by both companies (Hussey, 1981; Lyall, 1982) and academics (see for example Hilton, 1978; Hussey and Marsh, 1983; Maunders, 1984). The academic interest in employee reporting appears to have dwindled, if not disappeared, since the mid 1980s and this would seem to support the contention of Parker *et al.* (1989) that the historical development of reporting to employees has been 'characterized by countercyclical periods of interest from managers and accountants'. The information needs of employees were most widely discussed in the context of the content of employee reports and this led to a plethora of potential measures being suggested. These employee reports are used as the primary source here for potential measures of an organization's performance to its employees.

Specific Performance Measures for Employees

Employee remuneration is considered to be the single most important item by Trade Unions in collective bargaining situations (Foley and Maunders, 1977).[4] This does not mean that other aspects of employment are not important, but it is usually a fundamental component of any employment contract. Foley and Maunders continue that a change in the level of pay is supported by one or more of the following:

- Changes in the cost of living;
- Comparability;

- Productivity; and
- Ability to pay.

These four component parts of wage settlements are broadly consistent with the work of Ingram, Wadsworth and Brown (1999) that examined the influences on wage settlements in the UK in the period from 1979-1994. In addition they found that the state of industrial relations and the state of the labour market would be of importance. It can be seen from these influences that the level of an employee's remuneration is not set in isolation but is more a factor of societal and organizational factors. As this is the case it is necessary to consider levels of remuneration, and their appropriateness, in relation to these societal and organizational factors.

Factors other than remuneration are important when considering an organization's performance for its employees. Foley and Maunders (1977) argue that employee information needs fall into four major categories: job security; working conditions; achievement or performance indicators; and equity (between employees and shareholders, workers and management and between workers). This broadens the information needs of an employee to be more than purely relating to issues of level of remuneration. Specifically, job security and working conditions are not covered within the components of pay claims listed above, although achievement and equity were expressed in terms of remuneration comparability or productivity. Job security and working conditions will not have a direct impact on an employee's wealth or remuneration but will have a significant impact on his / her welfare.

Therefore it would appear that the key components of performance for an employee will relate to:

- Levels of remuneration, most importantly in relative terms to the cost of living and in comparison to other employees and other stakeholder groups;
- Changes in productivity as both an indication of the intensity of the work experience of employees and also as a component part of the drivers of changes in remuneration;
- Working conditions and job security.

The completeness and appropriateness of the list above can now be compared to the proposals for employee disclosure recommended by several organizations in the 1970s. Hilton (1978) produced a 'Summary Chart of Recommendations on Disclosure' that is reproduced below:

Table 4.1 Summary chart of recommendations on disclosure

Information heading	TUC	CBI	ACAS	100 Gp	DoT
Objectives	-	X	-	-	X
Employment	X	X	X	X	X
Pay, conditions	X	X	X	X	-
Productivity	X	X	X	X	-
Plans	X	X	-	X	X
Competition	-	X	-	-	-
Financial information	X	X	X	X	X
Unit-based reports	X	X	-	-	X

Source: Hilton (1978)

Hilton suggests that there is a consensus here which clarifies the appropriate content of an employee report. If we take a consensus to be where the majority of the five organizations believe that the information should be included, we are left with the following categories: employment, pay and conditions, productivity, plans, financial information and unit-based reports. Matching these to the key components suggested above again shows a level of consistency that is reassuring. Pay, conditions and productivity can be matched immediately. Further employment relates to details concerning manpower or personnel information that we will see are important as drivers of job security and job satisfaction. Plans are also important for the purposes of job security as any significant changes in business activity will almost always affect the employees. Financial information is important as it allows the employees to consider the strength of the organization as well as indicating whether the economic rewards of business are being distributed equally. Finally, unit-based reports are preferred when feasible, as they are more likely to be relevant and specific to the individual employee. If we can therefore accept that the three key components of an organization's performance to its employees are levels of remuneration, productivity levels and working conditions and job security we can next consider which specific measures will provide relevant information to employees.

Levels of Remuneration

As a complete stakeholder group employee remuneration can be measured as an aggregate measure and this information is provided in the annual reports of companies. This as a total can be compared to the rewards to other stakeholder groups in the form of a value added statement. As this is an aggregate measure it would not be possible to identify changes due to levels of employment nor differences between different groups of employees. An average remuneration per employee can be calculated in order to compensate for changes in employment levels. A breakdown of employee remuneration by job type and location, however, would be necessary in order to highlight distribution changes between groups of employees. A further comparison can be made with remuneration levels to similar employee groups external to the industry; for reasons of equity or parity one would expect levels of remuneration to stay in line with remuneration for equivalent work elsewhere.

The changes in the levels of remuneration discussed above would be in nominal or money terms rather than real terms and as such do not take into account the increased cost of living. Foley and Maunders (1977) state the Retail Price Index (RPI) is the most commonly used statistic by trade unions to measure changes in the cost of living. They further note that it should be net pay, after income tax and National Insurance Contributions, which is compensated for to meet changes in the cost of living.

The employee remuneration information considered here relates to the changes in the cost of living and comparability. In addition to these reasons for changes in levels of remuneration, Foley and Maunders (1977) also suggested that productivity and ability to pay would be influential. The ability to pay is dependent on the financial performance of the organization and as such can be measured in terms of the accounting measures and ratios discussed within the shareholder and investor sections above. The next section considers the importance of productivity levels for employee remuneration and more generally.

Productivity Levels

Productivity is the ratio of outputs to inputs, a deceptively simple concept according to Maunders (1984). Marginal productivity measures the increase in inputs necessary to increase outputs and is often problematic to measure. Productivity can be measured in terms of total factor productivity, where all inputs are considered, or in terms of a specific factor of production such as labour productivity. As we are concerned with employees here it is labour productivity which would appear most relevant. Maunders (1984) suggests that there is a fundamental problem with considering a specific factor of productivity in that labour, for example, will not have produced the output in isolation but in conjunction with the other factors of production. It is simply not possible to produce a unit of production without using other factors of production. The most obvious 'other factor of production' is capital and a change in capital employed may well lead to a change in the amount or type of labour required. Therefore in order to gain an appropriate understanding of changes in labour productivity it will also be necessary to consider changes in the other factors of production.

The numerator of a productivity calculation is output and this is preferably measured in terms of units of production rather than monetary value.[5] Monetary values are obviously affected by price changes and price discrimination and are not therefore an objective measure of output. Similarly sales (or turnover) is not an appropriate measure of output, as it will be related to the units sold in a period rather than the units produced. The key difference between production and sales is changes in the levels of stocks and this must therefore be taken into account in the calculation of output.

The denominator of a productivity calculation is the level of inputs and, as discussed above, in this case we are most concerned with the level of labour input. When considering an organization, or an industry as a whole, there are many different types of labour involved in the production process. Each employee will have different skills or tasks and cannot therefore be considered to be a standard unit of production. This suggests that it is not really appropriate to simply add different employee hours together. Parker and Martin (1995) argue that it is possible to simply use the level of employment in terms of hours or numbers of employees, assuming that there has not been a change in the quality or skills of the labour force. They argue that this is reasonable given the short time frame in their study. This meant four-year periods. If this cannot be assumed over the period of study it is necessary to find an alternative measure of employee inputs. The use of employee costs can be claimed to compensate for differences in quality or skill, although Maunders (1984) suggests that without the existence of a perfect labour market the costs may not accurately reflect the intrinsic value of the employee contributions. Having acknowledged this, it would appear that the weighting of different employees by their remuneration would appear to more accurately reflect their value than by simply considering different employees as equivalent.

Working Conditions and Job Security

This category broadens out the measures to include items that do not affect the employees' remuneration but are more associated with their overall welfare. Potential factors that affect an employee's welfare are many and are often extremely difficult to measure. For example, Hilton (1978) reports that within the second code of practice produced by the Advisory Conciliation and Arbitration Service, five areas are highlighted one of which is 'conditions'. The breakdown of factors suggests that conditions include:

- Recruitment;
- Redeployment;
- Training;
- Promotion;
- Equal opportunity;
- Appraisal;
- Safety, health, welfare;
- Redundancy; and
- Pensions.

Some of these factors, for example redeployment and redundancy information, may be more relevant to job security, but this shows the range of factors that are relevant but not related to remuneration. This is not the end of the story, as Maunders (1984) suggests under a category of Health, safety and welfare information that is potentially relevant, but not necessarily exhaustive, includes accident rates, occupational diseases, noise, temperature, lighting, protection from weather, vibrations, ventilation, dirt / cleanliness, humidity / wetness, smells, working space / overcrowding, air pollution – dust / fumes / smoke, radiation levels, exposure to chemicals, risks of biological infections, physical hazards from machinery etc, and fire hazards. Each of these influences are potentially important and therefore should not be ignored, but at the same time it could be argued that the majority of these items will not have changed significantly over a short time period.

  Job security is also rather intangible, as it will relate to the state of mind of an individual employee and the perception that they have of their future prospects within an organization. Having said this, there are certain pieces of information that will have a direct impact on this perception. Specifically, the financial strength and performance of the organization will be important, but probably even more important are the future plans for both the business and its employment levels. It is for this reason that it has been argued that employees specifically require information on financial performance and plans as was identified in the summary provided by Hilton and reproduced above. Further, it is for this reason that it is also important to the employee that the information is specific to his or her own place of work.

Overall Job Satisfaction

The measures of an organization's performance for an employee discussed above all consider factors that affect an employee's overall level of job satisfaction. This is to say that an employee's level of satisfaction will depend on their remuneration, level of productivity, working conditions and job security. As such these could be considered to be measures of inputs into employee satisfaction or welfare. An alternative approach is to measure the output, in this case the level of employee satisfaction. This can be done directly through the use of employee surveys into their level of satisfaction. The potential problems with this relate to the appropriate phrasing of a questionnaire to obtain unbiased and representative responses. A second way to measure job satisfaction is through the use of proxy measures. Maunders (1984) argues that the following measures could be used as output indicators of employee satisfaction:

- Accidents;
- Disputes incidence;
- Grievances;
- Absenteeism and poor time-keeping;
- Productivity;
- Employee wastage / stability;
- Disciplinary cases.

Each of these can be measured in absolute terms or relative to numbers of employees or time lost. According to Maunders (1984), the measure of labour wastage most commonly used is a variation of the 'annual labour turnover index' as expressed below:

$$\text{ALT} \quad = \quad \frac{\underline{\text{Numbers of leavers in year}}}{\text{Ave. no. employed during year}} \quad * \; 100$$

Bowey (1974) has claimed that this measure is biased toward the 'pull' process (attractions elsewhere) as opposed to the 'push' process (dissatisfaction with job). Bowey continues that the 'push' process is better measured by an index of labour stability such as:

$$\frac{\underline{\text{Present number of employees with 1 year's service or more}}}{\text{Total employed one year ago}} \; * \; 100$$

Both the 'push' and 'pull' process are evidence of the comparative attractiveness of an organization and therefore the ALT, which incorporates both, could be considered to be the more comprehensive and therefore the more appropriate.

Concluding Thoughts on Employee Measures

In order to measure the performance of an organization it is necessary to consider many different aspects of that organization's relationship with the employee. An organization has performed well for an employee if that employee is satisfied in their work. The difficulty encountered is in measuring the level of satisfaction of employees, which even when attempted through direct communication, can be problematic. As a result attempts have been made to produce measures that are proxies for employee satisfaction and these can be found in two forms; either input or output measures. In fact both can be considered to be complementary and can therefore be used in conjunction to gain an appreciation of an organization's employee performance. The input measures can be divided into four types that relate to remuneration, productivity, working conditions and job security. Each of these is considered above. In addition output proxy measures of employee satisfaction, that consider labour stability and turnover, can be used.

Customers

The satisfaction of customers is of fundamental importance to most organizations and is often measured directly through the use of customer surveys or questionnaires. Another output measure of customer satisfaction is the respective market share an organization commands within its given target market. This can also be considered over a period of time to identify changing trends. Such information would clearly need to be considered on a product by product basis.

We can also consider more detailed measures of consumer performance and these are most commonly related to the price that they are paying for the good or service and its quality. One of the difficulties here is obtaining the actual price and quality information. A specific issue is the inter-relationship between price and quality. It is clear that a different price can be charged for a different quality of product. Kaplan and Norton (1996a and b) recognized the importance of consumers within their balanced scorecard approach to performance measurement. The customer perspective was primarily interested in identifying customer needs. Within the balanced scorecard each perspective is operationalized through a number of key performance indicators. Again this could be distinguished between issues related to price and those related to quality.

In terms of price it is by no means always the case that organizations attempt to compete on price alone. Certain organizations attempt to signal quality or exclusiveness by setting high prices. Nevertheless for many products, most clearly in the case of necessities as opposed to luxuries, price is the single most important factor when making a consumption decision and therefore from a consumer's perspective comparative price will be important.

As mentioned above, however, price can not always be isolated from quality. The quality of a product is very much married to the nature of the product itself and therefore it is difficult to provide general quality measures. Perhaps the most common measures are customer retention and numbers of new customers. These two measures will clearly feed directly into the market share of an organization, as considered above. Customers may fail to return for a number of reasons such as the speed of service / delivery, the reliability of the product, or after sales service provided to name but a few. Each of these can be extremely important and will therefore require measurement, but perhaps here more than for any other stakeholder group the act of consumption is so individual to the consumer and to the specific product or service that it is difficult to generalize. Suffice it to say that price and quality are the key inputs, which can be compared with competitors, and the outputs are measured in sales achieved. One other measure of customer satisfaction is to monitor the number of customer complaints and this will also be considered.

Suppliers

This stakeholder group has similar information needs to those of the investor group discussed above. In fact within *The Corporate Report* (ASSC, 1975) the two groups were amalgamated into a single group, the loan-creditor group. Therefore it is reasonable to suggest that suppliers will be interested in the measures discussed in the investor group (i.e. bankruptcy and liquidity measures). In terms of more specific measures, the most widely used is creditor days. This is calculated using the following formula:

$$\text{Creditor days} = \frac{\text{Trade Creditors (excluding VAT)}}{\text{Annual Purchases}} * 365 \text{days}$$

This measure reflects the speed with which the trade suppliers to an organization are paid. Trade creditors are an often free, or cheap, source of funds to an organization and as such there is a possible motivation to delay payment. This is to the detriment of the suppliers' own cash flow and an ability to do this, without the supplier withdrawing supply, would suggest that the organization is in a position of power over the supplier.

The Environment

Involuntary stakeholders cover a wide variety of different stakeholder groups. For the purposes of this study the key interest is in the environment. Environmental accounting has been an incredibly popular subject amongst academics since the late 1980s. Some of the research has attempted to demonstrate a causal relationship between environmental performance, or disclosure, and financial performance (a recent example is Toms, 2000). Another important strand of the empirical research has been considering the change in volume of disclosure over a period of time (see Adams, Hill and Robert, 1995).[6] Relatively less has been written about what measures should be used to gauge environmental performance. There appear to be two distinct approaches. Firstly, environmental effects could be quantified into costs and benefits and somehow incorporated into an adjusted version of traditional accounting statements. Secondly, the impacts may not be quantifiable in money terms or at all (Boyce, 2000) in which case other quantitative data (but not denominated in monetary terms) and qualitative data would be seen as more relevant.

One advocate of a form of full cost, i.e. incorporating both 'public and private costs' is Mathews (1993). He terms this approach 'Total Impact Accounting' and this would necessarily involve transferring all effects of an organization's activities into monetary terms. An interesting attempt at this was made by Atkinson (2000). He used data from a variety of sources to consider the 'damage' caused by pollutants emitted and the estimates are summarized in Table 4.2 below:

Table 4.2 Marginal damage per tonne of pollutant emitted (£)

	SO_2	NO_x	PM_{10}	CO_2	CH_4
Health			19500-44800		
Non-health	300-670	200-280			
Total	300-670	200-280	19500-44800	12	80

Source: Adapted from Atkinson (2000) citing: Fankhauser (1994); European Commission (1995); Pearce & Newcombe (1998)

Corporate Social Performance: A Stakeholder Approach

These are drawn from an evaluation of energy externalities within the UK (European Commission 1995). The CO_2 and CH_4 estimates are from Frankhauser (1994). The rows of Table [4.2] represent 'receiving agents' (broadly conceived). These are the ultimate effects of polluting activities on human health (e.g. morbidity and mortality), and non-health (forest damage, material and building damage). Pollutants such as SO_2, NO_x and PM_{10} are implicated in significant damage to health (Maddison et al. 1995).

These estimations were then used to consider the 'green value added' and 'corporate genuine saving' (CGS) for the UK. electricity industry and Powergen respectively. The results are summarized in the tables below:

Table 4.3 Atkinson (2000): green value added for the UK electricity industry (£million 1990 prices)

	1987	1994
Value added (VA)	5600	6830
Environmental damage	2742	1955
% VA	49.0	28.6
Green VA	2858	4875

Source: Adapted from Atkinson (2000), citing Office for National Statistics (1998) and see also sources listed below Table 4.2

Table 4.4 Corporate genuine savings for Powergen plc (£million, current prices)

		1992		1996
Profit on ordinary activities		359		687
CO_2 damage	256		212	
SO_2 damage	279		162	
NO_x damage	43		27	
PM_{10} damage	491		215	
Total pollution damage		-1068		-616
CGS		-709		71

Source: Adapted from Atkinson (2000)

This improvement in environmental performance is the most dramatic in any industry, but under these accounting criteria Powergen plc did not make a CGS until 1996. This approach to accounting has two fundamental problems, both acknowledged by Atkinson. Transferring pollution details into monetary values involves a high level of estimation, which can provide significant doubts about the accuracy of any results. Secondly this approach would appear to suggest that if Powergen plc had higher profits then there would not be an environmental problem as there would be a corporate genuine saving. This is irrespective of whether any of this profit was used to tackle the environmental problems caused by the activities of the organization. For these reasons this does not appear to be an appropriate approach to environmental accounting.

The second approach identifies the key environmental issues facing an organization and then considers measures that appropriately incorporate performance on these issues. Gray, Bebbington and Walters (1993) suggest that the following environmental issues are key:

Table 4.5 Environmental issues

Crisis? What Crisis

• Thinning of the ozone layer	• Third world debt
• Global warming	• Deforestation
• Species extinction	• Waste disposal
• Habitat destruction	• Energy usage
• Acid rain	• Starvation
• Desertification	• Inequality
• Soil erosion	• Population
• Air pollution	• Water depletion
• Water pollution	• Toxic chemicals
• Land pollution	• Nuclear waste
• Noise pollution	• Ethnic peoples
• Resource scarcity	• Poverty

Source: Gray, Bebbington and Walters (1993, p.25)

Another source of environmental performance measures is provided by ISO 14031 (ISO, 1997) that has three basic indicator categories:

1. Environmental condition indicators – that track the environmental consequences of business activities. Bennett and James (1998) suggest that these often focus on receptor indicators such as impacts on air, water, land, flora and fauna, people and buildings.
2. Operational environmental performance indicators – this is split into 9 sub-categories:
    • Inputs of materials, energy and services
    • The operation of facilities and equipment and logistics
    • Outputs of products, services, wastes and emissions.
3. Management environmental performance indicators – that consider the implementation of policies and programmes, the conformity of organizational actions with requirements or expectations, community relations and environment-related financial performance.

Bennett and James have used this set of indicators and have organized these in terms of an 'environment-related performance diamond' (see Bennett and James, 1998 and 1999). There is a consistent message from these works: that the key issues are emissions, use of scarce resources, and waste.

Conclusions

This chapter has considered a wide variety of literature that is concerned with performance measurement. The insights from this literature have clarified the requirements of the stakeholder performance measurement model, although it is clear that there are a lot more measures for some stakeholder groups than others. Clearly shareholders, employee and the environmental measures have been the subject of much more detailed consideration that those of other stakeholder groups. Some of these are more relevant to certain organizations than others. Chapter 6 considers the importance of the measures identified to stakeholder groups within the specific case of the Electricity industry in England and Wales. Chapters 7 and 8 demonstrate how the measures identified may be used in practice to ensure that organizations remain accountable to the society within which they operate. It becomes clear within these chapters, however, that there are certain informational difficulties with some of these measures, which suggest that the performance of organizations to each of their stakeholders can not be measured to the same degree of accuracy nor with the same degree of confidence.

Notes

[1] Organization transformation is the ability of an organization to 'transform itself to meet future challenges.... The transformation processes pursued by a firm can be classified into two broad categories: adaptive specialization and adaptive generalization' (Chakravarthy, 1982, p.449.) Adaptive specialization is predominantly concerned with 'profitably exploiting the firm's current environment' (p.449). 'Adaptive generalization, on the other hand, is concerned with the investment of the firm's net surplus of "slack" resources (Cyert and March, 1963) for improving its ability to adapt to uncertain or even unknown future environments.' (p.449)

[2] To quote Bendheim *et al.* (1998) 'Data on CSP are from the social research firm of Kinder, Lydenberg, Domini (KLD). KLD rates corporate social performance of companies in the Standard & Poor (S & P) 500 listing along 10 dimensions, 4 of which are used for this study. KLD's ratings of employee relations, product (a surrogate for customer relations), community relations, and environmental responsibility were obtained for each year from 1990 to 1993. For details on the construction and empirical use of KLD data as a source of CSP assessment, please refer to Waddock and Graves (1997a, 1997b); Sharfman (1993); and Ruf, Muralidhar, and Paul (1993).' (pp.311-2.)

[3] This suggests that it is only possible to enhance value by spending money, whereas it is possible to spend money that destroys value and therefore would reduce market value.

[4] This is now rather dated, but the interest in employee reporting reduced in the early 1980s. This remains one of the most comprehensive texts in this area and the work of Ingram,

Wadsworth and Brown (1999) appears to support the continued importance of the areas identified.

[5] Maunders (1984) discusses the difficulties and benefits of using both monetary and non-monetary values and recognize that in practice both are problematic.

[6] See also Mathews (1997) for a useful review of the development of social and environmental accounting.

Chapter 5

Value Added Analysis

Introduction

The previous three chapters have in turn considered the role of business in society, social accounting and stakeholder identification and stakeholder performance measurement. The argument has been made that businesses, or organizations more generally, should be held accountable to the societies within which they operate. Therefore a number of metrics and tools of analysis have been considered in order to suggest how corporate social performance can be measured. In chapter 3 *The Corporate Report* was discussed as an interesting development from the accounting profession. Value added statements were commonly reported by UK businesses in the late 1970s and, as discussed in chapter 3, they were argued to show organizational truths that the more traditional profit and loss account could not. In fact it was argued that the value-added statement had the power to demonstrate the co-operative nature of production and the show how the fruits of this production was then distributed between the contributors. It is for these reasons that value added analysis is considered to be an essential part of corporate social performance within this work. In order to demonstrate the power of this analysis this chapter uses the electricity industry in England and Wales as an illustrative case. This industry is essential to the every day life of a modern society such as the UK and therefore it makes an especially interesting case to study. The remainder of this chapter is organized as follows. The next section introduces the case study industry briefly discussing its history and the period under study. There then follows a detailed value added analysis for the period from privatization in 1990/1 to 1997.

Privatization and the Electricity Industry in England and Wales

In order to operationalize this research the electricity industry in England and Wales was chosen as a case study. The importance of this industry to modern life can not be over-stated. People rely upon electricity to an incredible extent in their every day lives. The actual importance of the industry was vividly demonstrated recently. In August 2003 parts of the US and Canada experienced what some have called the worst blackout in North American history. It affected more than 40 million people and it took nearly 30 hours for power to be restored to many areas with some taking much longer than this. President Bush says it is a 'wake-up' call, that the US electricity network is 'antiquated' and that it must be upgraded. The economic cost of the blackout in New York City alone, approximately one fifth of the people affected, was estimated at over US$1billion in terms of lost economic activity and lost perishable goods, but this does not even begin to account for the effect on individual's lives. Within two weeks London was also hit by a power cut, which led Ken Livingston, the mayor of London, to state 'under-investment in the National Grid must not be allowed to cause this kind of chaos in a city like London.'

The recent history of the electricity industry in England and Wales is one of incredible change and immense challenges. In the 1980s UK government policy was, as mentioned earlier, heavily influenced by free market economics. As part of this broader ethos it was believed that the role of the public sector should be reduced. This was to be achieved through a privatization programme that Ogden and Anderson (1995) argued has been one of the most important and controversial policies of recent times. The privatization programme included the sale to the public of the utility industries, such as telecommunications, gas, electricity, and water. Marsh (1991) details the evolution of the policy, from before the 1979 election. The term privatization was not included in the 1979 Conservative manifesto and the policy was only followed to a limited extent in their first term of office. However, it became a major policy instrument in the second and third terms, and it is suggested that this increase in importance may be due to the failure of other economic policies. Marsh comments, therefore, that the privatization programme should not be regarded as a coherent policy. The first utility to be sold was British Telecom in 1984, early in the Conservative government's second term. Each of the utility industries sold contained a natural monopoly, which Foster (1994) defines as an industry where the most efficient supply of a service or product can be achieved through a single organization. This can be either on a national or local scale and is usually exemplified by the use of a grid or network. It has been recognized that the duplication of networks would be an expensive, inefficient and wasteful exercise. The concern with such industries is that the private companies whose primary aim is to enhance the welfare of their shareholders will abuse the inherent monopoly power. This could well be at the expense of consumers, or more significantly, as the products and services provided by the utilities are of such importance, could impact on all members of society. The economic rationality for and political motivations behind the sale of the utility industries has ensured that it is this element of the entire privatization programme that has attracted the most attention and resulted in the need for economic regulation.

There is a fundamental disagreement as to whether the policy was designed for economic or political purposes. Hodges (1997) and Hodges and Wright (1995) examine the reports produced by the National Audit Office (NAO) in reviewing the government departments responsible for 26 privatizations. The reports are a result of investigations, performed by the NAO, to assess the success of the departments responsible for the privatizations in meeting the government objectives for each one. The objectives have not been the same for each privatization but usually they would include a combination of some or all of the following:

- a timely sale;
- maximizing sale proceeds;
- minimizing costs;
- widening of share ownership; and
- the advancement of competition and efficiency in the industry.

Hodges and Wright (1995) note that these investigations found that sales proceeds were either not maximized, or it was uncertain as to whether they had been maximized, in more than half of these privatizations. Also in six of the seven privatizations which set a competition / efficiency objective it was uncertain as to whether this had been achieved. Of the other independent economic analyses of the process completed Vickers and Yarrow (1988) provide one of the most thorough examinations. Within their perceived government objectives they additionally include: reducing government involvement in the industries, reducing the Public Sector Borrowing Requirement (PSBR), gaining political advantage and the weakening of the public sector trade unions. These final two motivations have been studied in more detail. Holtham and Kay (1994) note that there has been a significant interest in possible political motivations, for example a political party's search for votes. McAllister and Studlar (1989) consider that the policy was primarily instigated by the government, as an 'elite interest', not by the electorate. However, they also conclude that the selling of shares to the public increased the Conservative vote, in the 1987 election, by 1.6 per cent. Privatization has had an ambiguous effect on industrial relations (Ferner and Colling, 1991, and 1993) and tends to depend upon whether the management have decided to attempt to maintain stability or take a stronger, more aggressive line. However, the privatized companies have diversified and it is becoming more evident that the employees within these new diversified activities are subject to a different, less unionized form of industrial relations.

Irrespective of the motivations behind the privatization programme, Vickers and Yarrow (1988) believe that its long term success or failure will depend on whether the policy has been successful in improving the efficiency of the respective industries. The question of the continued performance of the industries has become the domain of the individual industry regulators (for example OFTEL, OFGAS, OFFER,[1] OFWAT and ORR).

The economic argument for privatization is based upon an assumption that the private sector promotes efficiency and therefore creates value. However, it has long been argued that these gains are not actually generated through a change in ownership but more by the effects of competition normally faced by firms operating in the private sector. It was recognized at the time of the sale of the utilities that the natural monopoly nature of the industries was problematic. The response was two-fold in that firstly liberalization acts were passed and secondly regulatory offices were set up to 'hold the fort' until sufficient competition arrived (Beesley and Littlechild, 1983).

Regulation is still evident in all of the privatized utility industries. It is this regulatory regime which distinguishes these private sector companies from their counterparts on the stock exchange. The price-cap method of regulation has been adopted in all of these industries. This method was chosen as it theoretically provided the strongest incentives to improve economic efficiency. It attempts to replace and perform the same tasks as the missing competitive, or market, forces. Therefore, in theory, these regulated utility companies are operating under the same conditions as other private sector companies with the exception that the normally 'invisible hand' of the market is replaced by the more visible hand of the regulator. Cooper, Crowther and Carter (2001a, b) argue that there are two processes within the regulation of utilities in the UK an overt and covert review. The overt review is carried on through a formal discussion process and is mainly carried out through the media and public statements. In contrast the covert review is very much a 'private discourse and sharing of information' between the regulator and the companies, and this part of the process has been criticized for lacking transparency.

It can be argued that the privatization of the utility industries evolved through time. The earlier privatizations, namely telecommunications and gas, can be recognized as those where the industry was privatized into a single private sector company. Chronologically the next utility to be privatized was the water industry in England and Wales. At the time of its privatization it was separated into ten vertically integrated regional water and sewerage companies. This horizontal separation into regions may be considered to be an attempt to address one of the fundamental difficulties facing the regulators, namely information asymmetry[2] (Bishop and Kay, 1988; Jenkinson and Mayer, 1996; Vickers and Yarrow, 1988). The advantage of the industry being separated into several companies was the multiple sources of information they provide. The benefits to the regulator are derived from the ability to compare the similar companies and establish benchmarks and therefore implement yardstick competition. A further step was taken in the subsequent privatizations of the electricity industry in England and Wales and the railway industry as these were separated both vertically and horizontally. This is exemplified in the electricity industry in England and Wales, where the structure can be explained as follows:

- Generation, a potentially competitive industry and therefore not requiring formal regulation;
- The National Grid, a natural monopoly as the most efficient service is provided by a single organization (Foster, 1994), that requires regulation; and
- Twelve supply and distribution companies (the RECs), which at the time of privatization held regional monopolies. This regional separation enabled the regulator to use yardstick regulation with the intention of introducing true competition later.

The benefits of this vertical separation of the industry were seen to be the opportunity this provided to minimize regulation. For example, it was believed that electricity generation would not require regulation as it was potentially competitive, and competition was believed to provide the best incentive to efficiency. To this end the generators have never been subject to price-cap regulation, but they have been required to divest some of their generating capacity in order to enhance the competitive nature of this part of this industry. This point will be returned to within the analysis undertaken in later chapters. The only natural monopoly elements are the wires that transmit and distribute the electricity and these would always need to be regulated. Therefore since privatization there has also been a separation of supply from distribution, as it is believed that the supply industry is competitive and therefore not requiring price-cap regulation. To this end the regulator (OFGEM) has removed price-cap regulation from the supply companies. It can be argued therefore that the more separated industry structures are the most theoretically advanced, with the revised structure being based upon the experience gained from earlier privatizations.

The utility industries are of incredible importance in modern societies as they provide goods that are relied upon very heavily. As such they have great importance for the quality of every day life. It is perhaps not surprising that this public policy, of passing these industries from the state, elected by the demos to uphold societal norms, to private sector companies primarily required to satisfy the shareholder, was controversial. It is the combination of monopoly power, albeit potentially tempered somewhat by economic regulation, and private ownership that makes this an interesting case to study.

The Distribution of Value Added

In previous chapters *The Corporate Report* (ASSC, 1975) has been acknowledged as an earlier attempt to provide a report that addressed a wider range of users. These constituencies, or stakeholders, were identified and their information needs considered. An important conclusion was that a value added statement was important, as it would demonstrate how the value added by a company is distributed. Froud *et al.* (1998) suggest that

> the most obvious indicator of significance is the composition of internal costs after excluding purchases: since these costs are equal to value added. (p.113)

The value added analysis undertaken by Shaoul (1997) and Froud *et al.* (1998) very much concentrates upon the distribution of value added between shareholders and employees. Therefore it is primarily interested in the conflicting interest of capital and labour. As part of this conflict the role of capital equipment and expenditure is also considered, as labour can be replaced by capital (here meaning plant, machinery and equipment) in the production process. At the end of chapter 8 of this book the use of and expenditure in capital equipment within the industry is considered. The analysis performed in this book, however, goes further than that adopted in these studies due to its more specifically stakeholder approach. Therefore other stakeholder groups, most especially customers and the environment are given more emphasis than under these earlier value added analyses. Having said this it is important to reiterate that the analysis undertaken here owes much to the research method and insights of Shaoul (1997) and Froud *et al.* (1998).

The analysis undertaken in this chapter and the stakeholder analysis chapter relate to the period form privatization to the election of the Labour government in 1997. As mentioned above this is a period of immense change for the industry and hence makes a unique case study, which has been selected for in depth study. Tables 5.1-5.3 below provide a value added analysis for the three different elements of the electricity industry in England and Wales, namely Generation, Transmission and Supply and Distribution. The tables in this section include data that has been taken from the annual report and accounts for the fifteen companies, the two generators, the National Grid and twelve RECs, over the years 1990/1 to 1997. For each year the relevant data was extracted from individual company accounts and has then been summarized into the three sections of the industry. Firstly we consider the two generating companies together, then The National Grid is considered, and finally the twelve RECs are summarized. The nuclear element of the industry was not privatized until a later date and has therefore been omitted from the analysis performed in this and subsequent chapters.

The Generators

If we consider the generation of electricity since privatization the changes have been significant. Firstly the two generating companies, Powergen and National Power, have been required to divest some of their capacity since privatization. In 1990/1 the year of privatization Powergen and National Power generated 73.1 per cent (Source: CRI, 1998) of the electricity in England and Wales and this had fallen to 60 per cent (Source: Company accounts) in 1994/5 and further to 56.1 per cent in 1996/7 (Source: CRI, 1998). Therefore this is not a complete analysis of the industry. In 1990/1 the remaining capacity was provided almost exclusively by nuclear power, but by 1995 Powergen and National Power were no longer a duopoly in terms of non-nuclear generating capacity. By 2001 and the number of generators had increased again with seven companies providing 80 per cent of the capacity but a larger number of smaller companies providing the rest. Due to this enforced divestment and the mature nature of the industry (electricity demand is increasing in England and Wales, but only marginally as is demonstrated within the Environmental section of the stakeholder analysis chapter) the revenues of these two companies have been constrained. In fact by the end of the period under review the total turnover of these two companies has fallen by more than 10 per cent and this is nominal terms. The actual changes in electricity generated and prices is considered in more detail in the stakeholder analysis chapter, but it is crucially important to recognize at this point the constrained nature of the turnover for these two companies from their core activities over this period of time. Table 5.1 below provides a detailed breakdown of the value added by the generation companies in each of the years ending in 1991, the year of privatization, through to 1997.

Table 5.1 Distribution of value added by generation companies

	1991	1992	1993	1994	1995	1996	1997
	£m	£m	£m	£m	£m	£m	£m
Total Income	7,029	7,798	7,536	6,573	6,838	6,881	6,298
Purchases (materials and services)	5,746	6,098	5,711	4,658	4,715	4,611	4,139
Value added / internal costs	1,283	1,700	1,825	1,915	2,123	2,270	2,159
Gross labour costs	570	556	456	366	320	298	274
Charged to Balance sheet	-9	-12	-15	-4	0	-1	-2
Charged to profit and loss account	561	544	441	362	320	297	272
Depreciation	233	305	333	333	481	450	497
Net Interest	-112	-22	46	67	72	30	84
Tax	251	266	300	286	337	366	291
Dividends	113	188	217	259	300	418	1682
Retained profit	237	419	488	608	613	709	-667
Value added	1,283	1,700	1,825	1,915	2,123	2,270	2,159
	%	%	%	%	%	%	%
Total Income	100.0	100.0	100.0	100.0	100.0	100.0	100.0
Purchases (materials and services)	81.7	78.2	75.8	70.9	69.0	67.0	65.7
Value added / internal costs	18.3	21.8	24.2	29.1	31.0	33.0	34.3
Gross labour costs	44.4	32.7	25.0	19.1	15.1	13.1	12.7
Charged to Balance sheet	-0.7	-0.7	-0.8	-0.2	0.0	0.0	-0.1
Charged to profit and loss account	43.7	32.0	24.2	18.9	15.1	13.1	12.6
Depreciation	18.2	17.9	18.2	17.4	22.7	19.8	23.0
Net Interest	-8.7	-1.3	2.5	3.5	3.4	1.3	3.9
Tax	19.6	15.6	16.4	14.9	15.9	16.1	13.5
Dividends	8.8	11.1	11.9	13.5	14.1	18.4	77.9
Retained profit	18.5	24.6	26.7	31.7	28.9	31.2	-30.9
Value added	100.0	100.0	100.0	100.0	100.0	100.0	100.0

We can see from Table 5.1 above that over this period of time the value added as a percentage of turnover rose from 18.3 per cent to 34.3 per cent. This increase in percentage terms is accentuated by the fall in levels of turnover noted above, but does still indicate a significant decrease in the purchase of materials and services from £5,746million to £4,715million. Whilst turnover has fallen by approximately 10 per cent over the period the level of purchases has fallen by nearly 18 per cent. Therefore the increase in value added has been produced by the reduction in purchases, which would appear to be at the expense of the suppliers of materials and services to these companies.

The increase in the value added (from £1,283million in 1990/91 to a high of £2,270million in 1995/6) partly explains the dramatic fall in the proportion of value added relating to labour costs. In actual fact, whilst the absolute level of value added has increased by more than 68 per cent the total remuneration paid to employees has fallen, in absolute terms by almost 52 per cent (1991, £570m; 1997, £274m). The combination of the increase in value added and the fall in employee remuneration results in an amazing fall in labour's share of value added from 43.7 per cent to 12.6 per cent. This level of fall will be considered in more detail in the employees' section of the stakeholder analysis chapter later.

The level of depreciation in these companies has more than doubled over the period. Powergen has 'accelerated depreciation' in each year from 1995 onwards, and the amounts involved are £61 million in 1995, £57 million in 1996 and £98 million in 1997. This is to reflect 'the write-down of certain plant at coal and oil-fired power stations' (Powergen, 1997). Also, in 1995 the depreciation charge of National Power was significantly higher than in any other year, and this is only partly explained by 'a charge of £31million relating to the permanent diminution in the net book value of a power station' (National Power, 1995). These items explain the raised levels of depreciation in 1995 and 1997. The level of depreciation for these years is higher than in any other.

In 1991, the first year after privatization, both companies had net interest receivable and since this time there has been a shift towards net interest payable. This shift has resulted in both companies becoming net interest payers, although the level of net interest paid is very small and is never above 4 per cent of value added. This would appear to imply that debt is not an important source of finance in these companies, although it is being increasingly used. The tax charge has remained relatively constant over the period of time, although it has fallen as a percentage of value added.

The largest gain in share of value added has been that of the shareholders in terms of profit attributable to shareholders, which is made up of dividends and retained profit. The level of dividends has increased significantly and consistently each year until 1997. In 1997 the level of dividends increased due to a special dividend of £1,207m paid by National Power, and related to a 'major capital restructuring' (National Power 1997, p.5). Retained profit also increased markedly until 1997 when it is adversely affected by the level of dividends just mentioned. If dividends and retained profit are taken together this indicates an increase from 27.3 per cent in 1991 to 47 per cent in 1997. In absolute terms this increase in the shareholders' share of value added is even more dramatic. From a total of £350million in 1991 the amount of dividends and retained profit has effectively trebled to £1,127million in 1996 and £1,015million in 1997.

From the value added analysis of Powergen and National Power we can clearly see some significant changes over the period under consideration here. These changes are effectively redistributing the benefits from these companies between stakeholder groups. The most significant changes since privatization have been the fall, in absolute and relative terms, of labour costs and purchases of materials and services and the increase in dividends and retained profit. The increase to shareholders can not be seen as value created, as it has come at a time when revenues for these companies are falling. This clearly demonstrates a redistribution from the labour force and suppliers to shareholders. As mentioned above one way to reduce employees is to replace them with capital equipment. Therefore, as part of the broader stakeholder analysis undertaken in chapter 8, consideration is given to the levels of capital investment made by these companies over this period of time. Suffice it to say here that subsequent to privatization there has not been a marked increase in the levels of capital investment undertaken in the key areas of generation and transmission.

The National Grid

Data pertaining to the distribution of value added by The National Grid is given in Table 5.2. The National Grid was privatized in 1990/1, owned by the twelve RECs and then floated on the London stock exchange in November 1995. The National Grid's core business, from which it earns the majority of its income, the running of the transmission network, is subject to price-cap regulation. The National Grid's total income increased in each year from 1991 to 1996 such that in 1996 the level of total income was nearly 30 per cent higher than in 1991. There appears to be a change in the results of National Grid in the year 1996/7. Up to this time total income had increased every year and the percentage of value added had been relatively constant, although slightly increasing each year until 1994/5. This is the case because the absolute level of purchases had been increasing at a similar, but marginally lower, rate than revenues. In the year 1996/7 total income fell for the first time and the percentage value added rose significantly. The figures in fact suggest that purchases of materials and services fell by more than 50 per cent in this year from £525.6million to £258.3million. The most significant cause of the increase in value-added was that there was a 'profit on deconsolidation of a subsidiary undertaking' equalling £173.2m (National Grid, 1997). As this amount does not increase turnover, but is simply included as a profit figure, it effectively reduces the purchases figure. Therefore purchases before this deconsolidation profit is equal to £431.5million, which is equal to 30.6 per cent of turnover. This is still a reduction on the previous years, but is not of the same order as that suggested in the table below.

  This profit on deconsolidation also effects the levels of profit attributable to shareholders in 1996/7, which according to the table appear to be approaching 54 per cent. If this is recalculated without deconsolidaton profits we would see that the shareholders' share of value added is 46 per cent in 1996/7. This is relatively in line with the levels of 44.6 per cent and 45.3 per cent in 1995/6 and 1994/5 respectively, but this does reflect an increase when compared to the 36.0 per cent in 1990/1. In 1995/6 there is a very large dividend paid out to shareholders and this relates to 'the capital reconstruction which occurred during the year ended 31 March 1996' (The National Grid, 1997, p.12).

Table 5.2 Distribution of value added by The National Grid

	1991	1992	1993	1994	1995	1996	1997
	£m	£m	£m	£m	£m	£m	£m
Total Income	1144.3	1319.9	1391.8	1425.0	1428.3	1487.0	1408.4
Purchases (materials and services)	422.9	467.6	488.5	469.7	469.2	525.6	258.3
Value added / internal costs	721.4	852.3	903.3	955.3	959.1	961.4	1150.1
Gross labour costs	182.1	216.8	219.2	222.4	197.8	171.9	173.4
Charged to Balance sheet	-17.0	-16.8	-25.0	-27.2	-28.3	-22.6	-19.2
Charged to profit and loss account	165.1	200.0	194.2	195.2	169.5	149.3	154.2
Depreciation	91.6	93.5	116.3	129.6	144.6	147.4	134.5
Net Interest	79.0	60.9	59.6	51.0	34.4	40.6	51.2
Tax	126.2	163.2	151.9	139.7	175.8	195.5	188.8
Dividends	104.5	117.0	129.3	149.1	162.0	1957.0	190.7
Retained profit	155.0	217.7	252.0	290.7	272.8	-1528.4	430.7
Value added	721.4	852.3	903.3	955.3	959.1	961.4	1150.1
	%	%	%	%	%	%	%
Total Income	100.0	100.0	100.0	100.0	100.0	100.0	100.0
Purchases (materials and services)	37.0	35.4	35.1	33.0	32.9	35.3	18.3
Value added / internal costs	63.0	64.6	64.9	67.0	67.1	64.7	81.7
Gross labour costs	25.2	25.4	24.3	23.3	20.6	17.9	15.1
Charged to Balance sheet	-2.4	-2.0	-2.8	-2.8	-3.0	-2.4	-1.7
Charged to profit and loss account	22.9	23.5	21.5	20.4	17.7	15.5	13.4
Depreciation	12.7	11.0	12.9	13.6	15.1	15.3	11.7
Net Interest	11.0	7.1	6.6	5.3	3.6	4.2	4.5
Tax	17.5	19.1	16.8	14.6	18.3	20.3	16.4
Dividends	14.5	13.7	14.3	15.6	16.9	203.6	16.6
Retained profit	21.5	25.5	27.9	30.4	28.4	-159.0	37.4
Value added	100.0	100.0	100.0	100.0	100.0	100.0	100.0

Gross labour costs within The National Grid have fallen in absolute terms when comparing 1996/7 with 1990/1. This does not, however, accurately portray the whole story, as it can be seen that gross labour costs increased each year from 1990/1 to 1993/4 and since this time has fallen. Even in this first four years labour's share of value added was falling, but since 1993/4 this decrease has been more marked. Over the whole period labour's share of value added has fallen from a high of 25.4 per cent in 1991/2 to a low of 15.1 per cent in 1996/7. The figure in 1996/7, however, overstates the decrease somewhat due to the deconsolidation profit discussed above. If this profit is ignored then labour's share of value added remains more in line with the approximately 18 per cent recorded in 1995/6. The fall in labour's percentage of value added is significant, but not on the same scale as that noted in the case of the generation companies.

There is a significant fall in the levels of net interest paid between 1990/1 and 1994/5, from 11.0 per cent to 3.6 per cent and then the levels start to increase again. The increase is probably due to the capital restructuring mentioned above, which was undertaken after flotation in November 1995. Even after this marginal increase the net interest payable remains at a relatively low level of 4.5 per cent by 1996/7. Levels of depreciation do vary year on year, but with an underlying increase over the period. There is a fall in the year 1996/7, but if we ignore the deconsolidation profit the fall is not as significant. In terms of tax payable there has been some variation over the period but there is no discernible trend to these movements in relative terms. In absolute terms taxation has increased as the business has reported higher turnover and profits over the period.

As with the generation companies the largest gains are made by the shareholders and this is clearly the case in terms of both dividends and retained profit. One difference from the generating companies, however, is that in this case the increases to shareholders do not appear to be a redistribution from other stakeholders, although there is an element of this. In fact if we look at the absolute level of value added in the period from 1990/1 to 1994/5 we see that it has increased by £237.7million. Over the same period the profit attributable to shareholders has increased by £175.3million and therefore this could have been funded by the increase in value added. The story is less clear in the following two years due to the flotation, capital restructuring, special dividends and profit on deconsolidation.

The Regional Electricity Companies

Table 5.3 demonstrates the distribution of value added by the RECs. As with The National Grid, the RECs are subject to price-cap regulation on their core activities for this period of time. In the first years after privatization the RECs jointly owned the National Grid, but this changed in November 1995. The sale of the National Grid in the year 1995/6 has a significant effect on the figures reported in that year, as each of the RECs recorded exceptional items relating to the profits from that sale. As a consequence of the flotation of The National Grid the RECs were also obliged to provide a customer discount in the year and this explains why total income is lower in 1996 than in any other year except for the first. In fact in the first three years considered here the total income of the RECs increased by 13 per cent, was relatively constant for two years and then fell markedly in 1996. The level of total income does not return to its 1994/5 levels in 1996/7. This decrease may well reflect the price reviews carried out by the regulator of distribution businesses in England and Wales. In April 1995 there was a price review that, on average, required companies to make a one-off price cut of 14 per cent on the distribution element of their income and to reduce real prices by 2 per cent in future years. In April 1996, however, the regulator decided that these price controls had not been strict enough and therefore ordered a further one-off price cut of, on average, 11 per cent and an annual reduction of real prices by 3 per cent. This change of heart by the regulator was claimed to be a result of the take-over activity demonstrating that the RECs had greater resources at their disposal than had been originally thought. Therefore in the 1997 accounts of the companies the distribution price of electricity was required to be approximately 23.5 per cent lower than in the year ended 31 March 1995. The distribution business accounts for approximately one-quarter of the RECs turnover in both 1991 and 1997 (CRI, 1998). Therefore the effect of this reduction in distribution prices would be to reduce the turnover of the RECs by approximately 5 per cent and the actual turnover of the RECs fell by 4.5 per cent from 1994/5 to 1996/7. This decrease in the level of total income also explains the fall in the level of value added as a proportion of total income from 24.3 per cent in 1994/5 to 21.9 per cent in 1996/7. The level of purchases in 1996/7 is only marginally lower than in 1994/5 and therefore does not sufficiently compensate for the decrease in total income.

The other effects of the flotation are a dividend received from The National Grid, some tax effects and by far the largest is a 'Specie dividend on flotation of The National Grid Group plc' (Northern Electric, 1996, p30). In total in the year 1995/6 £5,120.9million were paid out to shareholders in dividends, more than five times the amounts paid out in the previous year.

The absolute level of employee remuneration falls from a high of £1,650million in 1991/2 to a low of £1,170million in 1996/7. This is a fall of approximately 29 per cent and when combined with the increases to value added this explains the very large reduction in labours' share of value added (53.7 per cent, 1991; 36.2 per cent, 1995). This decrease in employee remuneration is in contrast to increases in the absolute and relative terms of levels of depreciation, net interest and tax. In the case of depreciation we can see that the largest increase is in the final year and this is explained by the fact that some of the companies elected to accelerate depreciation in 1996/7. Net interest paid increases even more dramatically over the last two years of analysis and this is due to capital restructuring within the companies resulting in higher levels of debt. Until 1997 the net interest paid accounted for a small share of value added, but as the companies were taken over so debt levels have increased.

Finally we can consider the shareholders' share of value added. The level of dividends paid as a percentage of value added has risen significantly from 8.1per cent in 1990/1 to 25.6 per cent in 1994/5. As mentioned earlier there are special dividends paid in 1995/6 that explains the extremely unusual figures for that year. The dividend in 1996/7, however, remains more than 50 per cent higher than in 1994/5. If we consider profit attributable to shareholders, as consisting of dividends and retained profits, we see a familiar story, as the level rose every year in total from 28.3 per cent in 1990/1 to 40.1 per cent in 1994/5 and to 50.9 per cent in 1995/6. In 1997 profit attributable to shareholders falls back to 30.6 per cent. If we compare the absolute levels of profit attributable to shareholders in 1996/7 as opposed to 1994/5 we see a significant drop from £1,502.5million to £987.2million. The major explanatory factor of this decrease in profit attributable to shareholders is the £691.1million fall in total income as compared to a relatively smaller reduction in purchases (£161.4million).

Table 5.3 Distribution of value added by the RECs

	1991 £000m	1992 £000m	1993 £000m	1994 £000m	1995 £000m	1996 £000m	1997 £000m
Total Income	13.63	14.88	15.43	15.26	15.42	13.80	14.73
Purchases (materials and services)	10.79	11.43	11.88	11.64	11.67	9.16	11.50
Value added / internal costs	2.84	3.45	3.55	3.62	3.75	4.64	3.23
Gross labour costs	1.52	1.65	1.59	1.55	1.48	1.27	1.17
Charged to Balance sheet	-0.20	-0.21	-0.25	-0.26	-0.25	-0.28	-0.30
Charged to profit and loss account	1.32	1.44	1.34	1.29	1.23	0.99	0.87
Depreciation	0.35	0.37	0.42	0.45	0.47	0.50	0.55
Net Interest	0.04	0.17	0.12	0.07	0.06	0.12	0.27
Tax	0.33	0.41	0.44	0.46	0.49	0.67	0.55
Dividends	0.23	0.37	0.43	0.50	0.96	5.12	1.46
Retained profit	0.57	0.69	0.80	0.85	0.54	-2.76	-0.47
Value added	2.84	3.45	3.55	3.62	3.76	4.64	3.23
	%	%	%	%	%	%	%
Total Income	100.0	100.0	100.0	100.0	100.0	100.0	100.0
Purchases (materials and services)	79.2	76.8	77.0	76.3	75.7	66.4	78.1
Value added / internal costs	20.8	23.2	23.0	23.7	24.3	33.6	21.9
Gross labour costs	53.7	47.9	44.8	42.9	39.6	27.4	36.2
Charged to Balance sheet	-7.1	-6.0	-7.0	-7.1	-6.8	-6.1	-9.2
Charged to profit and loss account	46.6	41.9	37.8	35.8	32.8	21.3	27.0
Depreciation	12.1	10.6	11.7	12.3	12.5	10.9	17.1
Net Interest	1.4	4.9	3.3	1.9	1.6	2.6	8.3
Tax	11.7	11.9	12.5	12.7	13.1	14.4	16.9
Dividends	8.1	10.9	12.2	13.9	25.6	110.4	45.2
Retained profit	20.2	19.9	22.5	23.4	14.5	-59.5	-14.6
Value added	100.0	100.0	100.0	100.0	100.0	100.0	100.0

In this value added analysis of the RECs we see some familiar stories to those of the generators and The National Grid. We once again see a remarkable increase in the shareholders' share of value added, as the period progresses. This is partly explained by the increase in value added, but more significantly by the redistribution of wealth from labour. As is the case in the generating companies there is a dramatic decrease in the absolute levels of nominal employee remuneration that suggests a redistribution, as opposed to a creation, of value. The pattern of this redistribution is actually changed in the last two years of the analysis. Over this period the regulator recognizes the shareholder gains being made and acts to redistribute these benefits. The redistribution, however, is not back to the employees, but is rather passed on to the consumers through lower prices.

Conclusions from the Value Added Analysis

The value added analysis undertaken here covers a very turbulent time for the industry. Firstly the companies analyzed were privatized and subject to price-cap regulation. Then in 1995 the government disposed of its golden shares, which made the companies possible take-over targets and in fact all twelve RECs were subject to take-over bids in the two years from 31 March 1995 and 31 March 1997. The effect of this will be considered in more detail as part of the shareholder and stakeholder analysis chapters later. In addition that RECs disposed of their shares in The National Grid, which was floated on the London Stock Exchange. Finally, at the end of this period a general election was in the offing and it was widely predicted, and correctly so, that the UK would see its first Labour government for nearly two decades. This in itself brings risks to the privatized utility industries as there was, again correctly, talk of a windfall tax being levied upon them. There appears, within the period from privatization to 31 March 1997 to be two sub periods, which are distinguished by the government's sale of its golden share on 31 March 1995. In order to demonstrate this the first half of this conclusion will discuss the changes in the period from privatization to 31 March 1995 and then the final two years will be considered.

The two most significant changes in the period to 31 March 1995 that are consistent across all aspects of the industry are the increase in the shareholders' share of value added and the fall in labour's share in value added. In absolute terms the increase in profit attributable to shareholders has been dramatic as it has risen from £1,411.3million in the year ending 31 March 1991 to £2,580.3million in the year ending 31 March 1995. This represents nearly an 83 per cent increase in nominal terms in the period. This increase can also be expressed in real terms by adjusting for inflation in the period. The Retail Price Index (RPI) in the UK rose from 131.4 in March 1991 to 147.5 in March 1995 an increase of 12.25 per cent. This would suggest a real increase in profit attributable to shareholders of approximately 63 per cent. If we now aggregate employment remuneration in all fifteen companies we see that in the year 1990/1 total employee remuneration (including that charged to the balance sheet) was £2,276.5m and by the year 1994/5 this had fallen to £2,002.7m. This represents a 12 per cent decrease in absolute terms although in real terms, after taking into account inflation, the real decrease in employment remuneration is equal to 22 per cent. This level of reduction is significant and can be achieved in one of two ways, namely by reducing the number of employees or by paying the same number of employees a lower rate of pay. The exact nature of the changes in employment are considered in detail in the employees section of the stakeholder analysis chapter later.

This shift in value added from employees to shareholders is apparent, but this analysis is not sufficient to clearly portray how the other stakeholders have fared. From this analysis it is not clear how these companies have performed for their consumers, their suppliers[3] and the environment. It is especially important to remember that for this period of time consumers were effectively involuntary stakeholders as they had no choice of supplier and electricity is a pre-requisite for modern life. In order to get a fuller picture of the changes in performance over this period we will therefore also consider these stakeholders in the stakeholder analysis chapter.

In the two years from 31 March 1995 to 31 March 1997 there are some clearly different circumstances facing some stakeholder groups. For some groups these changes in circumstances simply reinforce earlier trends whereas in others it marks a change in fortune. Labour's share of value added has continued to fall, although perhaps not as dramatically. Shareholders appear to have continued to prosper, with exceptional dividends being paid out by the RECs, The National Grid and National Power. However, for the first time regulation appears to have made its presence felt with the reduction in the RECs total income in 1996/7 feeding directly through to the shareholders. In addition, capital restructuring has meant an increased role for debt in the industry and many of the companies have deemed it necessary to accelerate depreciation.

As a result of the changes in ownership of the companies the data for analysis also becomes more difficult to obtain and analyze. The RECs become parts of larger groups of companies and lost their stock market listing. In contrast The National Grid was floated on the London Stock Exchange for the first time. Important caveats are always necessary when discussing reported accounting results, but these must be made even more vociferously here. Firstly, the motivation for so-called creative accounting is high in this period, as the companies are threatened by take-over and government taxes. Secondly, for the RECs there are exceptional gains made on the sale of their holdings in the National Grid, and as they become incorporated into larger groups the difficulties of ring-fencing activities and ensuring accurate transfer pricing become more acute. These concerns with the data do not, I believe, detract from the story told here. The evidence presented above clearly shows a redistribution of wealth between certain stakeholder groups. This point, however, will be returned to where necessary in the stakeholder analysis chapter.

Notes

[1] OFFER and OFGAS have now been merged to form OFGEM.

[2] Information asymmetry is where one group, in this case the managers, has more information than another group, in this case the regulator. Where information asymmetry exists it is possible for the group with the additional information to mislead the other group. The ability to do this, it is argued, is reduced where there are other sources of information, such as other companies in similar circumstances.

[3] The increase in value added, and hence the decrease in purchases, would suggest that suppliers have been squeezed since privatization.

Chapter 6

Stakeholder Performance
Measurement in Practice

Introduction

Chapter 4 considered the accounting and performance measurement literature in order to identify relevant measures for each of the stakeholder groups identified in chapter 3. This chapter seeks confirmation of the importance of these measures in the post-privatization electricity industry in England and Wales. Therefore it documents a series of interviews that were, on the whole, undertaken over a period from June 2000 to March 2001. The first round of interviews was with representatives of the stakeholders identified. The aim of these interviews was to uncover what each stakeholder group considered to be the key issues in the industry. Further, it was then hoped to see how these issues were managed and corporate performance measured by each of the stakeholder groups.

The findings from these interviews were used in conjunction with the reviewed literature as a basis for a model of stakeholder objectives and drivers of performance. This model was then used as a starting point for the interviews with the organizations operating in the industry. Representatives of one organization from each of the vertically distinct parts of the industry (i.e. generation, transmission, distribution and supply) were interviewed. These interviews were rather more structured, as the developed model was discussed. Finally, interviews were held with the secondary social stakeholders government and regulators, as their influence had been emphasized by both the stakeholders and the companies. This is to say that one way in which the stakeholders and companies tried to manage stakeholder issues was through government or regulator lobbying. In addition an exploratory interview was held with a representative of the regulator at a much earlier stage in the research.

Stakeholder Interviews

Interviews were chosen as the method of data collection, as it was felt that this would give a more comprehensive insight into the pertinent issues. Interviews were preferred to questionnaires because this enabled a greater richness of data. It is acknowledged that this method enforces a smaller sample and can be questioned on grounds of objectivity. Questionnaires, however, often with worryingly low response rates, can also be subject to bias. For example it is only those recipients with strong views that respond. The interviews were separated into three distinct phases. Firstly, stakeholder representatives were interviewed in an attempt to discover what they considered to be the key issues in the industry. Interviews were then carried out with representatives of companies operating in the industry and finally representatives of the regulator and the government. First contact was made by letter to an appropriate person in the relevant organization. In this respect websites were extremely useful and it was possible to identify an appropriate person. The response to these letters was disappointing and in fact it was the follow up phone calls where agreement to be interviewed was reached. Having said this, it was still useful to have sent the letters so that when the phone call was made the person had, usually, some vague recollection of seeing something about it.

As a very large number of individuals make up each of these stakeholder groups it was decided to interview representatives from organizations that had a specific interest in the needs of these stakeholders. Therefore representatives from the following types of organizations were interviewed as proxies for the stakeholders themselves:

Table 6.1 Stakeholder representatives

Stakeholder group	Organizations visited
Shareholders	Institutional shareholders (A)
	Brokers (B)
Employees	Unions (C and D)
Consumers	Consumer groups (E, F and G)
Suppliers	Organizations supplying primary fuel (H and I)
The environment	Environmental pressure groups (J and K)

A specific problem with this approach is that the representative of the stakeholder group may have different or additional goals to those of the stakeholders themselves. As mentioned above, this type of bias has been addressed by ensuring that more than one stakeholder representative, always from different organizations, was visited for each stakeholder group. In the table above each interviewee is represented by a letter and these are used to distinguish between interviewees where quotations from interviewees are given later in this chapter.

The second stage of interviews was with representatives of the companies. A representative from a company operating in each of the elements of the industry, namely generation, transmission, supply and distribution was interviewed. Gaining access to the company management was more difficult than for stakeholder representatives and required significant time and confidentiality restrictions, as well as questions such as 'What's in it for me?' This is not a problem unique to this research and Easterby-Smith *et al.* (1991) note that as managers are busy and powerful people they will not allow research access 'unless they can see some commercial or personal advantage to be derived from it.' Further they note that the 'more the company gives, in time and money, the more it expects in return.' In this case the contribution required from the representatives was kept to a minimum with one member of staff interviewed at their place of work. In order to obtain this level of access it was necessary to offer both confidentiality and also findings from the research. The access obtained was at the level just below the board and the managers interviewed were obviously adept at public relations and handling face-to-face interviews.

During the stakeholder and company interviews the importance of the government and regulator was regularly reiterated and so the final interviews carried out were with these secondary stakeholders. In addition the very first interview undertaken, whilst the research was still being scoped, was with the regulator (OFFER as they were at that time). This interview was most valuable in gaining an understanding of the role of the regulator, the workings of the industry, and the level of interest in stakeholders.

The interviews were, on the whole, undertaken over a period from June 2000 to March 2001. In total representatives from 17 different organizations were interviewed and this resulted in an extremely wide-ranging sample of the industry. Due to this breadth of coverage it was not considered possible to obtain a greater depth of access than a single interview with each organization. The exception to this is the regulator, who was visited at a very early stage in the research and then revisited at the end. The majority of organizations were also only willing to agree to a single visit and therefore this limited the opportunity for further interviews with multiple representatives of the organizations. It is felt that the coverage obtained is significant, but to reiterate, attempts to triangulate the findings from these interviews have been made.

The stakeholder interviews were very open and semi-structured in that the initial letter had detailed four or five issues that could be discussed. So for example the letter sent to the unions, as a proxy for employees, suggested that the following issues would be discussed:

- the information presently available to employees and their representatives;
- the information needs of employees;
- employee remuneration in the privatized electricity companies;
- employee welfare in the privatized electricity companies; and
- the performance of electricity companies since privatization.

Each of these areas could be considered to be a 'topic guide' (Jones, 1985) and this enabled a framework for the interviews. The use of semi-structured interviews was considered appropriate as the interviews wanted to 'understand the constructs that the interviewee uses as a basis for her opinions and beliefs about a particular matter or situation' and because the subject matter was in some cases confidential (Easterby-Smith *et al.*, 1991). The interviews with the representatives of the companies, the regulator and the government used the stakeholder performance model developed from the literature and the stakeholder interviews as the starting point. In addition to the broad questions some organization-specific questions were also asked. The reasons for this were threefold. Firstly, such knowledge was perceived as important to demonstrate to the interviewee that some understanding had already been obtained and as such I was 'on the ball'. Secondly, the questions related to specific instances relevant to the themes discussed and as such increased the richness of the data. Finally, as the interview time was so restricted it was important that not too much time was wasted going over information already in the public domain.

All except one of the interviews were carried out face-to-face. The one exception was an environmental group where the interview was carried out over the telephone. It is not believed that this weakens the evidence from that interview, although it is recognized that certain subtleties can be lost over the telephone. Also, for this interview, as with all of the interviews, summary interview notes were written up and sent to the interviewee. This was done to enable the interviewee to review my understanding of what was said and to correct any misinterpretations that might have been made. Each interviewee was made aware that this would be done at the start of the interview and it is hoped that this enabled the interviewee to feel more comfortable about the process and more trusting of me. In the same vein the interviews were not tape recorded as it was felt, due to the confidential nature of some of the material, that this might be counterproductive. Easterby-Smith *et al.* (1991) also note that tape recording interviews can result in the loss of 'potentially revealing insights', as the interviewee may be conscious of the tape.

The following section takes each of the stakeholder groups in turn and from the interviews identifies stakeholder issues, objectives and drivers of performance.

Shareholders

Shareholders are often seen as the privileged stakeholder group in many large companies, where some explicitly adopt a 'shareholder value approach' (see for example Rappaport, 1986). This is also reflected in accounting, where it is thought that the annual report and accounts is specifically designed and targeted at shareholders and, some may say, other providers of capital. It is therefore interesting to consider how important the actual annual report and accounts of a company are to shareholders. Interviews were held with supposedly sophisticated investors or users of financial information, as opposed to the 'private shareholder' (Lee and Tweedie, 1977 and 1981). The importance of this distinction is '[t]hat sophisticated shareholders use available financial information more intensely, and have a greater understanding of it than private shareholders' (Lee and Tweedie, 1981, p.3). The specific aim of the sophisticated users is to reach an investment decision as to which shares to buy, hold, sell or to recommend. Interestingly both of the interviewees (an institutional shareholder and a broker: see Table 6.1) suggested that much of the information contained within the annual report and accounts were of limited use, with one suggesting that 'sometimes there is something tucked away but generally not' (B). Both saw that the main purpose of reviewing the annual report and accounts was to ensure that the message is consistent with their own understanding of the situation and to gain data for their valuation models.

The actual numbers from the accounts are important and are used in developing valuation models for the companies. These valuation models are considered to be extremely important in making the investment decision or recommendation. One analyst suggested that a company's worth 'distils down to a DCF [discounted cash flow] model' and that effectively you are trying to 'crystallize what drives the business into five or six things' (B). These things change depending on the nature of the business being considered and therefore what is considered key for a generator within the electricity industry will not necessarily be the same as for a supplier of electricity, let alone companies in completely different industries. Therefore information such as customer base, cost control and efficiency gains are important. A key element of these discounted cash flow models is the discount rate and the greater this is the less influence the future has. As we shall see later, it is this discounting of the future that other stakeholder groups are most concerned about.

As well as the accounting based information discussed above, the more strategic plans of the company are also considered fundamental. The primary source of this information is not the annual report and accounts but press releases and meetings and briefings with the company's management. Effectively, according to one interviewee, if you are an institutional shareholder or analyst with a large investment bank 'access is not a problem' and 'if the company is too busy to see you then you know that they are up to something' (B). For the analysts these meetings present an opportunity to gain as much information as possible, although the company is obviously extremely aware as to what it is legal to do and say. As this is the case the analysts are trying to 'read between the lines' (A) and to infiltrate the CEO's mind to 'see what he's thinking, what he's seeing, where he sees it going' (B). Specifically, signals are looked for in terms of how the companies are going to 'get bigger'. This growth can be either international or domestic in nature, but either way is considered crucial.

As well as the company-specific considerations of financial models and strategy, both analysts stressed the importance of macro factors. The institutional investor stated that it is 'best not to go into too much detail' as the 'macro influences can be huge' (A). The mood of the market, in terms of wanting, say, high-tech shares, has in the recent past had a significantly dampening effect on the value of defensive stocks such as utilities. Other macro effects such as interest rates were quoted as having significant influence. Then there are also industry-wide influences, most obviously in the electricity industry the actions of the regulator and the advent of competition.

The interviewees consider the impact of the companies on other stakeholders where relevant. In terms of consumers this is only considered a key driver, perhaps not surprisingly, at the consumer end of the industry, i.e. in supply. Here, increasing the customer base is seen as a key objective, although no distinction was apparent as to whether this was achieved organically or through acquisition. Customer satisfaction will be more important as the industry becomes more competitive. The changing conditions for employees in the industry, in terms of reductions in employee numbers, is considered to be the 'inevitable end' as the nationalized industry was, to quote one interviewee 'overmanned and overpaid'

(B). He continued that announcements of job cuts are considered to be 'healthy' as the 'older generation' need to be replaced by 'younger people to innovate' and the other shareholder interviewee suggested that 'it can only be good news for consumers' (A). Both analysts felt that the environment should be important and that it was increasing in importance but that 'it still takes a poor second place to economics and politics' (B). Poor environmental performance would lead the institutional investor to write to the management to 'express concerns', but it is only in 'exceptional circumstances', such as 'Shell and Brent Spar', that the shares will be sold (A).

Employees

Employee representatives see employee welfare as key and this is influenced by many factors. Employee satisfaction surveys are used infrequently by the Union; rather the information is gathered more informally from the stewards who are in constant contact with the work force. Since privatization the decreased level of job satisfaction is almost 'universal, almost like teachers demoralizing' (C). This is attributed to an increase in job insecurity plus an increase in stress and pressure in terms of workload. This increased stress and pressure is exacerbated for many employees by the nature of the work in terms of the health, safety and security issues.

Job insecurity in the industry is high, as there has been a large decrease in the number of direct employees and the previous belief that a job in the electricity industry was a 'job for life has gone' (D). It is acknowledged that increased efficiency and productivity, '40 per cent since privatization' is a 'valid element' (C), as there was some 'slack in the system', which was a result of the 'philosophy of security of supply' (D). There is now a concern that this has gone too far. It is believed that these reductions will have serious long-term implications, not least in terms of 'the threat to health and safety' (C). The report of the NII (Nuclear Industry Inspectorate) has been seen to offer some hope for the future as it is one of the first official documents that actually reports 'links between over-cutting employees and the threat to health and safety' (C). As well as the health and safety the union is also concerned that standards are falling and they suggest that the distribution network is 'now at a point of crisis' (C) in terms of the ability to repair lines. This problem is accentuated in certain geographical areas, where the weather is more likely to damage the network, and by the increased use of sub-contractors, who are often thought to be less skilled, less motivated and less well remunerated. Similarly, introducing new working practices such as multi-skilling has also left employees with a feeling of job insecurity, and 'bad management of [this] change' (C) has not helped. As price controls increase pressure on companies the Unions interviewed feel that it should not always be jobs first. This is considered a 'short-term approach to take' (C) and it would be better in the long-term if sometimes profits were cut and not jobs.

Remuneration in the electricity industry is still 'pretty good' (C) and the reductions in employee numbers have, to date, been managed through voluntary redundancies, which have also been on 'good' terms. This does not mean that there have not been changes since privatization, and negotiations are now company-wide or even by individual function within a company, as opposed to industry-wide. In addition the structure of pay is now very different with, for example, PRP and individual bonuses becoming more important and therefore the single percentage deal means less than before. From the Union's perspective negotiators are provided with the deals to date in other companies and will use these to negotiate their own settlement. In addition the negotiators will seek advice on an average deal 'below which they wouldn't go' (C). The negotiators also like to have as much information on the company as possible. The annual report and accounts is important and especially last year's profitability. A final factor in negotiations is changes in working practices that have resulted in improved performance.

The Unions interviewed recognize the needs of other stakeholder groups, namely shareholders and consumers, but feel that there needs to be a balance. At the moment it is felt that the needs of 'employees are overlooked and ignored' (C). In contrast it is felt that the shareholders have 'done very nicely' (D), has too much influence and this results in companies making short-term decisions. This 'will always be bad for employees', but also results in lower investment and maintenance as 'shareholders don't want to see investment in the long-term' (C). Once again it is believed that the problem is that when 'companies are asked to cut prices they cut employees and capital expenditure' (C), never profits. The Union feels that there should be more 'common ground' between consumers and employees as both have an interest in the 'good long-term future' of the industry and a 'safe and secure supply' (C).

Consumers

The price and quality of supply are consistently given as the key objectives of the electricity industry. As mentioned, it was recognized at the time of privatization that regulation would be required to protect consumers' interests. Also, due to the essential nature of electricity to the everyday life of people in the UK, consumers are effectively an involuntary stakeholder group; until recently it was not possible for domestic users of electricity to choose their electricity supplier. The transmission, distribution, and supply[1] elements of the industry are price-controlled and the regulator monitors conformity across customers and across companies. Also the regulator monitors 'guaranteed' and 'overall' standards of performance and arguably the most important of these relate to the 'reliability and availability' of the supply. This is also monitored through the number of customer minutes lost. The regulator also monitors the number of customer complaints as an 'indication of satisfaction'.

The price of electricity has fallen in real terms since privatization, although the reason for this is far from clear. One interviewee suggested that prices were 'jacked up by 30 per cent before privatization and since then came down by 30 per cent' (G). The information provided by the regulator has been criticized by consumer bodies, as it does not provide a breakdown of the causes of changes in prices. This is to say, how much of lower prices are caused by 'changes in world energy prices, decreases in the fossil fuel levy, changes in generation and the pool, and then regulation' (E). In addition after privatization due to 'very clever gaming by the generation companies' there were 'price spikes' where the price could change from '£100 compared to 2p' (per kWh) (F). Some consumer bodies believe that people are 'still paying too high a price' (E) for their electricity. In the first two years since privatization 'the price of electricity increased by 13 per cent' (E) and this is not justified when considering the returns earned by the companies over the same time period. The National Consumer Council (NCC) (1997) argues that domestic consumers had, between privatization and 1994, 'paid the companies some £650 million more than necessary', and this had risen to £949 million by 1995.

Overall in the electricity industry 'quality probably has improved' (E), and this is demonstrated by the statistics relating to the regulator's guaranteed and overall standards. There is a suggestion, however, that with 'technological improvements' quality 'would have improved anyway' (E). Also the guaranteed and overall standards are not considered ideal. These standards 'focus on certain things' and, for example, 'didn't care about poorer customers' and they are also criticized because of the 'minimal' cash penalty imposed if companies fail to meet a standard (E). An important and difficult problem facing consumer associations is the balancing of the interests of present and future consumers. Concern was voiced as to whether companies have been investing enough as an inevitable effect of this would be supply interruptions in the future. This again suggests concerns that the privatized companies are too focused upon the short-term and that it is in the long–term that other stakeholders may lose out.

In terms of other stakeholder groups, it is felt that the shareholder has had more than a 'fair share' as the companies were 'sold too cheaply' (F), and then made 'colossal profits for seven or eight years' (F). In the words of another interviewee, shareholders 'did really well for a number of years and then sold for a high price' and this is in a 'low risk' industry (E). In comparison it is felt that consumers have paid too much toward new investments and there have been very few, or no, rights issues in the industry to finance activities. There is a concern also that job cuts may have gone too far and this may affect the quality of service. Little consideration has been given to the issues of primary fuel or environmental issues, although it is felt that energy conservation and efficiency is desirable. There is also concern that on privatization 'nobody took responsibility for social effects' (E). Therefore there have been concerns over fuel poverty, and although there has been a decrease in the number of disconnections the problem remains. In response to these concerns the regulator has recently introduced a new standard relating to prepayment meters and has produced a 'social action plan', but it is debatable whether this will resolve the problems. There is another, even broader, concern that there is 'still a great reliance on competition working' and a 'trend to deregulation too quickly' (E). This is considered premature, as there is still some uncertainty as to whether competition will be sufficient given the small margins in the industry.

Suppliers

As mentioned in the Employees section above, there has been a dramatic increase in the use of external service providers, or sub-contractors, in the industry. This is an interesting development and one that is returned to in chapter 9, but interviews were not carried out with external service providers. The interest here was to talk to a supplier of the key raw material in the industry (i.e. the primary fuel used to generate electricity). Since privatization there have been changes in the type of primary fuel used to generate electricity in the UK. The Department of Trade and Industry (DTI, 2000b) publish the Digest of United Kingdom Energy Statistics. This includes a breakdown of the 'Fuel used in electricity generation, electricity supplied basis' which shows that in the UK the following changes occurred between 1994 and 1999:

Table 6.2 Fuel used in electricity generation, electricity supplied basis

Type of fuel	1994	1999
	%	%
Gas	15.0	38.5
Coal	48.0	28.0
Nuclear	25.0	24.5
Imports	5.0	4.0
Other fuels	1.5	2.5
Oil	4.0	1.5
Hydro	1.5	1.0

Source: Digest of United Kingdom Energy Statistics, 'Fuel used in electricity generation, electricity supply basis' (DTI, 2000b)

These changes in primary fuel are not inconsequential and the replacement of coal by gas has significant impacts on the coal industry and certain communities that have relied heavily upon that industry for employment. Also it is important to recognize that the primary fuel used to generate electricity significantly influences the environmental impact of the industry. The environmental impacts of the industry, in terms of the perceived dangers of emissions as well as the future implications of nuclear power, are significant and manifold as discussed in chapter 4. Representatives from the coal and nuclear industries were interviewed and it is their views that are discussed below. Unfortunately it was not possible to interview a representative of the gas industry.

The 'dash for gas' has been somewhat 'fortuitous on environmental emissions' but has not been 'economically ideal' (H). RJB mining, the largest coal producer in the UK, produce figures on their web site (www.rjb.co.uk) suggesting that the first generation of gas fired power stations produce electricity at 3.2p per kWh as compared to coal at 1.6p per kWh. These figures compare the cost of continued operation of the coal-fired power stations at higher levels, as they are presently operating far below their potential, with the cost of the new gas fired stations. In these calculations the total cost for the gas-fired stations includes the capital cost, as these would not have been necessary if the coal-fired stations had been used instead. One consequence of this shift has been a continued decline in the UK coal industry. This has seen the number of direct employees fall from 240,000 in 1977 to 10,000 in 1999/2000. The future of the coal industry in the UK does not look especially promising, but it is believed that the other primary fuels are problematic. Firstly, the coal industry argue that proven gas reserves are less than 10 years, the proven and probable are less than 15 years and the maximum is less than 20 years (H). As a result of this the coal industry believes that gas could very well be expensive in 20 years time and the UK could be importing 90 per cent of its gas requirements by this time. In comparison, according to one interviewee, coal is a 'long-term resource ... almost limitless in current terms' (H). Also new clean coal technology is being developed and coal stations being built today are operating at much higher levels of efficiency. At present the efficiency of coal fired power stations in the OECD averages 38 per cent and it is believed that with the use of new advanced materials with pulverized power plants this could be raised to 55 per cent. Such a 50 per cent increase in efficiency would reduce carbon dioxide emissions by one-third. In fact it is argued that in order to meet the Kyoto target reduction 'you would only need to increase the efficiency of the world's coal-fired power stations by 1 per cent' (H).

Another possibility for the future would be to increase the proportion of electricity generated from nuclear fuel and this would certainly result in a reduction in greenhouse gas emissions, but this has very little political support. At present nuclear is actually 'the biggest single source in the UK' (I), but its contribution is set to fall in the UK in the near future. Plans are already in place for the 'cessation of electricity generation at the eight [Magnox] stations' (BNFL, 2000, p.16) that presently contribute approximately 8 per cent of UK electricity. Within the nuclear industry it is felt that environmental pressures will leave nuclear and renewable supplies as the future of electricity generation. It is felt that a new generation of nuclear plants will be very different to those presently being used that were built in the 1950s and 1960s. A lot more is now known about nuclear energy and the reasons why this is not being more seriously considered are the two big issues of 'safety and waste management'. In terms of safety 'people do worry that it could blow up' and this can be debated and it is felt there are 'convincing arguments' to allay these fears (I). Waste management, however, deals with the 'legacy of nuclear waste' and this is much more complex as it concerns moral and emotional issues. There are experts who say that the waste can be contained for thousands of years, whereas others say, 'you can't predict what the future holds' such as earthquakes or even ice ages. Despite this it is 'inevitable' that nuclear will have a future, although this will only be accepted with 'reluctance' (I).

As mentioned above, a further option is to dramatically increase the use of renewable energy sources, but even the target of 10 per cent by 2010 is considered optimistic as this would require 'an area the size of the Peak District to be covered in windmills' (I). In addition these renewable energy sources are not price-competitive at present. A further problem is that there are risks attached to having a larger supply of renewable energy, more so even than nuclear. In the UK winter there is a tendency toward cold days with little wind and if electricity is being generated from wind and waves this is a huge problem. If renewable energy counted for more than 10-15 per cent of supply there would be 'too much variation' and the resultant lack of electricity 'could kill hundreds of thousands of people' (I). This would be a disaster on a completely different scale even to the damage caused by the Chernobyl accident. Ultimately, therefore, there are thought to be limits to how far renewable sources can go. The only other option is to 'stop people burning electricity' and this is 'not going to happen globally as living standards rise' (I).

As can be seen from this discussion, one of the primary determinants of the primary fuel used in future electricity generation is environmental issues and the next section considers these same issues, but from the standpoint of environmental stakeholder groups.

The Environment

As noted above, the recent history in the UK shows that there has been a significant shift in the fuel used from coal and oil to gas. This is an interesting environmental development as gas is cleaner and technically more efficient than both oil and coal in electricity generation. This means that as a result of this shift there will be lower emissions of greenhouse gases, however this is not seen as a long-term answer to environmental concerns as gas generation does still make significant emissions. The key strategies of environmentalists are to try and influence legislation and consumers to enforce a move toward a greener energy society. In 1999 the renewable sources supplied approximately 3 per cent and the UK government has targeted 5 per cent by 2003 and 10 per cent by 2010. In contrast to these targets Friends of the Earth (1997), applying their 'environmental space' methodology, 'suggests targets of 22 per cent reduction [in CO_2 emissions] by 2010 and a longer-term target of 89 per cent by the year 2050' (pp.62-3) are necessary. The achievement of these targets is difficult to envisage unless great developments are made in renewable energy sources in the near future. Therefore environmental lobby groups see investment in such projects as key, but these are often rejected on financial (DCF) grounds.

Another important area is that of energy efficiency and there are Energy Efficiency Standards of Performance (EESOPs) that are 'returning to the political domain' (J) i.e. they will be the Minister's responsibility not the regulator's. As with the consumer group, environmentalists felt that the regulator was very much an economic regulator who saw social and environmental considerations as an 'add on' that were 'difficult to deal with' (J). Having said this, there is a levy for energy efficiency and this is to be increased from £1.20 to £7.20 per annum per dual fuel household. This money is used by the companies in energy saving schemes that must be approved by the Energy Savings Trust (EST). Another important change would be to see the supply companies move away from being purely sellers of units of electricity. This provides the wrong sort of incentives in terms of energy savings and efficiency. Therefore companies that offered a more complete service, selling energy-saving equipment and advice, would be preferred.

As can be seen from the above discussion, the arguments concerning electricity generation and environmental effects are complex. A clear message, however, is that the key environmental issue for this industry, at the present time, is greenhouse gas emissions. As a representative of the coal industry put it, we are 'not bothering with the argument as to whether the greenhouse effect is real. The UK government sees it as real and so [we] see it as real' (H). The concentration on a single issue such as greenhouse gas emissions, as the stakeholder representatives see this as key, simplifies matters greatly. In the language of ISO14031 (ISO, 1997), this would put emphasis upon a single environmental condition indicator, namely the impact of emissions on global warming and climate change. The relevant operational measure would be the input of the primary fuel into electricity generation and the efficiency of the generation and use of electricity.

Discussion of Stakeholder Interviews

Gray, Owen and Adams (1996) suggest that 'accountability involves two responsibilities or duties: the responsibility to undertake certain actions (or forbear from taking actions) and the responsibility to provide an account of those actions' (p.38). Providing an account to stakeholders, in the form of a corporate social report or a social account, should form an essential part of the accountability process. The table overleaf provides a broad framework, a starting point, for what a social account, which would indicate corporate social performance, could focus upon in the electricity industry in England and Wales.

This framework is not suggested as being relevant to all industries or companies, although parts of it could be. This is because an important aspect of a social account should be a stakeholder dialogue identifying the specific issues most relevant to the company and industry, although industry-wide frameworks and standards should be possible. This table of objectives and drivers of performance was sent to each of the interviewees from within the industry and used as a starting point for discussions concerning stakeholder management and measurement. In the next section we shall consider the evidence from the interviews undertaken with representatives of the management within four privatized companies from within the industry.

Table 6.3 Stakeholder objectives and drivers of performance

Stakeholder group	Objective(s)	Drivers of performance
Shareholders	Wealth maximization	Customer base
		Cost control and efficiency gains
		Cost of capital and interest rates
		Strategic intent
		Stock market mood
		Regulation (including price)
Employees	Remuneration	Comparative levels of pay
		Ability to pay
		Productivity levels
	Welfare and job satisfaction	Employment levels
		Health and safety
		Job security
		Training
Consumers	Price	Absolute and relative prices
		Levels of profitability
	Quality	Reliability and availability of supply
		Issues relating to fuel poverty
		Investment in and maintenance of the network
The environment and suppliers	Reduction in greenhouse gas emissions	Primary fuels used
		Efficiency of electricity generation
		Efficiency of electricity use
		Investment in renewables
		Policies in terms of using renewables

Industry Interviews

Having completed the stakeholder interviews, companies within the industry were then approached to discuss the stakeholder issues and drivers of performance identified. The interviewees were representatives of companies within generation, transmission, distribution and supply. As such these companies do not operate in the same business and it is therefore to be expected that they have different stakeholder relationships. This is to say that a generator would not necessarily identify the same key stakeholders as those identified by a supply company. Having said this, similar approaches to stakeholder management were apparent and these similarities are discussed first.

Firstly, at an operational level it is interesting to note that the different stakeholder relationships tend to be managed in separate departments. Therefore the investor relations department specifically deals with shareholder issues and the human resources department with employee issues. It also appears that it is primarily at the executive level that, as the supply company suggested, the 'different stakeholder opinions are brought together'. As this is the case it is important that the executives are close to the issues and it was suggested that a key part of the executive role is to build and maintain stakeholder relationships. This appears especially important in relations with the government and the regulator. Each of the companies, including the generator, who is not actually subject to regulation, recognized that the government and regulator were key stakeholders. In fact the generator suggested that the government and regulator are absolutely key as they 'can stop us operating and add costs to our business'. Therefore a consistent theme was the desire to be 'aligned' with government and to be 'the partner of choice' of the regulator. The desire to work closely with these bodies was specifically seen as a tool to get them 'on our side'. This is a longer-term strategy, and it is felt that if the company is helpful, or in line, now then the company's influence will be greater in the future. For example, this may enable the company to influence decisions such that future 'criteria set are the right ones from [our company's] point of view'.[2]

Another consistent theme throughout the interviews was the importance of 'managing perceptions'. The interviewees suggested that the industry is not well understood and therefore it is important to 'inform stakeholders about the issues'. It is believed that if the stakeholders better understood the issues their opinion towards the companies would be more favourable. It is perhaps for this reason that external communications are considered key to the stakeholder process, and this is in terms of getting both the timing and external message right. What is also of particular interest is that this message is not necessarily the same for all stakeholders. Therefore one interviewee specifically stated that there were different messages for employees and shareholders. This appears to be an example of de-coupling as per institutional theory (DiMaggio and Powell, 1991), and this will be further examined in chapter 9.

In terms of actually managing conflicting stakeholder interests there do appear to be different approaches being undertaken. In one company it was clearly stated that there was no 'standard hierarchy' of stakeholders. Therefore stakeholder issues were discussed at the executive level and the competing interests were considered and the final decision would depend on the specific circumstances. In contrast, each of the other companies had made some attempt to consider the relative importance of different stakeholders. The approaches taken to prioritize stakeholders vary. One company's approach was to look at the evidence on how successful the stakeholders have been in achieving their goals and to use this to assess their importance. The following example was given:

> If you look at Friends of the Earth, they have 'been partially successful' and so you then 'look at it and see what they want and make an assessment of how effective they can be.'

A second company also considered stakeholders' 'Degree of influence'; however, a distinction was made between 'direct' and 'operational' influence. This approach resulted in a matrix of degrees of influence. This is a very instrumental approach to stakeholder management, as it is only if the stakeholder group can bring about change that they are considered important. Therefore this would appear to be more consistent with Mitchell, Agle and Wood's (1997) 'stakeholder salience' than a more normative approach to stakeholder management. Finally a third company, the supplier, was a subsidiary of a larger energy group and guidance was given as to a stakeholder hierarchy. It was clear from the group's strategy that profits, customers, and the government were the three most important stakeholders and, further, that at this time primacy was given to increasing the customer base over all other things.

The actual stakeholders identified by each company were very much in line with those anticipated, although some differences are noted. Most importantly, in addition to the list of stakeholders identified in Table 6.3 all of the companies stressed the importance of the regulator and the government (in its many forms). As a consequence of this interviews were held with the regulator and a government department in order to gain an insight into their roles and views on the stakeholder issues identified. In addition the media was recognized as an important stakeholder as, not surprisingly, companies want to avoid 'bad press'. In contrast it was apparent that suppliers, or external service providers, were not considered as important as the other stakeholders in the model were. In fact only one company specifically mentioned suppliers and this is reflected in the degrees of influence matrix mentioned above where external service providers (ESPs) are considered to have high operational influencing ability, but low direct influencing ability. This company believed that ESPs were important as they were considered to be partners and the hope was that joint cost reductions could be achieved by working closely together. Each of the remaining stakeholder groups is now taken in turn to consider how the companies themselves measure the stakeholder performance.

Shareholders

Shareholders were considered key by all of the companies, irrespective of whether they were a subsidiary of a larger group or a separately listed company. In each case traditional accounting measures were seen as a key determinant of how well the company was performing for its owners. Therefore profit and return on capital employed were specifically mentioned as key performance indicators for shareholders. This profitability measure was always supplemented by other measures such as cash flow, share price, dividend, and for the supply business customer measures (specifically mentioned were customer base and customer service indicators). This appears to provide some confirmation of the service profit chain (Heskett *et al.*, 1994), in that in service organizations there is perceived to be a link from customer performance into financial performance. If these measures are compared to those mentioned in Table 6.3 we see some similarities, although what appears to be missing is the cost of capital and the more market / economy-wide drivers of performance identified. It may be that these are believed to be outside the control of the organization. Therefore, although they do impact on a company's shareholder performance, there is perceived to be little that the company itself can do about them.

Employees

Employees were recognized as an important stakeholder by each of the companies interviewed. Each of the companies performs regular employee surveys in order to discover levels of (dis)satisfaction. In addition each company felt that there were sufficient 'other' ways for employees to feedback their feelings, at briefing sessions and the like. In addition great store was put in the ability of the company to achieve the 'softer' measure of Investors in People, although two of the companies visited had tried and failed in this respect.

On another level, there have been significant changes in the remuneration of individual employees in the industry. The shift toward PRP and individual remuneration packages is seen as a key development. In fact the move to rewarding people for extra effort is seen as a central part of the new ethos of the industry. Further, as this is coupled with reduced staffing levels, it is now felt that staff are asked to work harder and take more responsibility, but this results in a more rewarding work experience, both in terms of satisfaction and remuneration. One company suggested that this was reflected in the surveys produced, as employee satisfaction has consistently improved from 'the most dire time' in 1992/3, when levels of redundancy were high.[3]

Therefore, in comparison to Table 6.3, we see that the companies consider remuneration to be key, but that there has been a shift to more individual pay and this might hamper comparisons. Also employee satisfaction is important, but the companies have the ability to measure this directly and therefore do not need to resort to proxy measures. Employee satisfaction surveys were popular, but one company recognized that the collection of this data was a difficult process and as yet 'not very advanced'.

Consumers

The generating company did not specifically identify customers as a key stakeholder. This company is the most removed from the final consumer and, on the whole, is generating electricity for a relatively faceless electricity pool. Each of the regulated companies did identify customers as a key group, although the actual customers were either distribution companies, supply companies or the final users. For the supply and distribution companies, which are subject to yardstick competition, relative performance on the regulator's measures, including minutes lost per customer and restoration times, was considered important. Also the company's ranking against its competitors on guaranteed and overall standards as well as complaints were seen as key. It is interesting to note that despite the importance placed on these measures it was recognized that the statistics produced by the industry are 'not very good'. Even more interesting is the desire expressed to be 'in the middle of the pack' or just better than average in these standings. This is to say that these companies are not aiming to be the best as this may single them out for specific attention. The fear is that if too high a level of performance is achieved the regulator may decide that this company is over-resourced and therefore it would be struck with more stringent price-controls in the future.

In terms of the other drivers of performance identified in Table 6.3, it was suggested that profitability really should not be any concern of consumers. Also investment levels in the industry were not highlighted, as the emphasis very much appeared to be on today's consumers. These 'objective' measures of performance were also supported by customer satisfaction surveys, although again one company suggested that these are problematic. In addition to these formal measures there was a belief that consumer problems would also be detected informally, because the company has 'such a close relationship with our customers that we would detect unhappiness' if something is wrong. This is dependent on the relationship that the company has with its customers and a key factor here is the number of customers. At the supply end of the industry, where the larger companies have upwards of 3 million customers, it is not so easy to have an intimate customer relationship. It is also the case that it was also only at the supply company that price was mentioned as an important factor. Therefore the supply business is concerned with sending a 'savings message' to potential customers.

The Environment

This was recognized as important by each of the companies, although it was noticeable that it was given more attention in the Generation company. This is not surprising as the earlier discussion highlighted the fact that it is the primary fuel used in generation that has the most significant environmental impact. The generator recognized that there is a 'clear environmental threat' to their business and that therefore emissions are important. Having said this, it was felt that the primary fuel used to generate electricity in the UK should be a government, not a company, policy decision. The company itself also recognized the importance of security of supply and as such has a company policy of maintaining a balanced portfolio of generating facilities.

At the supply and distribution end of the industry the interest was much more focused upon energy efficiency, and for the supply company there was also the development of green products. It was felt that in many ways the companies were being forced to do things by the Government. For example, the Government has control over the Energy Efficiency Standards of Performance (EESOPs), the climate change levy, and the level of renewable sources to be used in the market. In this last instance, since privatization a number of companies have produced green products and tariffs as innovations, but this now appears to be out of their hands as the government has legislated levels of renewable sources to be used in electricity generation in the future. In this way it appears that it is the government that is controlling environmental developments as opposed to the companies.

On a more practical note, all of the companies had achieved, or were attempting to achieve, ISO 14001. It appears that in the UK electricity industry this is seen as a useful environmental standard and, as environmentally aware companies, something in which they should be at the forefront.

Secondary Social Stakeholders

Finally I consider the issues raised by the interviews with the government and the regulator. As mentioned above, it was made apparent during the earlier interviews that the relationship with government is a key one for all interests. In its legislative capacity, as in the case of the Utilities Act, the government is able to provide the framework for the industry and can therefore make a huge difference to each of the interests. It is therefore not surprising that each of the stakeholder groups and the industry organizations cited the importance of keeping in close contact with the government so that their views were taken into account. Also the regulator was seen as a key stakeholder for each of the companies in the industry interviewed, as it retains certain powers and duties.

The Regulator

The regulatory role is set out in legislation and has from the beginning been split between primary and secondary duties. The primary duties have included 'keeping the lights on', ensuring that the private companies are financially stable and promoting competition. The reliability and availability of the transmission and distribution networks is fundamental and this is monitored through the measurement of customer minutes lost per customer. Financial stability has been taken to mean that the companies must be able to finance their activities. One way in which the regulator can assist in this respect is to ensure that the industry is considered to be low risk. If the companies are perceived as low risk, and regulatory risk is an important determinant of this, then the companies should be able to get better financing terms. Finally, the regulator has taken an extremely active role in promoting competition in both the generation and supply aspects of the industry. Therefore the supply market has been progressively opened to competition and the incumbent generators have been encouraged to divest their capacity. The regulator monitors the level of competition within the industry through a variety of measures for different groups of customers in different areas and these include market share, the range of prices and the arrangements for transferring from one supplier to another. At present the twelve original supply companies still maintain 60-70 per cent of the market in their regions, but the major concern to the regulator is whether this is resulting in anti-competitive behaviour. It is accepted that in the future there may be as few as five or six large supply companies and this is not seen as a problem by the regulator.

       The secondary duties of the regulator relate more specifically to customers, health and safety and the environment. The actual importance placed on these secondary duties appears to vary significantly. The customer concerns are firmly entrenched in the workings of the regulator, through guaranteed and overall standards and monitoring of customer complaints, and these are discussed in the Consumers section above. The close monitoring of these measures has become an integral part of the work of the regulator and reports are produced annually on the comparative performance of the different companies. In contrast the involvement in health and safety issues is limited to considering whether the companies have appropriate 'machinery in place to limit incidents'. In fact the regulator sees their role in this area as secondary to that of the Health and Safety Executive (HSE). The environmental responsibilities of the regulator have actually decreased over time, as the Energy Efficiency Standards of Performance (EESOPs) have become the responsibility of government. Despite some minimal administrative duties in this area, it is clearly felt that environmental issues are the domain of government. This is exemplified in that ofgem has 'nothing to do with the nuclear industry' and there are no objectives relating to the emission of greenhouse gases. This is also reflected by the fact that it is the government, not the regulator, which consents, or does not consent, to new generating capacity. As mentioned earlier, it is this policy that has the most significant environmental impact.

In contrast to the reduced involvement in environmental issues, the regulator has recently adopted a more 'focused' approach to social issues and this has been achieved through the publication of the 'Social Action Plan'. Actually it is not felt that this has meant that the regulator is now performing a more social role, but simply that this is now more effectively communicated through the plan. The plan provides a more focused approach to how the regulator is dealing with disadvantaged groups. As with the environmental issues, the regulator's role in social issues, such as fuel poverty, is still seen to be secondary to that of the government, who are seen to be the real drivers of change.

The Government

The role of government is not unitary as there are influences from the DTI, the DETR, central government and the EU. These government bodies are concerned with 'the complex issues' raised by the industry. In this sense the government deal with the 'intractable problems' in that they concern conflicting interests that are 'not resolvable'. An example of such conflict is the competing social and environmental considerations of energy prices. Therefore low prices are seen as beneficial, in that they reduce the number of people in fuel poverty, but they also send the wrong signal in terms of energy efficiency and the need to meet environmental emission targets. This problem needs to be managed and is resolved by running separate programmes, one for fuel poverty and one for environmental emissions. Another intractable problem is the need for primary fuel in the future. As UK natural resources run down and the Magnox nuclear fleet are closed down this suggests that the UK needs to find alternative fuel sources. One 'obvious' answer is to build new nuclear capacity, as this does not contribute to global warming, but within the EU Germany has a stance of 'no nuclear and meeting Kyoto'. Another alternative will be to import primary fuel, but this dependence would be a 'real risk', as opposed to a 'financial risk', and as such you 'can't insure against' these.

It would therefore appear that the companies are left to operate in their own way for the short-term, but the longer-term problems remain with government. At present there is a debate within the UK government, and at a European level, as to how far into the future plans should be made. As yet there is no answer, but it is recognized that, given the nature of the long-term issues highlighted above, there are potential environmental and supply problems in the future.

Conclusions

This chapter documents the findings of interviews with stakeholders and companies in the electricity industry in England and Wales. The initial purpose of these interviews was to discover the stakeholder issues, objectives and drivers of performance within the industry. The findings from the stakeholder interviews in this respect are summarized in Table 6.3 and these have been contrasted to those measures considered important by the sample of companies in the industry. Based on the findings from these interviews and the review of the performance measurement literature in chapter 4 it is now intended to suggest a provisional corporate social performance measurement model, or social accounting framework, for the industry. Therefore I shall once again consider each of the key stakeholders in turn and identify specific performance measures that will form part of the final model.

Shareholders

In chapter 4 it was concluded that the following measures are important:

- Return on Equity;
- Return on Capital Employed;
- Return on Sales; and
- Total Shareholder Returns (TSR) as adjusted for risk and market-wide factors.

If these measures are compared to the drivers of performance in Table 6.3 and those identified in the company interviews we find significant agreement. Profitability and Efficiency as measured by the accounting measures are also considered important in practice. There is again agreement between the literature and the interviewees that market-wide and industry-wide factors are important. This is difficult to incorporate in specific measures, but the cost of capital will be considered as the interviewees suggested this. It was also apparent from the interviews that the companies' future intentions, specifically in terms of future growth, are important and therefore in addition to the measures identified in the literature the growth in revenues of the companies will also be considered. Finally, cash generation is important and therefore the cash flow return on investment (CFROI), a measure argued to be consistent with shareholder wealth maximization, will be included.

The shareholder representatives did not mention the market-based measure of TSR, probably because they are trying to identify future returns and the historical return is not considered important for this. One company, however, did suggest that dividends and share price are important and together these comprise TSR. In fact TSR is a measure of shareholder wealth creation, and the other measures are seen as important because they are drivers of this performance. Therefore TSR will be considered in the shareholder analysis chapter that follows this one.

Employees

There is agreement between the literature and the interviews that the key objectives for employees are employee remuneration and welfare. Further, it is also agreed that it is comparative remuneration that is most important. Therefore average remuneration per employee will be compared with changes in other industries through 'Income Data Services', which is considered by one interviewee to be the 'Bible' on such things. As mentioned earlier, employee welfare is less easily measured. The stakeholder representatives use informal feedback to gauge this and the companies all use satisfaction surveys, the design and results of which they were not willing to share. This therefore means that, as discussed in the literature, proxy measures will need to be used. From the stakeholder interviews it was apparent that employment levels, health and safety, job security and training were perceived as being the most important drivers of employee welfare. Therefore the following measures will be used:

- Changes in employment levels;
- Numbers of Accidents;
- An 'annual labour turnover index' (a proxy for job security as discussed in chapter 4); and
- Expenditure on employee training.

Customers

Again, there is agreement that the final customer is interested in price and quality of supply. Therefore changes in prices to consumers will be considered and this will be contrasted with changes to other customers, both within the UK and globally. In terms of quality of supply, the industry appears to be in agreement that customer minutes lost per customer, the number of complaints and OFFER/OFGEM'S guaranteed and overall standards of performance are relevant, although the accuracy of the statistics reported is questioned. This is because the data is provided by the companies and there is some scope for flexibility in the definitions of the figures to be reported. It is intended to use company performance in these respects to analyze performance for customers.

Suppliers

Little was gained in terms of performance measures specifically for creditors and it is therefore intended to use measures of creditor days and liquidity (i.e. a current ratio) as identified in chapter 4. Changes in the mix of primary fuel supply will be considered as evidence of the specific fuel industries gaining or losing. This will also be of importance when considering the environmental effects.

The Environment

A clear message was received from all stakeholders and companies that it is emission of greenhouse gases from the industry that is the single most important environmental issue. As this message was so strong the performance measurement model here will be purely based on factors affecting these emissions. This is not to suggest that other areas of environmental concern are insignificant, but that they are overshadowed by this much larger problem. As mentioned above, this also has the benefit of simplifying the number of measures to be used and so it is that the key factors influencing emissions are:

- Total and mix of primary fuel used in generation;
- Efficiency of generation;
- Total electricity supplied.

The Model

Therefore, from the literature reviewed and the interviews performed, the measurement model is summarized in Table 6.4. This will be used to analyze how the various stakeholders have benefited or lost since privatization. This stakeholder analysis will provide further detail to the conclusions from the value-added analysis performed in the previous chapter. This analysis suggested a redistribution between certain stakeholder groups, but it is hoped that the model developed here can provide further information about the nature of any redistribution.

The availability and ease of access to the information required will be discussed as part of the analysis chapters. This is important as one of the aims of this book is to identify gaps in corporate information that would be required to provide a more complete picture of corporate social performance.

Table 6.4 The stakeholder performance measurement model

Stakeholder group	Stakeholder measures
Shareholders	Return on equity
	Return on capital employed
	Return on sales
	Growth in revenues
	The cost of capital
	Cash added value
	Total shareholder returns
Employees	Average remuneration
	Changes in employment levels
	Numbers of accidents
	Annual labour turnover index
	Expenditure on employee training
Customers	Average prices
	Customer minutes lost per customer
	Numbers of complaints
	Performance against OFGEM'S guaranteed and overall standards
Suppliers	Creditor days
	Current ratio
	Mix of primary fuel
The environment	Total and mix of primary fuel used in generation
	Efficiency of generation
	Total electricity supplied
	Annual emissions

Other Findings

Another important finding to become apparent from the interviews was that each of the companies was undertaking some form of stakeholder management. This stakeholder management appears rather instrumental in nature, as the stakeholders' influence over company performance is the determinant of their perceived importance rather than any moral or ethical stance. Beyond this it is less easy to generalize, but it was reassuring to note that the stakeholders identified by the companies were in line with those identified in the literature. In fact these interviews did emphasize the importance of the regulator, the government and the media in addition to the primary stakeholders already identified.

It has been argued (Carter and Crowther, 2000) that the privatization of the UK electricity industry has resulted in a shift from an engineering led industry, where primacy was given to the technical aspects of security of supply, to a more financially oriented one.[4] This may well be in order to reflect that, arguably, the most important stakeholder, the shareholders, are primarily concerned with financial performance and that this is best reflected in discounted cash flow models. By their nature these models discount the future and place greater importance on the short-term. It is this short-term perspective that appears to be at the heart of the key concerns of the other stakeholders. Consumers are concerned that not enough is being invested today to ensure reliable supply in the future. Employee representatives claim that the cut in employee numbers raises concerns about the reliability of supply and further that the changes to the industry will also result in a skills shortage in the future. The number of electricians being trained by the industry has fallen dramatically and the age profile of qualified electricians is getting older and older. Also recent history shows that the primary fuel used in electricity generation has shifted to gas, the majority of which the UK will need to import within the foreseeable future. Reliance on imports for such an essential commodity again raises concerns about future supply. The difference in temporal perspectives is perhaps most apparent when considering the environment. The environmental problems connected with the industry are extremely long-term and the solutions are not to be found easily or quickly. Friends of the Earth are suggesting there is a need for dramatic reductions in emissions by the year 2050, which is significantly past the planning horizon of the industry: the regulator works in 5-yearly cycles. Even this does not compare to the need for nuclear 'spent fuel management' that requires the safe management of radioactive waste for hundreds of years into the future. The short-term perspective of the industry could be storing up problems for the future, and this is certainly a consistent message from stakeholders. The companies also recognize these potential long-term threats to the industry. Interestingly their response appears to be that these are government, rather than corporate, policy issues. Therefore the buck is firmly being passed to, and apparently accepted by, government to find solutions for the 'intractable' problems. Whether the government can find appropriate solutions to these long-term problems is debatable and only time will tell.

Notes

[1] Subsequent to the period under consideration here the supply industry has been further opened up to competition and the level of direct regulation relating to this aspect has fallen as a result.

[2] The regulator and government are not included in the Clarkson (1995) model and are considered to be secondary stakeholders by Wheeler and Sillanpaa (1997). Therefore they were originally excluded from this model, however, these interviews made it clear that in this industry they are of primary importance and therefore interviews with a relevant government department and the regulator were carried out.

[3] Unfortunately the company was not willing to provide a copy of either the surveys or the results.

[4] Ogden (1995) also notes a change in the UK water industry, whereby the use of accounting vocabulary assisted a culture shift to cost and then profit orientation.

Chapter 7

Shareholder Analysis

Introduction

Chapter 6 reported on interviews undertaken with stakeholder representatives of the electricity industry in England and Wales. These interviews, in conjunction with the earlier discussion in chapter 4, provide a model for analyzing the performance of different stakeholder groups. Such analysis augments the value added analysis undertaken in chapter 5. The value added analysis provides an indication that shareholders have benefited from privatization, as a greater proportion of value added has been distributed to shareholders through the period. This does not, however, sufficiently explore how this has been achieved. Therefore this chapter looks in more detail at how the specific shareholder measures identified in the earlier chapters can help to explain a company's shareholder performance.

Chapter 6 concluded that in terms of shareholders the most important objective is wealth maximization. In order to achieve this the literature reviewed and the interviewee responses suggested certain key indicators that help to manage and measure this performance. These measures are as follows:

- Traditional profitability measures;
- Accounting Return on Capital measures;
- Cash flow measures; and
- Market performance measures

Each of these measures is discussed below and calculations performed to demonstrate their value using the electricity industry in England and Wales as a case study. In addition to these measures size and growth were recognized as important factors. The issue of size and growth were discussed in chapter 5 as part of the value added analysis. Finally the cost of capital is important and this is considered in the sections as appropriate.

The period under consideration here, as in the value added analysis chapter, is from privatization to 1997. There is, however, a very important change in the ownership of the majority of these companies in the period from 31 March 1995 to 31 March 1997. The catalyst for this change was the sale by the government of its 'golden share' in the RECs and the flotation of the National Grid. Therefore this chapter separates the longer period of analysis into two sub-periods, privatization to 31 March 1995 and then the period from 1 April 1995 to 31 March 1997.

The Period from Privatization to 31 March 1995

Traditional Profitability Measures

Absolute levels of profit attributable to shareholders and levels relative to value added have been calculated and discussed above in chapter 5. In the value added analysis we noted the increase in shareholders' share in value added. This is augmented here by a consideration of return on sales and earnings per share. Both of these measures are widely used in practice and are considered important indicators to the market as to the financial performance of the company. For the purposes of this chapter Return on Sales has been defined as:

$$\text{Return on Sales} = \frac{\text{Profit before interest and tax}}{\text{Turnover}} * 100\%$$

In summary the following returns on sales were achieved:

Table 7.1 Return on sales (1991-1995)

	1991	1992	1993	1994	1995
	%	%	%	%	%
Generators	9.5	11.0	14.0	18.4	19.3
National Grid	40.6	42.3	42.6	44.2	47.5
RECs	9.2	11.3	11.9	12.4	13.8

These simple averages show a very consistent picture of an increasing profitability in the industry. These increased levels of profit throughout the industry suggest that, as the period of time has progressed, so the companies have been able to reduce their operating costs and hence increase margins. From our earlier value added analysis we can suggest that the major cost savings have been in terms of labour costs.

Earnings per share (EPS) are required to be published in sets of accounts. Since the introduction of FRS 3 in the UK the definition of EPS has been made more stringent and this is:

$$\text{Basic Earnings per share} = \frac{\text{Profit attributable to shareholders}}{\text{Weighted Average no. of ordinary shares}}$$

The profit attributable to shareholders is specifically defined to reflect profit after extraordinary and exceptional items and this definition of profit has been used here. For simplicity the simple average of the number of ordinary shares, at the beginning and end of the accounting period, rather than the weighted average has been used. An exception to this is in the year ended 31 March 1991, where the year end number of ordinary shares is used as it is in this year that the shares were issued.

Table 7.2 Earnings per share (1991-1995)

	1991	1992	1993	1994	1995
	£	£	£	£	£
Generators	0.17	0.30	0.35	0.43	0.47
National Grid	0.65	0.84	0.95	1.10	1.08
RECs	0.41	0.55	0.66	0.68	0.77

The improvement in EPS is consistent across all of the distinct parts of the industry, although it is not the case that every single REC showed an improved EPS each year. Also it is worth noting that the majority, but not all, of the RECs reduced the number of shares by approximately 10 per cent in the year ending 31 March 1995. This means that in total the average number of ordinary shares used in the 1995 calculation was approximately 3-4 per cent lower than in the 1994 calculation. If this change had not occurred the EPS for the RECs would still have increased, but not as much, to approximately 0.74.

The traditional profitability measures appear to tell a story of a financially successful industry with steadily improving prospects. This is to say that profitability was improving throughout the period. One problem with these measures is that it is difficult to say whether these returns are sufficient to reward the shareholders for their investment. In order to be able to do this we need to be able to compare the returns with an appropriate cost of capital. Therefore in the next section we consider the returns and costs of capital for these companies.

Accounting Return on Capital Measures

The return on capital employed (ROCE) is considered here. ROCE relates to the returns made to all providers of finance. ROCE is a measure of the efficiency with which the companies turn their capital into profits and is defined here as:

$$ROCE = \frac{\text{Profit before interest and tax}}{\text{Capital + Reserves + Loans due in > one year}} * 100\%$$

The table below summarizes the ROCE generated by the distinct parts of the industry in each of the five years. These results below do not at first sight appear as clear cut as those produced by the traditional measures calculated above, but there still appears to be an improvement in ROCE through the period. There appears to be no obvious trend to the National Grid's performance whereas for the generators and the RECs there does appear to be a definite year on year improvement with the exception of 1994 where the levels dropped.

Table 7.3 Historic cost return on capital employed (1991-1995)

	1991	1992	1993	1994	1995
	%	%	%	%	%
Generators	18.4	20.3	22.2	21.2	25.0
The National Grid	27.6	31.9	28.9	26.9	29.2
The RECs	18.6	22.8	23.0	21.4	24.8

However, this is not the end of the story as we should remember that these are the returns and they should therefore be compared to the cost of capital. ROCE is a measure of return to all of the providers of finance and we should therefore compare it to the Weighted Average Cost of Capital (WACC). Edwards, Kay and Mayer (1987) consider the use and relevance of returns on capital as a measure of performance. They argue that:

> the accounting rate of return over a segment (of whatever size) of an activity's lifetime provides information which, in a great many cases, is directly relevant for economists, investors, regulators and others who are concerned to assess the performance of activities. (p.63)

They conclude that a comparison of the return on capital to the cost of capital provides evidence on performance, but this must be in current cost terms to be of value. As such they suggest the appropriate formula is:

$$\text{The accounting rate of profit} = \frac{\text{Real profit}}{\text{Net worth}}$$

Where real profit is equal to nominal profit (the profit as calculated using value-to-the-owner rules) less the rate of inflation multiplied by the net worth. The net worth is also calculated using value-to-the-owner rules. Value-to-the-owner rules:

> stipulate that if the replacement cost of the firm's assets exceeds their net realizable value on disposal then the assets of the firm should be valued at:
> i   Net realizable value if the value of the firm's assets in their current use falls short of their net realizable value on disposal
> ii   Replacement cost if their value in current use exceeds the cost of replacing the firm's assets with assets that generate an equivalent stream of services
> iii   Present value of future earnings if the value of the firm's assets in their current use lies between net realizable value and replacement cost. (p.123)

This value-to-the-owner valuation is not provided by the electricity companies, but current cost information is available. Therefore it is intended to use this current cost information to calculate a current cost ROCE (CCROCE) that can then be compared to the real WACC. The tables below document the current cost return on capital employed for each of the companies based on the following formula:

$$\text{CCROCE} = \underline{\text{Current cost PBIT (after gearing and inflation adjustments)}} * 100\%$$
$$\text{Current cost capital employed (including current cost reserve)}$$

Table 7.4 CCROCE for RECs (1991-1995)

	1991	1992	1993	1994	1995
	%	%	%	%	%
East Midlands	0.2	5.3	8.2	0.3	10.3
Eastern	-2.3	3.0	6.5	7.0	4.2
London	-2.3	2.8	5.5	6.3	5.5
Manweb	-3.0	4.2			
MEB	-1.8	3.7	7.9	8.1	
Northern	-0.6	4.6	7.4	7.8	7.8
Norweb	-4.2	5.0	8.1	8.0	8.4
Seeboard	-3.0	1.6	5.5	5.7	6.6
Southern	-1.7	4.8	8.0	7.9	5.2
Swalec	-0.7	3.4	5.9	6.5	
SWEB	-1.8	3.0	6.6	6.3	4.9
Yorkshire	0.6	4.3	6.2	5.2	8.3
Simple Average	-1.7	3.8	6.9	6.3	6.8

Table 7.5 CCROCE for National Grid and the generators (1991-1995)

	1991	1992	1993	1994	1995
	%	%	%	%	%
National Grid			6.0	6.1	5.9
National Power		0.9	4.0	5.0	3.5
Powergen	-5.3	1.6	4.6	5.3	4.5

In order to discover whether these companies have created value for their capital providers we need to calculate the cost of capital. The cost of capital can be calculated as the weighted average of the cost of debt and equity. The cost of capital is the normal returns that are required by the providers of that capital. If these returns are not forthcoming the providers of capital are not being sufficiently recompensed for the risks that they are taking in investing in this specific company. Modern finance theory suggests that the investors should be rewarded for investing in risky assets, but only for the market not the total risk. It is argued that investors can reduce / eliminate unique or unsystematic risk by investing in a diversified portfolio. Companies generally, and indeed in the electricity industry, have two primary sources of finance, namely debt and equity. These different types of finance have different costs as they contain different risks, with the equity investor, the shareholder, seen to take the greater risks as there are fewer guarantees of payment. In chapter 4 we considered the measurement of the costs of equity and concluded that the Capital Asset Pricing Model (CAPM) is most commonly used to calculate the cost of equity and can also be used to calculate the cost of debt. This is reflected in the following formulae:

The cost of equity = Risk free rate + Beta * (equity risk premium)

The cost of debt = Risk free rate + Beta * (debt risk premium)

In this case, as we are considering the current cost returns after adjusting for inflation, we must consider the real WACC. This is to say that the cost of capital must not include inflation. Firstly we need to calculate the real risk free rate. This was calculated by reference to the return offered by government bonds and securities as quoted on DATASTREAM. The following information was gathered for the years ending in March of the year quoted:

Table 7.6 Returns on government bonds and treasury bills (1991-1995)

	1991	1992	1993	1994	1995
	%	%	%	%	%
UK GOVT BOND YIELD - LONGTERM	10.89	9.75	8.94	7.44	8.46
UK TREASURY BILL RATE	13.55	10.25	7.85	5.05	5.46
UK BOND YIELD GOVT.10 YR(ECON) - MIDDLE RATE	11.07	9.76	8.87	7.40	8.49
UK TREASURY BILL DISCOUNT 1 MTH - MIDDLERATE	14.02	10.58	8.15	5.41	5.37
UK GOVT BOND YIELD - MEDIUM TERM	11.63	9.99	8.23	6.49	8.44
Lowest nominal rate	10.89	9.75	7.85	5.05	5.37
Inflation as calculated by change in RPI March to March	8.24	4.03	1.90	2.30	3.51
Implied risk free rate	2.4	5.5	5.8	2.7	1.8

Source: DATASTREAM

The real rates for the years ending in 1992 and 1993 appear out of line with the other years. This seems to be caused by the rate of inflation falling at a quicker rate than the returns offered by the government. Another approach is to consider the returns offered on Index Linked Gilts (ILG) as these are protected from inflation risks. Evidence on the level of returns offered by ILGs is considered by OFGEM (2001) and they note that the implied risk free rate fluctuates: 3.1 per cent (January 1998), 1.8 per cent (April 1999), 2.2 per cent (March 2001), 2.6 per cent (June 2001). In addition OFGEM (2000) determined a risk free rate of 2.5 per cent to

2.75 per cent based on a study of spot yields on UK ILGs with greater than 5 years to maturity. This evidence seems in line with the rates calculated for the years ending in 1991, 1994 and 1995 above and it would appear that the other two years are overstated. Based on this the best estimate of the risk free rate for the period appears to be of the order of 2.5 per cent (the average for the 1990/1, 1993/4 and 1994/4 above is 2.3 per cent).

If this is our best estimate of the risk free rate we then need to calculate Beta * Equity risk premium. Again there is significant disagreement on both the level of Beta and the level of equity risk premium. If we consider the level of Beta for the electricity industry the Monopolies and Mergers Commission (MMC) and the regulator consistently suggest a range of 0.55 to 0.75. In comparison Datastream (a financial information package) suggests Betas of 0.44 and 0.31 for electricity companies. There is also disagreement as to the level of equity risk premium. Watson and Head (2001) report that empirical studies by Dimson and Brealey (1978), Allan *et al.*, (1986) and Ibbotson Associates (1990) all suggest equity risk premiums of approximately 8-9 per cent. They further note that Jenkinson (1994) recalculates the equity risk premium using a geometric mean and this suggests that the previous studies overstate the premium. Jenkinson's work has also been used by the MMC and the regulator, and the MMC (1997) state:

> The question of whether to use arithmetic or geometric means remains one of debate, mainly reflecting different views as to how best to characterize the process assumed to generate returns over time. In the short term it is conventional to assume that annual returns are independent which would suggest using arithmetic means. But it has been argued that this assumption is implausible over the longer term, and the alternative view has been employed to justify the use of geometric means. We see no reason, in the light of the present state of the debate, to depart from the use of geometric means, noting that this gives an overall range of the WACC consistent with that has been used elsewhere. (p.15)

Two comprehensive studies of the equity risk premium are the Barclays Capital (2001) 'Equity-Gilt Study' and Dimson, Marsh and Staunton (2001) in their book 'The Millennium Book II: 101 years of Investment Returns'. These two studies consider the equity risk premium over the 100 years of the twentieth century and suggest an equity risk premium of 4.6 per cent and 4.5 per cent respectively. The MMC has used a range of 3.5-4.5 per cent and the regulator suggesting a similar, although slightly higher, range going up to 5 per cent. Given this shift toward acceptance of the geometric mean and the range of values suggested it would appear that a best estimate for the equity risk premium would be 4.6 per cent. Given this is consistent with the OFGEM and the MMC it would appear sensible to also use the middle of the range Beta as suggested by them of 0.65. This suggest a real post-tax cost of equity can be calculated as follows:

Real post-tax cost of equity = 2.5% + 0.65 * 4.6% = 5.49%

It must be remembered that returns calculated above are before tax and therefore this post-tax cost of equity needs to be increased by the effective tax rate for the companies. The marginal corporate tax rate is 30 per cent and the regulator uses this in its calculations despite acknowledging that the effective tax rate is less than this (OFGEM, 1999). The Competition Commission (2000) used an effective corporate tax rate of 20 per cent in calculating the pre-tax cost of capital for Sutton and East Surrey Water and this would appear to be a more realistic approximation for the electricity companies. This results in a pre-tax cost of equity of approximately 6.9 per cent. This is of the same order as that suggested by the regulator since privatization.

In terms of the Debt risk premium * Beta, the MMC (1997) report an analysis of debt undertaken by electricity companies in the years 1995 and 1996. This records 17 loans and 14 of these show a debt premium between 0.4 per cent and 0.8 per cent. Therefore the cost of debt can be estimated using a debt risk premium of the order of 0.6 per cent. This gives us an estimated cost of debt of:

Cost of debt = 2.5% + 0.6% = 3.1%.

Finally the costs of debt and equity can be combined to produce the Weighted Average Costs of Capital (WACC). The weightings of debt and equity were calculated based on the average of the RECs capital structure as per their year end accounts. The use of accounting figures can be criticized for not reflecting the market values of the debt and equity, although in this case due to the low levels of debt, between 11 per cent and 17 per cent, the difference is not likely to be that significant. If we suggest that the average is approximately 14 per cent for the five-year period we calculate:

The real pre-tax WACC = 0.14*3.1% + 0.86*6.9% = 6.4%

This figure needs to be treated with quite some caution. Numerous estimates and assumptions are made to calculate this cost and changes to these would obviously result in a different cost of capital. For example assuming that the equity risk premium is 5 per cent, the Beta is 1.0 and the tax increase should be 30 per cent would result in a cost of equity of 10.7 per cent and a WACC of 9.6 per cent.

If we consider the performance spread (i.e. the CCROCE – the real pre-tax WACC) we should get a fuller understanding of these results and this is represented in Table 7.7 below.

Table 7.7 CCROCE – real pre-tax WACC (1991-1995)

	1991	1992	1993	1994	1995
	%	%	%	%	%
Generators		-5.5	-1.4	-0.8	-1.7
National Grid			-0.4	-0.3	-0.5
RECs	-8.1	-2.6	0.5	0.0	0.4

This would suggest that competition and the price-cap were at appropriate levels for this five-year period as the companies produced real current cost returns in line with the cost of capital. More recently shareholder value advocates have suggested that it is appropriate to consider cash flow as opposed to current cost returns and so in the next section we consider this.

Cash Flow Measures

The cash generated by the companies was highlighted as an important part of their performance to shareholders and in addition it is seen as less easy to manipulate cash figures as compared to profit figures. In order to consider the cash generating ability of the companies Cash Flow Return on Investment has been calculated. Firstly a very basic measure of CFROI has been calculated. Braxton Associates (1991) suggest that a basic version of CFROI can be calculated using the following formula:

$$\text{CFROI} = \frac{\text{Real cash flow}}{\text{Gross operating assets (current prices)}} * 100\%$$

Real cash flow = Profit after tax + depreciation and amortization + interest + operating lease rental + deferred tax charge + stock adjustment

Gross operating assets (current price)
= Book value of total assets + accumulated depreciation + fixed asset inflation adjustment + stock adjustment + capitalized operating leases + other off balance sheet assets - non-debt liabilities – goodwill

Figures are available in the accounts of the electricity companies for most of these items. Virtually all of the electricity companies produce current cost balance sheets and these were used to calculate the fixed asset inflation adjustment. Adjustments could not be made for operating leases, off balance sheet assets and stock adjustments and it is hoped that these omissions are not material. The results of these calculations are as follows:

Table 7.8 Basic CFROI (1991-1995)

	1991	1992	1993	1994	1995
	%	%	%	%	%
Generators	6.4	11.1	11.1	12.5	13.8
National Grid	12.8	13.2	12.9	13.1	13.3
RECs	9.2	10.9	11.5	11.2	12.1

Once again these returns are difficult to comment upon without comparing them to the relevant costs. In this case the returns here are after tax, but are also in real (not nominal) terms and must therefore be compared to the companies' real WACC (Cornelius and Davies, 1997). We calculated the real WACC above as 6.4 per cent and if this were used again it would suggest that in each year the companies, on average, are creating cash flow returns in excess of the cost of capital.

The measure of real cash flow suggested by Braxton Associates is in reality a halfway house between profit and cash. Therefore it was decided to also calculate the CFROI using operating cash flow – tax paid. This is closer to a true measure of the cash generating ability of the companies from their operating activities. The findings are:

Table 7.9 Operating CFROI (1991-1995)

	1991	1992	1993	1994	1995
	%	%	%	%	%
Generators	12.5	11.5	10.5	10.5	19.2
National Grid	12.1	14.4	12.8	12.7	14.7
RECs	2.7	11.3	12.6	18.8	7.6

These results also show that for the Generators and the National Grid were generating cash flow returns in excess of the real WACC (6.4 per cent) in every year. This same is true for the RECs with the exception of 1991. Unlike the results using the current cost return on capital employed this suggests that the companies are generating returns in excess of the cost of capital. This does not paint a clear picture of returns to the shareholders and so it is interesting to see whether the actual returns to the shareholders, in terms of dividends and capital gains, have been higher than the cost of equity or not. These market returns to shareholders are what we now consider.

Market Performance Measures

In chapter 5 share price was mentioned as an important measure of performance, but this fails to include the dividend element of returns to shareholders. Therefore rather than considering purely share price, total shareholder returns (TSR) are used to capture the full benefit of share ownership. In order to calculate the TSR the

Return Index from Datastream has been used. This calculates the total benefits to shareholders assuming that they reinvest dividends into the shares of the company. As The National Grid was owned by the twelve RECs and not listed on the London Stock Exchange it is not possible to calculate a separate TSR for this company. However, as it was owned by the twelve RECs we can say that its performance and value should increase the value of the RECs in the period. The following TSRs were calculated.

Table 7.10 TSR (1991-1995)

	1991	1992	1993	1994	1995
	%	%	%	%	%
Generators	17.4	2.5	78.0	53.9	-7.7
RECs	37.1	5.3	66.7	38.6	-0.7

These results fluctuate much more than those calculated earlier. It is important to remember that the results for 1991 are for the period from privatization until 31 March 1991. They therefore relate to three and a half months for the RECs and just three weeks for the Generators. These can be seen to be part of the under valuation of the companies by the Government at the time of privatization. The reasons for this are discussed earlier in chapter 5, but are primarily believed to have been to ensure that the flotations were successful. If we assume that the shareholders are long-term investors we can consider that an annualized return would be of most interest. If we calculate the annualized returns to shareholders for the four years from 31 March 1991 to 31 March 1995 (hence excluding the one-off gains made in the first few weeks for the under valuation at privatization) we see an average return of nearly 27 per cent for the shareholders of the generators and nearly 25 per cent for the shareholders of the RECs.

Again we need to compare this with the appropriate cost of capital. These returns are in nominal terms and therefore we need to compare these returns with the nominal cost of equity. We can use Fisher's equation to convert the real cost of equity calculated earlier to the nominal cost of equity as follows:

$$(1+m) = (1+r) * (1+f)$$ where m = nominal cost of equity as a decimal
r = real cost of equity as a decimal; and
f = rate of inflation

If we calculate the nominal cost of equity for each year we get:

1990/1 nominal cost of equity = 1.064*1.0824 = 1.152; = 15.2%
1991/2 nominal cost of equity = 1.064*1.0403 = 1.107; = 10.7%
1992/3 nominal cost of equity = 1.064*1.0190 = 1.084; = 8.4%
1993/4 nominal cost of equity = 1.064*1.0230 = 1.088; = 8.8%
1994/5 nominal cost of equity = 1.064*1.0351 = 1.101; = 10.1%

These costs of equity are far below the annualized total shareholder returns calculated above and this demonstrates that the shareholders of electricity companies have received returns in excess of those expected given the risks attached.

Finally it might be that these excess returns relate to the performance of the market rather than the specific shares. Therefore it is also worthwhile comparing the TSR of electricity companies to those achieved by the market as a whole or a comparable set of companies. If we consider the 'Total Return Index' from Datastream for the FTSE all share index over the same period (i.e. 31/31/91 – 31/3/95) we see a return of approximately 11.5 per cent per annum. This means that the, supposedly low-risk, shares in the electricity companies offered returns more than double those offered by the Stock Exchange as a whole over the period 1991-1995.

Concluding Thoughts on the Period Privatization to 31 March 1995

Prior to privatization the government owned the electricity industry and hence shareholders are a new stakeholder group. The analysis of total shareholder returns suggests that shareholders, a group with no interest in the industry pre-1991, have received benefits far in excess of their related risk. The returns through dividends and gains in share price are far higher than the cost of equity capital calculated. The actual cause of these returns is less clear. The strongest message appears to come from the historical cost accounts, which show high returns on capital employed and improving earnings per share. Also the cash flow return on investment suggests that there are returns in excess of the cost of capital. This evidence is contradicted by the current cost return on capital employed as recommended by Edwards, Kay and Mayer. This measure shows the companies achieving returns in line with the cost of equity. The level of gains made by the shareholders would appear to support the literature suggesting that there is a 'functional fixation' with earnings per share and historic cost returns (see for example Hand (1990, 1991) and Day (1986)). Also, the nature of the information provided by the annual reports and accounts of the companies has changed over this period. Thompson (1993) suggested that there was a dramatic decrease in disclosure on privatization and changes in disclosure have continued. It is interesting that one of the results of privatization has been that the companies have shifted away from current cost accounting, as favoured under public sector ownership, in their annual report and accounts despite the need to provide current cost regulatory accounts. By 1995 three of the twelve RECs were not providing current cost information, and the others were soon to follow this lead, as is seen in the analysis of the next two years below.

The Period 1 April 1995 to 31 March 1997

The shareholder analysis performed for this period of time will be a simplified version of that performed above. The profitability and accounting return on capital measures will be calculated in the same way, but the cash flow measures are not included. This is because the RECs have tended not to produce cash flow figures for the period subsequent to take-over, as they are no longer required to do so. This analysis is still performed for the generators and the National Grid. Most analyses of take-overs adopt either a market approach (see for example Franks and Harris, 1989), that consider the market returns for a period of time before and after the take-over date, or a profitability approach (see for example Ravenscroft and Scherer, 1987). Therefore for each of the RECs the market performance will consider the increase in value to the shareholders of the RECs prior to the take-over and the market performance of the acquiring company both before and after. In addition, the profitability of the RECs will be considered both before and after the take-over.

Traditional Profitability Measures

The definition of return on sales and earnings per share are the same as those used above. In the period from privatization to 1995 we saw a very consistent picture of increasing profitability. In the years 1995 to 1997 the companies, with the exception of The National Grid, had an increase in exceptional (exc.) and extraordinary (ext.) items. Therefore for the Generators and the RECs the return on sales is quoted both before and after these items.

Table 7.11 Return on sales (1995-1997)

	1995	1996	1997
	%	%	%
Generators after exc. and ext. items	19.3	22.3	21.5
Generators before exc. and ext. items	19.7	20.3	21.8
The National Grid	47.5	45.8	45.4
The RECs after exc. and ext. items	13.8	23.9	12.7
The RECs before exc. and ext. items	15.0	16.8	14.6

If we include the exceptional and extraordinary items the largest anomaly is the comparatively high return on sales made by the RECs in the year ending in 1996. This is caused by the large profits made by the RECs on the sale of The National Grid in this year and the lower turnover caused by the customer discounts mentioned in the value added analysis in chapter 5. In 1997 the regulated elements of the industry, transmission and supply and distribution, show a reduction on profits as compared with the year ending in 1995. This, I believe, is due to the new price controls enforced by the regulator at this time. The effect of the price controls is to restrict turnover and this feeds through to a proportionately greater reduction in profit before interest and tax. Therefore turnover in 1997 is lower than 1995 and this has also resulted in lower profits. Table 7.12 shows how the price controls have become stricter over the period.

Table 7.12 Price control reviews in the electricity industry in England and Wales

Date	Price control review
April 1990	Transmission RPI – 0
	Distribution RPI + 1.3 (average)
	Supply RPI – 0
April 1993	Transmission RPI – 3
April 1994	Supply RPI – 2
April 1995	Distribution one off 14% and RPI – 2
April 1996	Distribution one off 11% and RPI – 3
April 1997	Transmission one off 20% and RPI - 4

The largest changes relate to the distribution aspect of the industry. Large one off cuts from the distribution price reviews came into effect in both April 1995 and April 1996. These were required as the regulator recognized that these companies had significant financial strength and had been able to make efficiency gains at a faster rate than those implied by the earlier price-cap. The percentage of a consumer's final bill that relates to distribution varies between 19 per cent and 29 per cent for large and domestic customers respectively. Therefore the effect of these changes on the real price of electricity (between the year ending 31.3.1995 and the year ending 31.3.1997) of the RECs would be somewhere in the region of 4-7 per cent (19 to 29 per cent * 14+11 per cent). The actual fall in turnover between the two periods is 4.5 per cent. The fall in return on sales in transmission might also, in part, be explained by the tightening of the price-cap in 1993, although the levels of profits remain extremely high. It is therefore not surprising that the regulator also chose to enforce a much more stringent price-cap in April 1997, including a one-off cut of 20 per cent.

In terms of earnings per share we also require information both before and after exceptional and extraordinary items. This is presented in Table 7.13 below.

Table 7.13 Earnings per share (1995-1997)

	1995	1996	1997
	£	£	£
Generators after exc. and ext. items	0.47	0.62	0.57
Generators before exc. and ext. items	0.48	0.54	0.58
The National Grid	1.08	0.40	0.24
The RECs after exc. and ext. items	0.77	1.31	0.51
The RECs before exc. and ext. items	0.87	0.72	0.64

If we consider EPS before exceptional and extraordinary items the results are similar to those for return on sales. The generators have continued to improve earnings per share, whereas the RECs have suffered a decline. For most of the companies this is caused by a fall in profits, but for MEB and Southern the decline is accentuated by the number of shares being doubled. Similarly, when the National Grid was floated on the London Stock Exchange the number of shares in issue was increased four-fold and the fall in profit is relatively speaking less significant.

Accounting Return on Capital Measures

As in the earlier period both the historical cost and current cost returns on capital employed will be considered. Table 7.14 below summarizes the historical cost return on capital employed for the industry in the period showing both before and after exceptional and extraordinary items for both the generators and the RECs. As can be seen from these figures the levels of returns on capital employed have remained high in the industry. The figure after extraordinary and exceptional items for the RECs in the year ending in 1996 is high due to the profits made on the sale of The National Grid.

Table 7.14 Historic cost return on capital employed (1995-1997)

	1995	1996	1997
	%	%	%
Generators after exc. and ext. items	25.0	25.9	21.3
Generators before exc. and ext. items	25.4	23.6	21.3
The National Grid	29.2	31.0	30.2
The RECs after exc. And ext. items	24.8	44.3	25.1
The RECs before exc. and ext. items	26.8	26.0	27.9

As mentioned above, according to Edwards, Kay and Meyer it is inappropriate to compare the historic cost ROCE with the cost of capital. Instead current cost is required. The necessary information is not available for ten of the twelve RECs in the year 1997. In addition the information is only available for six RECs in 1996, but these figures are again distorted by the sale of the National Grid. It is therefore not intended to include these results here. For the generators and the National Grid the following calculations were possible.

Table 7.15 Current cost return on capital employed (1995-1997)

	1995	1996	1997
	%	%	%
National Grid	5.9	7.3	n.a.
National Power	3.5	5.8	n.a.
Powergen	4.5	7.2	10.6

An improvement is seen in the current cost returns in 1996 over 1995. If compared to the WACC, as calculated earlier in this chapter at 6.4 per cent, we see that National Power remains below the WACC, but the other two companies are providing returns above the costs.

Cash Flow Measures

As mentioned above, once the RECs became subsidiaries of larger groups they were no longer required to publish cash flow information. It has been decided to not attempt to create a cash flow statement for these companies as the assumptions required are too great and the other measures calculated are already providing significant evidence as to the level of performance for shareholders. The cash flow return on investment has been calculated for the generators and the National Grid in the same way as was done above. The basic CFROI and the operating cash flow – tax CFROI are presented below in Tables 7.16 and 7.17 respectively.

Table 7.16 Basic CFROI (1995-1997)

	1995	1996	1997
	%	%	%
Generators	13.8	18.7	15.0
National Grid	13.4	12.7	13.0

Table 7.17 Operating CFROI (1995-1997)

	1995	1996	1997
	%	%	%
Generators	19.2	14.6	11.0
National Grid	14.7	8.7	19.2

Overall we can say that these cash flow returns appear to demonstrate that the companies are achieving returns in excess of the cost of capital (6.4 per cent). The question remains, however, as to how the market has viewed these different performance signals. We will now consider this in the next section.

Market Performance Measures

As mentioned above shareholders benefit from dividends and increased share prices. The generators have been listed on the London Stock Exchange throughout the period and therefore we can consider the total shareholder returns for these companies. The other companies in the industry all changed ownership in the period and will need to be considered individually.

Table 7.18 Generator's TSR (1995-1997)

	1995	1996	1997
	%	%	%
National Power	-4.6	14.0	45.9
Powergen	-10.9	19.9	17.0

We discussed the negative shareholder returns in the year ending in 1995 in the earlier part of this chapter. If we consider the following two years the returns to the shareholder are in excess of the maximum cost of equity of 13.1 per cent. Therefore it would appear that the abnormal accounting and cash flow returns have indeed followed through into the actual returns to shareholders.

Table 7.19 The National Grid's TSR (1995-1997)

	1995	1996	1997
	%	%	%
National Grid	N/a	-6.7	15.8

The National Grid was floated on the stock exchange in December 1995. The initial response was poor and the returns were actually negative in the period up to March 1996. It certainly seems that the National Grid was not unduly under-priced at the time of flotation, as there were very little gains to be made. In this case the strong returns suggested from the accounts and the cash flows do not appear to have benefited the new shareholders. This poor early response may also be in response to the large specie dividends paid to the former owners (the RECs) at the time of flotation. This left the National Grid in a less financially secure position than would otherwise have been the case. The returns to the shareholders continued to be negative and the return index is at it lowest in September 1996. In the six months after this the returns to the shareholders were strongly positive and in excess of the cost of equity.

If we now turn to the RECs the picture is made less clear by the take-overs in the period. The government redeemed its golden share in the RECs on the 31 March 1995 and this therefore opened the way for take-overs / mergers in the industry. The table below details the developments in the two-year period under consideration here. The dates followed by a tick (✔) represent the date of the successful take-over. As can be seen from this table, ten of the twelve RECs were successfully taken over by 31 March 1997. The exceptions are Southern, who were subject to a take-over bid by National Power that was not allowed, and Yorkshire, where the take-over was successfully completed one day later.

Table 7.20 Take-over activity

Company name	Take-over bid	Outcome
Eastern	31/7/95 – Hanson plc	18/9/95 ✔
East Midlands	13/11/96 – Dominion Resources	13/1/97 ✔
London	18/12/96 – Entergy Corporation	7/2/97 ✔
Manweb	24/7/95 – Scottish Power	12/10/95 ✔
MEB	18/9/95 – Powergen	24/4/96 FAILS
	7/5/96 – Avon Energy Partners	7/6/96 ✔
Northern	14/12/94 – Trafalgar House	2/6/95 FAILS
	28/10/96 – Calenergy	24/12/96 ✔
Norweb	8/9/95 - North West Water	8/11/95 ✔
	28/9/95 - Texas Energy Partners	
Seeboard	6/11/95 – Central and South Western	11/1/96 ✔
Southern	2/10/95 – National Power	24/4/96 FAILS
Swalec	4/12/95 – Welsh Water	29/1/96 ✔
SWEB	13/7/95 – Southern Electric	18/9/95 ✔
Yorkshire	24/2/97 – American Electrical Power	1/4/97 ✔

We shall now consider what effect the above take-over activity has on the shareholder returns for these companies.

Table 7.21 Datastream return index for RECs

Company name	31/3/95	Day before bid	End of bid day	Successful completion or 31/3/97
Eastern	297.9	379.7	493.1	525.1
East Midlands	315.7	532.5	542.5	580.0
London	304.7	499.2	508.7	526.1
Manweb	333.3	390.0	490.0	533.8
MEB	316.8	505.5	525.1	651.3 – 587.9
	587.9	670.3	686.1	703.6
Northern	391.9	496.5	618.7	608.2
Norweb	315.9	521.1	538.7	637.0
Seeboard	354.9	567.9	671.6	676.2
Southern	303.9	483.0	520.2	572.7 – 522.6
				524.9
Swalec	331.1	595.9	626.5	630.8
SWEB	327.4	484.1	489.8	520.5
Yorkshire	364.5	679.1	731.7	764.9

Table 7.21 reports the Return Index for each company at the start of this period, i.e. the day the government sold its golden share, and either on the day the

take-over was successfully completed or 31 March 1997 where this was not the case. As can also be seen from this table for some companies the announcement of a take-over bid makes a very large difference and the returns to shareholders on the day are extremely high. Chronologically the first bid after 31 March 1995 was for SWEB. There is little increase on the day of the announcement, but if we consider that the return index two weeks prior to the announcement was 347.3, in this two-week period there is a 41 per cent return to shareholders. Manweb and Eastern were the next RECs to receive bids and on the day of the bid the return index suggests returns in excess of 25 per cent. Not all of the companies experience such large increases in the period leading up to and including the announcement. It may be that the increase was incorporated once it became obvious that the RECs would be subject to take-over speculation and that the government would not block these.[1] This would suggest that somewhere between 31 March 1995, when the government redeemed its golden share, and the time of acquisition (or 31 March 1997) this fact should be incorporated into the returns to shareholders. To measure the extent of the effect of this information the following table records the total returns to shareholders for the period from 31 March 1995 to either the acquisition date or 31 March 1997 whichever is sooner.

Table 7.22 TSR for RECs (1995-1997)

Company name	Increase in return index	Period of time
Eastern	76.3%	5 months and 18 days
East Midlands	83.7%	1 year, 9 months and 13 days
London	72.7%	1 year, 10 months and 7 days
Manweb	60.2%	6 months and 12 days
MEB	122.1%	1 year, 2months and 7 days
Northern	55.2%	1 year, 8 months and 24 days
Norweb	101.6%	7 months and 8 days
Seeboard	90.5%	9 months and 11 days
Southern	72.7%	2 years
Swalec	90.5%	9 months and 29 days
SWEB	59.0%	5 months and 18 days
Yorkshire	109.8%	2 years

As can be seen from this table the returns to shareholders in this period are extremely high and far in excess of the cost of equity, which has a maximum of around 13 per cent. The actual annualized shareholder returns are at least double this and in some cases very much higher still. The shareholders that held shares throughout this period made huge gains and this added to the gains that were made in the period from privatization to 31 March 1995 further emphasizes the fact that these shareholders really have won as a result of privatization.

The shareholders of the acquired companies certainly appear to have benefited from this take-over activity. It is also interesting to consider whether the acquiring companies' shareholders benefited. This is not easy to ascertain, although the results are considered below. Return index information was found for six of the ten companies acquiring RECs before 31 March 1997.

Table 7.23 Datastream return index – acquiring companies

Company name	31/3/95	Day before bid	End of bid day	Successful completion	31/3/97
Hanson (Eastern)	161147.8	161577.0	160476.6	155817.8	118133.2
Dominion Resources (East Midlands)	583.4	712.3	723.5	715.2	673.6
Entergy (London)	406.8	604.1	615.1	587.6	547.4
Scottish Power (Manweb)	155.6	153.6	150.2	178.5	196.0
United Utilities (Norweb)	317.4	369.1	372.1	358.9	421.0
Hyder (Swalec)	353.4	397.9	416.3	443.0	501.9

Over this two-year period these companies will have undertaken many different activities and we can not suggest that any returns relate specifically or wholly to the purchase of a REC. The three RECs bought by UK utility companies (two water companies and a power company) have all seen positive returns since the announcement of a take-over. In the cases of Scottish Power and Hyder these post acquisition shareholder returns appear to be in excess of the cost of equity, although this is not the case for United Utilities. The two US companies and the conglomerate have all provided negative shareholder returns after the announcement of the acquisition and have therefore failed to provide adequate returns. Again it must be stressed that this is not necessarily a result of the acquisition, but we do appear to be able to say that shareholders in these companies have not fared as well as the shareholders of the RECs. This would appear to provide some evidence that it is the shareholders of acquired companies, as opposed to the shareholders of the acquiring company, that benefit from take-overs. This is consistent with the findings of many studies into the shareholder returns from mergers and acquisitions.

Concluding Thoughts on the Period 1 April 1995 to 31 March 1997

Historical cost returns still appear high for the privatized companies, although the RECs have experienced a fall in profits in this period as tougher regulation is introduced. The analysis of current cost and cash flow information is restricted by a change in disclosure by the companies. This leaves limited analysis that suggests an improvement in returns for the generators and the National Grid. The shareholders of the RECs continued to benefit from extremely high market returns up to the time when they were taken over. The story is not so clear cut for the acquiring companies. The RECs continue to make excellent historical cost returns, but the actual returns to shareholders have not been consistently high. It is worth remembering, however, that the new owners have benefited from high levels of dividends from the RECs. Four take-overs (Eastern, Manweb, Norweb, and South Western) were all completed before the flotation of the National Grid and so the specie dividend was paid to the new owners. For example, on '23 April 1996 the Company [Eastern] paid a dividend in Specie to Hanson' equal to £416.8million. Also the levels of dividends in 1996/7, when most of the take-overs had been completed, was more than 45 per cent of value added as compared to 25 per cent in 1994/5. So the acquiring companies have been able to use the RECs as a source of dividends, but the shareholders do not appear to have benefited as much as the owners of the RECs before the take-overs.

Conclusions

In chapter 5 we saw that there appeared, from the value added analysis, a large benefit to shareholders as a result of an increase in value added and a redistribution from other stakeholder groups, most clearly the employee group. This chapter has documented some more detailed shareholder analysis that enables further comment on the post-privatization benefits to shareholders. The historic cost accounts show that the privatized companies are very profitable with high historic cost returns on capital and sales. Edwards, Kay and Mayer (1987), however, argue that current cost information provides a more accurate prediction of returns. The current cost analysis is far less convincing and does not appear to demonstrate overly generous returns. Therefore there remains the question as to why the returns to shareholders, in terms of dividends and share price appreciation as measured by total shareholder returns, has been so large. It would appear that these returns are based on the historic cost information provided to the shareholders via the annual report and accounts. As mentioned earlier this would appear to support the literature suggesting that there is a 'functional fixation' with earnings per share and historic cost returns (see for example Hand (1990, 1991) and Day (1986)).

It must be stressed here that many of the calculations included in this chapter are based upon estimates and subjective judgements. The data itself has been obtained from publicly available sources and therefore could have been manipulated, or creatively accounted, before publication. Therefore this analysis can not claim to give the true, or the only, representation of performance in this industry for this period of time. It can be said, however, that in terms of actual returns received over the period the shareholders have done very well and certainly have received greater returns than those available on the stock market generally. Similarly when considering the risk undertaken by the shareholders, as measured here by the CAPM, the TSR are far in excess of those expected. It should be remembered that part of the regulator's primary duties is to ensure that the companies are financially viable. This, therefore, appears to reduce shareholders' risks below that experienced when investing in most private sector companies. Further, the interview with the regulator undertaken in this research it was clearly stated that the regulator wanted the industry to be seen as a low risk industry so that the companies have access to finance.

Note

[1] The timing of the returns to shareholders in these companies would make an interesting study that could provide some evidence with regard to market efficiency. An event study methodology could be adopted to analyse exactly when the market incorporated the industry and company specific information.

Chapter 8

Stakeholder Analysis

Introduction

The previous chapter showed a detailed analysis of shareholder performance in the Electricity Industry in England and Wales for the period from privatization to 31 March 1997. This analysis supported the conclusions from the value added analysis that shareholders had benefited significantly since privatization. This was most clearly demonstrated by the very large shareholder returns in the form of dividends and share price appreciation over the period. The value added analysis suggested that at least part of this wealth was a redistribution from other stakeholders, most clearly in the case of employees. This chapter analyzes the performance to a number of other stakeholder groups. The purpose of this is to better understand whether there has been a creation or redistribution of wealth and what the implications of this may be.

This chapter is separated into four main sections, one to deal with each stakeholder group: employees, consumers, suppliers and the environment. Each section considers the performance of the electricity industry for these stakeholder groups and discusses its implications.

Employee Analysis

From chapter 4 we saw that employee and employment reporting were at their height of popularity in the late 1970s and this resulted in a great number of employee-related measures being reported. Through the interviews held with representatives of employees, in chapter 6, the following issues were highlighted as the most important to the employees in this industry and have therefore been considered here. This does not mean that there would not be a benefit from a more complete consideration of other employee-related issues and measures.

- Employee remuneration;
- Job security; and
- Health and Safety.

Since the decrease in interest in employee reporting the level of detail of employee information within annual reports has reduced and is now consistent with those required by accounting standards and company law. There is no segmental information, either geographically or by job type, and this means that the analysis performed can only be at a very overall level and this raises questions as to its ability to fully detail what has happened. It would be much better to be able to consider the remuneration, security and health and safety of employees by location and job type, but this information is no longer available. In addition the level of employee training received was identified as a key driver of employee satisfaction. The companies provide no such information, although the Electricity Association (1997) report that an Electricity Training Association survey:

> revealed that the estimated spend [on training by Electricity companies] in 1995/96 was more than £1000 per employee with approximately six days per head of off-job training. These figures are far in excess of the national average. (p.55)

Employee Remuneration

Firstly if we consider the remuneration information provided by the companies the only distinction that can be made consistently across the companies between different employees is between employees and directors. The executive directors have been analyzed separately to all other employees as they can be considered to be a distinct stakeholder group, but the results are shown with those of the other employees for comparison.

Table 8.1 Average remuneration in generation

	1991	1992	1993	1994	1995	1996	1997
	£	£	£	£	£	£	£
National Power	22,833	26,276	29,198	31,281	32,522	33,810	33,476
Powergen	23,600	26,192	28,432	30,176	33,102	31,095	35,028
Total – Employees	23,109	26,245	28,918	30,831	32,774	32,558	34,142
Total – Executive Directors	148,400	220,900	230,800	272,500	315,900	342,900	436,100

The average level of remuneration in the generating companies has increased markedly over the period. In fact the average remuneration has increased by nearly 48 per cent over the period in nominal terms. The retail price index has increased by 18.3 per cent between March 1991 and March 1997 and so the average remuneration in the generators has significantly increased in real terms. This increase has come at a time when the employee numbers have fallen dramatically. It may well be that this increase in average remuneration suggests that the staff made redundant were lower paid and this means that there is a higher proportion of more highly paid staff in 1997 as compared to 1991. As the employee information is not segmented by job type it is not possible to answer this question from the information available in the annual reports of the companies.

In comparison the executive directors have seen their average remuneration increase by nearly 194 per cent over the period. This is significantly higher than the increase in the cost of living and the increase given to employees.

This means that the gap in salary between the executive directors and the other employees is growing. In the year ending in 1991 the executive directors earned 6.4 times the average employee, but by 1997 this had increased to 12.8 times.

Table 8.2 Average remuneration in National Grid (NG)

	1991	1992	1993	1994	1995	1996	1997
	£	£	£	£	£	£	£
NG - Employees	27,802	29,677	31,804	33,392	34,921	34,136	35,366
NG – Executive Directors	N/a	N/a	N/a	N/a	218,800	228,200	223,000

Average remuneration in the National Grid has increased over the period. In the years ending in 1992 –1995 the severance costs that were reported by the company as part of employment costs have been excluded. It is not clear whether severance costs were included in the 1991 total. Therefore if we just consider the years 1992 to 1997 we see a 19.2 per cent increase in average nominal remuneration. At the same time the retail price index increased by 13.3 per cent and so the average real remuneration has increased.

The executive directors were not remunerated until the year ending 31 March 1995 and so no comparison can be made. In the three years that remuneration was paid there is no clear pattern, although the level of remuneration in the year ending in 1997 is higher than that ending in 1995. We can also see that on average the executive directors are paid 6.3 times the amount that the average employee is paid.

Table 8.3 below shows that the average employee remuneration in the RECs as a whole has increased each year. If we consider the trend REC by REC there has also tended to be a year on year increase, although this is the not the case in every year. Regional differences are noted, and some of these are as expected: for example London is consistently above average and Norweb is consistently below average. Perhaps the most surprising result is the high levels of average remuneration provided by Swalec in 1992 and 1995. In the year ending in 1992 an exceptional item of £10.5million was included in the employee remuneration reported and if this is excluded the average remuneration falls to £21,552. In the year ending in 1995 severance costs of £10.1million were included and if this is excluded the average remuneration falls to £23,202. The effects of these on the overall averages are approximately £200 and do not therefore significantly alter the results. There are some specific anomalies relating to Manweb, MEB and Swalec in 1996. These are caused by severance payments and changes to pension schemes and the net effect is very small. The average level of remuneration has increased in nominal terms by approximately 29.5 per cent over the seven years analyzed here and so again we can say that the real average levels of remuneration have increased, but not by as much as in the generating companies.

Table 8.3 Average remuneration in RECs

	1991	1992	1993	1994	1995	1996	1997
	£	£	£	£	£	£	£
East Midlands	18,044	19,610	20,039	22,116	23,153	24,095	25,061
Eastern	17,330	18,569	19,393	20,674	22,735	22,987	26,981
London	21,103	22,735	21,726	23,920	26,145	24,079	24,708
Manweb	17,214	19,785	20,507	21,245	20,976	25,302	23,496
MEB	18,553	22,112	20,787	22,019	22,627	15,686	21,392
Northern	17,455	19,308	21,907	21,641	22,449	22,584	23,590
Norweb	16,698	18,157	18,894	20,240	19,504	22,209	27,456
Seeboard	18,734	20,313	20,870	20,025	22,256	23,117	21,557
Southern	20,311	21,055	21,958	20,721	21,884	22,514	21,904
Swalec	20,643	24,443	22,937	23,581	26,341	29,393	25,144
SWEB	19,149	21,604	22,148	24,771	25,644	25,816	22,635
Yorkshire	17,536	19,141	19,672	22,037	23,097	23,845	24,332
Total – Employees	18,456	20,331	20,683	21,746	22,760	23,028	23,903
Total – Executive Directors	109,770	143,710	152,640	165,860	192,780	N/a	N/a

The average remuneration for executive directors in the industry has also increased each year. In total it has increased by 75.6 per cent in the period 1991 – 1995 and this is much higher than the increases to employees and the increases in the cost of living. As was the case in the Generators, this means that the spread between the average employee and the average executive director in the RECs has increased. In 1991 the average executive director earned nearly 6 times as much as the average employee, but by 1995 this had increased to approximately 8.5 times. Due to the fact that the RECs were taken over in the period from 1995 to 1997 the information relating to directors' remuneration is no longer reported in sufficient detail. In addition the benefits to the directors from the sale of the National Grid and changes in directors as a result of the take-overs make a simple comparison difficult. It can be said, however, that the directors appear to have been rewarded handsomely irrespective of whether they continued to work for the new group of companies or not. The increases in pay to executive directors in the privatized utility industries have been controversial and the directors were labelled fat cats by some commentators in the press. The counter argument has been given that these directors are now operating in a very different environment, with regulation and capital markets to contend with, and that as a result of this their salaries should be equivalent to the market rates for private sector executive directors. It is not intended to say here which of these points of view is correct, simply to say that executive directors have benefited in terms of pay and prestige from the privatization of the industry.

If we now return to the main body of employees, another source of evidence for the changes in levels of earnings are the New Earnings Surveys produced by the Department of Employment that show the following changes in the period being analyzed:

Table 8.4 Changes in pay for full-time employees on adult rates April to April

	1990/1	1991/2	1992/3	1993/4	1994/5	1995/6	1996/7
	%	%	%	%	%	%	%
Production and distribution of electricity	9.3	13.1	5.9	4.0	-2.6	8.5	5.5
Matched sample	10.8	15.3	6.7	6.7	1.2	6.4	7.3

These statistics would suggest an increase of 51.8 per cent in the period, but suggests that the increase is below that of a matched sample in nearly every year. This suggests that the remuneration earned by employees in this industry were rising, but not as quickly as those experienced by equivalent employees in other industries. This does provide supporting evidence that remuneration has increased at a faster rate than inflation over the same period. The New Earnings Survey also provides some evidence on how the levels of pay are distributed between the employees and these are detailed in Table 8.5 below:

Table 8.5 Distribution of pay for full-time employees on adult rates (£/week)

	10 % earned less than £/week	% change from previous year %	10% earned more than £/week	% change from previous year %
1991	200.4	N/a	530.4	N/a
1992	220.6	10.1	592.2	11.7
1993	234.2	6.2	624.7	5.5
1994	235.0	0.3	716.0	14.6
1995	239.9	2.1	643.0	-10.2
1996	257.4	7.3	712.8	10.9
1997	257.8	0.2	771.6	8.2

Over the whole period the increases are 28.6 per cent for the lowest 10 per cent limit and 45.5 per cent for the highest 10 per cent limit. The lowest 10 per cent limit has not quite increased as quickly as the average or as the highest 10 per cent limit.

Overall the average levels of remuneration, in both nominal and real terms, have increased in the period of time since privatization. This is supported by the Unions who suggest that the remaining employees are earning the same real level of remuneration, as was previously the case in the nationalized industry. With the publicly available information it is difficult to say why this is the case, although an IDS (1995) report 697 appears to hint that an element of this is 'to buy change'.

The type of change is not mentioned in this report, but from the interviews with the Unions reported in chapter 6 it is clear that:

- the nature of the jobs have changed such that individuals are now expected to perform higher skilled or multi-skilled jobs; and
- the level of productivity expected from individual employees has increased due to the fall in levels of employment (see below).

Job Security

In chapter 4 we considered measures that relate to job security such as the 'annual labour turnover index'. This requires the number of leavers in a year to be divided by the average number of employees therefore giving a proportion of employees that leave the organization. The higher the index the less secure the job. Unfortunately this can not be calculated, as the number of leavers in the year is not known. The annual report of the companies provides information on levels of employment, but this only provides evidence on the size of the workforce and not whether people have left and been replaced. As this is the case the following analysis will look at the levels of employment and how they have changed over the period as this still gives us some indication of job security, although it is accepted that this is not a true measure of labour turnover. The table below identifies the employment levels for the period under consideration here.

Table 8.6 Employee numbers

	1991	1992	1993	1994	1995	1996	1997
Generators	24,553	21,048	15,649	11,737	9,618	8,996	7,841
National Grid	6,550	6,217	5,666	5,127	4,871	4,565	4,414
RECs	82,144	80,621	76,651	70,834	64,804	57,188	48,180
Total	113,247	107,886	97,966	87,698	79,293	70,749	60,435

As can be seen from a cursory examination of these numbers the decrease in numbers has been dramatic. The average decrease in employee numbers in these companies is nearly 47 per cent. The decrease is most significant in the generators, although it must be remembered that these companies now account for a smaller proportion of the total electricity generated in England and Wales than previously. This reduction from 73.1 per cent to 56.1 per cent of generation turnover (a 23 per cent fall), however, does not fully account for the 68 per cent decrease in employee numbers. The National Grid and the RECs also record significant reductions of 32.6 per cent and 41.3 per cent respectively. If we consider the case of the RECs we can see that the most dramatic reductions have occurred in the last two years. This is perhaps not surprising, as cost savings, through employee reductions, are often the motivation for take-overs. In fact if we consider the RECs that made the largest reductions over the period we can see that the five largest reductions are all made by companies that were successfully taken over by the end of January 1996, namely SWEB, Eastern, Manweb, Norweb, and Swalec.[1]

In their report the Electricity Association (1997) suggested that the reductions in employee numbers were due to:

> significant restructuring and cost cutting' and that it 'has been achieved almost entirely through natural wastage, early retirements, and voluntary severance supported by counselling and outplacement services. (p.54)

This does not, however, answer the question as to how the industry continues to operate with these levels of employment. It is suggested here that there are four possible ways by which these reductions have been made:

- employees have been replaced by technology;
- the industry was previously over staffed (or 'inefficient');
- certain work is now performed by sub-contractors to the industry; and /or
- certain work is no longer being performed.

From communications with the major unions in the industry it was confirmed that there have been dramatic changes in the employment practices within the electricity industry. Since privatization there has been a large decrease in the numbers of direct employees, there has been an increased use of sub-contractors, and employees have been subject to new working practices, such as multi-skilling. The decrease in employee numbers is a concern and although it is acknowledged that increased efficiency and productivity is a 'valid element', there is a concern that this has now gone too far.

There has been an increased use of sub-contractors, specifically, work such as canteen services, meter repairs and reading, and security are now sub-contracted. Therefore the same work is now being performed by an outside agency at a reduced price or with greater flexibility. As these are all labour intensive activities, it can only be assumed that these cost savings have been achieved through lower staff numbers or reduced rates of pay. This again raises concerns about the quality of service provided. The final possible explanation for the decrease in employee numbers was that certain work might not be performed now which previously was. Ferner and Colling (1991, 1993) recognized that if this was the case then there should be a subsequent effect on the quality of service provided. If this is the case this should become apparent in the consumer analysis below.

Overall it would appear reasonable to suggest that job security in the industry must be low throughout this period. This analysis confirms that the real reduction in total employee remuneration is explained by the reduction in employee numbers not by the levels of individual employee remuneration. The need to maximize shareholder wealth, the reality of regulation, and the potential of competition have had a dramatic impact.

Health and Safety

Health and safety concerns were expressed in interviews with Unions and this is obviously a key issue for employees. The Electricity Association (1997) reported on the safety records of the companies in the UK electricity industry, and on page 55 they state that: 'The chart below shows the improvement in three-day accident rates over the last 10 years.' Interestingly they note that the 'spread of accident incidence rates among member companies ranged from 0.22 to 3.06', which suggests that there is quite a disparity between the best and worst performing companies.

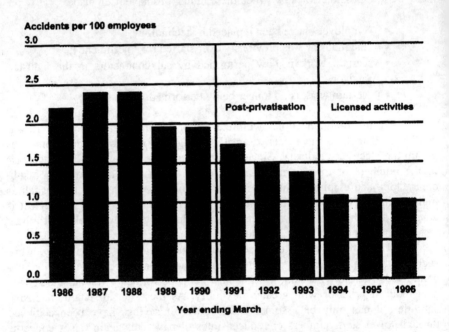

Figure 8.1 Accident rates in the electricity industry

Source: EA (1997)

The statistics reported by the EA relate to injuries that require an absence of over 3 days. The Health and Safety Executive also report on 'all reported injuries' for the 'production and distribution of electricity, gas and other forms of energy'. The figures reported by the Health and Safety Executive for the period are included in Table 8.7 below. Unfortunately the Health and Safety Statistics do not separately report on the electricity industry, but the downward trend reported in this broader category appears consistent with those published by the Electricity Association above.

Table 8.7 All reported employee injuries – rate per 100,000

	1990/1	1992/3	1993/4	1994/5	1995/6	1996/7
Production and distribution of electricity, gas and other forms of energy	1942.1	1533.8	1363.0	1181.8	1,225.9	1,475.6
Total manufacturing industries	1268.2	1229.4	1174.0	1200.4	1,199.0	1,210.3
Construction	1907.0	1602.8	1311.8	1315.0	1,262.0	1,508.8
All industries	818.0	739.5	720.9	723.6	685.4	698.6

Over the period to 1994/5 it is worth noting that the reported levels of accidents have fallen more quickly in energy production and distribution than in any of the other categories used for comparison above. It is clear, however, that across all industries and especially non-service industries the levels of reported accidents have also fallen over this period. In 1995/6 the category was changed from 'Production and distribution of electricity, gas and other forms of energy' to an 'Electricity, gas and water supply' section. This reflects the changes in Standard Industrial Classification between 1980 and 1992, but makes it impossible to compare the figures in 1995/6 with those from earlier years'. The figures also appear to suggest a jump in accidents and injuries in the year 1996/7. The following caveat, however, is placed upon the statistics:

> 1996/97 injury figures, excluding fatalities to workers cannot be directly compared to previous years figures as they were reported under different legislation (see Introduction and Revision of RIDDOR '85 to RIDDOR '95). (HSE, 1997, p.134)

Therefore this tells us very little about changes in the health and safety performance of the industry. It is, however, an example of how changes to reporting can make the figures / statistics reported worthless. Without comparability these figures are difficult to discuss.

Concluding Thoughts on Employee Analysis

Labour's share of value added fell dramatically in the period from privatization until March 1997. The reason for this fall was the significant reduction in numbers of employees. In the industry total employment fell by approximately 47 per cent and this dramatic reduction in numbers following year on year must result in increased job insecurity in the industry. The change is made more stark by the fact that previously the industry had been considered one of employment for life. Privatization and subsequent regulation has also resulted in higher expectations of productivity such that any slack has been reduced and employees are required to work harder to ensure that the work is completed. Having said this, the remaining employees have benefited from good levels of remuneration and 'increased responsibility' (Company interview). Also, over this period of time Health and Safety levels have improved, although Union interviewees suggest that this trend will reverse if employees continue to be asked to be ever more productive.

Consumer Analysis

In chapter 4 it was suggested that consumers' primary concerns (as consumers) are price and quality. The attention here is on the consumer, the end-user, of the product and so as it is the RECs, the supply companies, that are the contact point for these consumers the analysis necessarily concentrates on these companies. Given these objectives the following measures of performance for consumers are considered:

- Average prices;
- Minutes lost per customer;
- Performance against the regulator's guaranteed and overall standards; and
- Numbers of complaints.

Given the nature of these measures, the majority of the information is not required to be published in the annual report and accounts of the companies, although companies can choose to do so voluntarily. In practice the reports produced by the regulator are an important source of information for this analysis. Such valuable information is not so readily available in other, unregulated, industries and so at present such an analysis would be much more difficult to achieve elsewhere.

Average Prices

Table 8.8 below summarizes the developments in the regulatory price-cap.[2]

Table 8.8 Price-cap regulation

Date	Part of industry	Price-cap
April 1990	Transmission	RPI – 0
	Distribution	RPI + 1.3 (average)
	Supply	RPI – 0
April 1993	Transmission	RPI – 3
April 1994	Supply	RPI – 2
April 1995	Distribution	One off 14% cut and RPI – 2
April 1996	Distribution	One off 11% cut and RPI - 3
April 1997	Transmission	One off 20% cut and RPI - 4

The Conservative government, in April 1990, set the first price-cap for all regulated elements of the industry. We saw in chapter 5 that the advancement of efficiency is only one of several objectives set at the time of privatization and it should be recognized that not all of the objectives would lead to a similar level of X being set. For example, a lenient X would be more conducive to a successful and timely sale than it would to maximizing the efficiency incentive.

The first post privatization review undertaken by OFFER in England and Wales was performed on the transmission element in 1993. This saw a tightening of X from 0 per cent to 3 per cent and the review of the supply element of the industry in 1994 saw a similar tightening of X from 0 per cent to 2 per cent. The real change, however, occurred in the price reviews from April 1995 onwards where the regulator recognized that the companies had built up significant levels of financial strength and therefore we see much more stringent reviews. These price cuts were sufficient to impact upon the final price to the consumer, as discussed in chapter 7.

Not every element of the industry is regulated and therefore the actual final price to the customer may not necessarily move in line with the price-cap levels set by the regulator. Some electricity is supplied at a standard price to anyone requiring it, while some is delivered according to pre-agreed contracts, at a lower price. Such contracts relate to large customers, and the opportunity of providing such negotiated supply to large customers at a lower price is of course greater in the more industrialized regions.

The Electricity Association (1999) has considered electricity prices in the UK as compared to world and EU prices. Further, this data distinguishes between domestic and industrial electricity prices. Table 8.9 provides a summary of this data. The domestic price changes in the UK, as opposed to other EU countries, for this period suggest that benefits gained by consumers in England and Wales have been in line with, and in fact marginally better, than gains in other countries. The UK price has consistently been the fourth cheapest of the twelve EU countries for which data was given in every year until the last two years when it became the third cheapest. In the first year shown here, 1/1/1991 – 1/1/1992 the price of domestic electricity increased by 15.2 per cent and this is greater than the increase in the retail price index over the same period. This increased price is further accentuated if we extend the analysis back one more year. As at 1 January 1990 the domestic price of electricity in England and Wales (note that in this year it is not the UK price that is quoted) was ranked the second cheapest in the EU at a price of 7.26p/KWh. Therefore the ranking slipped two places in the year leading up to privatization. This suggests a nominal increase in domestic electricity prices of 9 per cent in the year, which exactly equals the increase in the RPI for the year. In the subsequent years the price for domestic electricity has varied between 9.00p/KWh and 9.29p/KWh. Over this period 1/1/92 – 1/1/97 the real domestic price of electricity of electricity was falling. In the final year it would appear that the stricter price controls are beginning to take effect, as there is a nominal decrease of 2.4 per cent, but this is more in the region of 7 per cent in real terms.

Table 8.9 EA electricity prices

	1/1/91	1/1/92	1/1/93	1/1/94	1/1/95	1/1/96	1/1/97
UK – Domestic prices (p/KWh)	7.81	9.00	9.29	9.01	9.23	9.23	9.01
Domestic EU ranking	4/12	5/12	4/12	4/12	4/12	3/12	3/12
Domestic World ranking	11/21	12/21	11/21	11/21	11/21	10/21	9/21
UK – Industrial prices (p/KWh)	4.79	5.18	5.29	5.29	5.29 / 4.56	5.29 / 4.53	5.29 / 4.14
Industrial EU ranking	8/12	8/12	7/12	7/12	7/12 / 3/12	6/12 / 2/12	8/12 / 2/12
Industrial World ranking	15/21	15/21	14/21	14/21	14/21 / 9/21	13/21 / 9/21	15/21 / 9/21

Source: Adapted from EA (1999)

If we now consider the industrial electricity prices we see that two prices are quoted for 1 January 1995 onwards. The higher of these is the price available 'based on published tariffs' and the lower price is the 'estimated price available under contract'. In previous years it is only the price based on published tariffs that is shown, except in 1994 when the comment is made that 'contract prices at this load are expected to be approximately 12 per cent lower'. This represents the opening up of the market for industrial users and the opportunity to contract / negotiate with the electricity companies for electricity. If we simply consider the published tariff prices, the nominal increase is 10.4 per cent over the period and hence there was a real decline in industrial electricity prices over the period. This increase is one of the lowest in the period as compared to the other twelve EU countries. If we consider the contract price, the performance is even better as the nominal price of industrial electricity actually falls by nearly 14 per cent. If we extend the analysis back one year, at 1 January 1990 the price in England and Wales was 4.51p/KWh and was ranked the fourth cheapest of the twelve countries. This represents a 6.2 per cent increase, below the rate of inflation, but sufficient for the ranking in the UK to slip from fourth to eighth.

Overall the real price of industrial electricity has fallen over the period and the gap between industrial and domestic prices has increased. By 1 January 1995, and subsequently, the price of electricity for domestic consumers is twice the contract price for industrial consumers. From this it would appear that industrial users have benefited more than domestic consumers. This could have been anticipated, because the industrial market has been opened up for competition, so the price will be competed down and levels of cross subsidies can change. Therefore, if industrial consumers were previously subsidising domestic consumers, as has been suggested was the case, then one way for electricity companies to become more competitive by offering lower prices is to reduce that cross subsidy. It is not easy to say whether consumers have benefited in terms of price. Industrial users have, as it is now cheaper in real terms, but whether it was necessary to privatize the industry to achieve this is unlikely. Similarly, domestic users end the period with a similar real price of electricity and the same effect could definitely have been achieved within the public sector.

Minutes Lost per Customer

This was acknowledged as the key service standard measure within the industry. EA (1997) report the following:

> the guaranteed standards introduced by OFFER after privatisation have put new emphasis on maintaining continuity of supply. Companies monitor their performance very closely by keeping a weekly track of every job carried out. Minutes lost, or availability, have improved for all companies, partly due to shorter, less frequent planned outages. The average minutes lost per connected customer due to pre-arranged outages has more than halved over the last five years from 35.5 minutes in 1991/2 to 17.0 minutes in 1995/6.

The chart below shows the average minutes lost per connected per connected customer for the years ending in March 1986 to March 1996. This chart shows that in eight of the eleven years reported here the level of faults have been of the same scale falling between 65 and 85 average minutes lost per connected customer and this suggests that electricity was available on average for 99.98 per cent of the time. The other three years show much higher levels of faults and presumably these will have been caused by bad weather conditions. Interestingly, if we exclude the three exceptional years, the four years with the highest average customer minutes lost are the four most recent years. Therefore it would appear that in years where there are no exceptional circumstances the minutes lost due to faults were actually marginally lower before privatization than after. In terms of the scheduled outages, the lowest levels are found in the last three years (1994-1996) and there does appear to be a reduction over this period. The level in 1994 is very marginally lower (1 or 2 minutes) than the levels achieved in 1986-88, and in fact the worst two years are those ending March 1991 (during which year privatization occurred) and March 1992, the first full year after privatization. The falls in scheduled outages in 1994-1996 appear to equal the increases in faults and therefore the performance could be said to have slightly worsened as one would imagine a consumer is happier with a scheduled outage, with warning, than a fault. Actually, the lowest total average minutes lost appear to be in 1986 and 1987, although the years 1986, 1987, 1989, 1994, 1995 and 1996 all have very similar levels of total average minutes lost, ranging from 95-98 minutes.

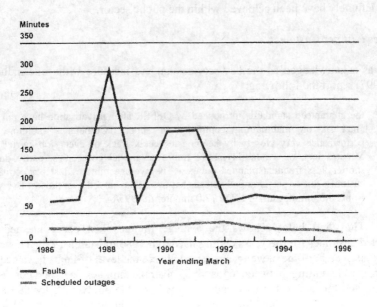

Figure 8.2 Average minutes lost per connected customer

Source: EA (1997)

     This consideration of the statistics provided by the EA would suggest that, if we exclude the exceptional years, the performance in the pre and post privatization periods have been very similar. In fact, if anything there appears to have been a shift from scheduled outages (the lower line) to faults (the upper line), which can only be considered to be a negative effect. If we were to continue the analysis further (see EA, 2001) we would see that in the years 1996 and 1997, the customer minutes lost due to scheduled outages continued to fall and have done so year on year up to and including 2000. The time lost due to faults remains less clear, although since 1996, which was the worst year since 1991, the trend does appear downward. It is clear that in 1997 the total minutes lost is lower than in any other year since privatization and that this is improved upon in both 1999 and 2000. This would appear to suggest a definite improvement, although it still does not provide us with the reason for this improvement (i.e. is it because of technological improvements or improved performance or improved weather).

Performance Against the Regulator's Guaranteed and Overall Standards

A deterioration of service levels would directly affect consumers and therefore OFFER introduced Standards of performance for the companies in 1991 (these are either guaranteed standards (GS) or overall standards (OS) and have been updated in 1993 and 1995) (OFFER, 1997). The standards are detailed below in Tables 8.10 and 8.12.

Table 8.10 Guaranteed standards

Service	Performance Level
1. Respond to failure of a supplier's fuse	Within 4 hours of any notification during working hours
2. Restoring electricity supplies after faults	Must be restored within 24 hours
3. Providing supply and meter	Arrange an appointment within 3 working days for domestic customers (and 5 working days for non-domestic customers)
4. Estimating charges	Within 10 working days for simple jobs and 20 working days for most others
5. Notice of supply interruption	Customers must be given at least 2 days notice
6. Investigation of voltage complaints	Visit or substantive reply within 10 working days
7. Responding to Meter problems	Visit within 10 working days or substantive reply within 5 working days
8. Responding to customers queries about charges and payment queries	A substantive reply within 5 working days
9. Making and keeping appointments	Companies must offer and keep a morning or afternoon appointment, or a timed appointment if requested by the customers
10. Notifying customers of payments owed under Standards	Write to customer within 10 working days of failure

Source: OFFER (1997)

We now consider the performance of the companies against the guaranteed and overall standards set by the regulator that came into force on 1 July 1991. The total number of failures against the guaranteed standards are set out in Table 8.11 below. The figures stated here for 1991/2 actually relate to the 9 months from 1/7/91-31/3/92, therefore the decrease in payments between 1992/3 and 1991/2 is more marked than would appear. In 1991/2 by far the largest number of payments related to GS9 – Appointments, and GS5– Notice of Supply interruption, and there have been definite improvements against these standards. In fact it is the improved performance against these standards that explains the vast majority of the fall in total failures. Having said this, failures against most standards have clearly improved over the period. This is not really the case for GS2 – Restoring electricity supplies after faults, GS7 – Meter problems, GS8 Charges and Payments queries and GS10 – Payments owed under standards. In these cases the improvements only seem to be made in the last two years of the period under consideration. In fact the reduction in payments under guaranteed standards has been impressive and almost across the board in these last two years. The only blemish is an increase in payments under GS2 in 1995/6.

Table 8.11 Total payments made for failure against GS

	1991/2	1992/3	1993/4	1994/5	1995/6	1996/7
GS1	134	82	38	43	41	11
GS2	525	358	500	377	466	153
GS3	113	179	42	22	16	6
GS4	326	200	75	19	18	32
GS5	2090	1931	1296	828	638	339
GS6	43	28	24	25	12	2
GS7	85	115	80	92	19	6
GS8	438	593	239	473	189	119
GS9	6870	6023	4195	2637	1899	1111
GS10	296	315	194	444	167	132
Total	10920	9824	6683	4960	3465	1911
Total – GS5 – GS9	1960	1870	1192	1495	928	461

Source: OFFER (1992, 1993, 1994, 1995, 1996, 1997)

Given the 'emphasis' placed upon security and availability of supply, perhaps this (GS2) is the most important guaranteed standard. There is no clear downward trend in failures against this standard over the period, although the largest problem was in 1991/2 especially when it is remembered that this is a 9-month period. Also by far the lowest number is in the last year. The regulator comments that the majority of the incidents in 1995/6 (331) relate to lightning storms and snowfalls in two specific regions. This demonstrates that to some extent these figures are not entirely under the control of the companies. From the interviews with consumer groups the following issues relating to the reporting of standards were also raised. There is a severe weather exemption that allows the companies to not make GS payments, although they do usually make ex-gratia payments. OFFER have said that they will revisit the severe weather exemption and this may become increasingly important if such conditions become more frequent due to climate change. A further issue is that there is a measurement problem when companies make ex-gratia payments, as opposed to GS payments. Ex-gratia payments are good for consumers, but they distort the statistics, as they are not reported as GS payments, and therefore make the statistics less reliable. It must be remembered that the statistics are 'manifestly a load of rubbish' (according to a Consumer group representative). Another example of the statistics providing incomparable data was when Scottish Power reported 619,000 queries about bills as opposed to another company reporting 2. The collection and reporting of this data requires auditing and a more precise definition of terms. This problem will also arise with the Consumer Satisfaction measure that is to be reported from April 2002, as this will be based upon the number of complaints and this will need to be carefully defined.

If we now turn our attention to the overall standards these are detailed in Table 8.12 below:

Table 8.12 Overall standards

1. Minimum percentage of supplies to be reconnected following faults within 3 hours and minimum percentage within 24 hours.
2. Minimum percentage of voltage faults to be corrected within 6 months.
3. Connecting new tariff customers' premises to electricity distribution system. Minimum percentage of domestic customers to be connected within 30 working days and minimum percentage of non-domestic customers to be connected within 40 working days.
4. Minimum percentage of customers who have been cut off for non-payment to be reconnected before the end of the working day after they have paid the bill or made arrangements to pay.
5. Visiting to move meter when asked to do so by customer within 15 working days in minimum percentage of cases.
6. Changing meters where necessary on change of tariff within 10 working days of domestic customers' requests in minimum percentage of cases.
7. Ensuring that the company obtains a firm reading for customers' meters at least once a year in a minimum percentage of cases.
8. Minimum percentage of all customers letters to be responded to within 10 working days.

Source: OFFER (1997)

The information provided by OFFER against the Overall Standards changes in the year 1993/4. In 1991/2 and 1992/3 details of the number of services and failures were provided and then performance, as a percentage, calculated. In 1993/4 only percentages are reported. This lessening of information makes it significantly more difficult to comment on the overall performance of the companies. For example, we could again argue that OS1A and B are the most important overall standards as they relate to failure to reconnect customers within a given time period. The percentage performance is calculated as follows:

$$\text{Actual performance} = \frac{\text{Number of customers reconnected within time limit}}{\text{Number of supplies lost during the period}} * 100\%$$

This means that a company's percentage performance can be 'improved' despite a greater number of supplies being lost during a period. This appears to give the companies a motivation to let the system fail as long as it can be repaired quickly i.e. within 3 hours for OS1A. For this reason the total number of failures and losses of supply are valuable pieces of information in their own right, but are no longer provided. For the two years where the information is available we see:

Table 8.13 Supply failures and reconnections

	1991/2	1991/2 * 12/9	1992/3
No. of customers not reconnected within 3 hours	1,165,031	1,553,375	1,780,703
No. of customers reconnected within 3 hours	10,173,212	13,564,283	15,640,076
No. of customers not reconnected within 24 hours	6,420	8,560	18,574
No. of customers reconnected within 24 hours	11,331,823	15,109,097	17,402,205
No. of supplies lost	11,338,243	15,117,657	17,420,779
OS1A	89.7%	89.7%	89.8%
OS1B	99.9%	99.9%	99.9%

Source: OFFER (1992, 1993)

  In 1992/3 the supply was restored within 3 hours 89.8 per cent of the time and within 24 hours 99.9 per cent of the time. This performance appears, as reported by OFFER, to suggest constant or marginally improving performance, but in actual fact the system has failed to supply customers more times and it has failed to reconnect a greater number of people within the specified time limit. Due to OFFER's failure to report this data in later years we can not say whether the number of interruptions has continued to increase or not, but this certainly questions whether an increased percentage under OS1A and B is actually good or bad. Table 8.14 below records changes in levels of performance against the overall standards by simply averaging the percentage performance of each of the twelve RECs. Although this is not ideal it should still give an indication of changing performance over the period.

Table 8.14 Performance against overall standards

	1991/2	1992/3	1993/4	1994/5	1995/6	1996/7
OS1A	88.8	89.1	88.8	89.2	89.2	90.1
OS1B	100.0	99.9	100.0	100.0	99.9	99.9
OS2	94.5	94.1	97.2	99.2	99.2	99.0
OS3A	97.1	98.1	99.9	99.9	100.0	100.0
OS3B	98.0	98.9	N/a	N/a	N/a	N/a
OS4	97.8	99.7	99.4	100.0	100.0	100.0
OS5	96.0	98.1	99.5	99.6	99.9	99.9
OS6	94.0	96.5	98.2	98.5	99.4	99.7
OS7	96.4	97.8	98.7	98.6	98.7	98.8
OS8	98.7	99.3	99.8	99.9	99.9	99.7

Source: OFFER (1992, 1993, 1994, 1995, 1996, 1997)

  Given this average performance by the companies it seems quite clear that performance against these overall standards has improved. The poorest performance is against OS1A where for most of the period the companies failed to reconnect more than 10 per cent of customers in less than 3 hours after supply has been lost. In fact it is only the last year of this period that OS1A is above 90 per cent. The problems with this measure have been discussed above, but this marginal change in addition to the evidence provided above would suggest that security of supply has marginally improved since privatization. Clearly this allays some of the fears expressed by consumer and employee groups concerning the security of supply. Their main concerns, however, relate to the long-term security of supply rather than present performance.

Numbers of Complaints

The number of complaints is recorded by the regulator as another form of monitoring customer satisfaction within the industry. The data reported by OFFER relates to the number of complaints made to the regulator and the consumer councils by customers. These customer complaints are those that have been previously raised with the company, but the customer is not satisfied with the response. Therefore it does not reflect the total number of complaints made to the companies. Table 8.15 shows the number of complaints over the period.

Table 8.15 Numbers of complaints

	1991/2	1992/3	1993/4	1994/5	1995/6	1996/7
Total number of complaints	14,771	13,934	9,567	8,741	6,904	6,119

Source: OFFER (1992, 1993, 1994, 1995, 1996, 1997)

This table shows a reducing number of complaints being made to the consumer councils and the regulator and would therefore indicate either an improvement in the customer performance or improved complaints handling processes by the companies.

Concluding Thoughts on the Consumer Analysis

If we split the period under analysis into the two sub periods used in the previous chapter, i.e. privatization to 31 March 1995 and then 1 April 1995 to 31 March 1997, we can see that there is a change in performance. Up to 31 March 1995 real domestic electricity prices increased and at the same time the quality of service provided, primarily concerned with security of supply, has not noticeably improved in terms of average customer minutes lost or performance against relevant GS and OS for reconnection of supplies. Having said this, performance against most other standards and the number of complaints have improved and this would appear to show an improvement in customer service. The number of complaints does not really provide evidence on whether the security of supply has improved because only a minority of complaints actually relates to this. In 1991/2 a total of 1,081 complaints, 7.3 per cent of total complaints recorded by OFFER, related to 'supply interruptions and the quality of supply'. Unfortunately, this detailed breakdown of the reasons for complaints was not provided in later years and therefore we can not see whether the number of complaints relating to quality of supply has improved in line with the total. In the two key measures, quality of supply and price, domestic consumers do not appear to have benefited greatly in the first years after privatization. Industrial consumers, however, have experienced a price reduction.

In the last two years analyzed, 1 April 1995 to 31 March 1997, there does appear to be an improvement in price and in the quality measures reported by the regulator. As noted earlier, the accuracy of these statistics can be and have been questioned. Nevertheless, given the decrease in real prices and in customer minutes lost, there does appear to be an improvement in customer performance. This is clearer than in the first post-privatization period and does appear to suggest that the regulator and/or competition is starting to protect the consumer.

Supplier Analysis

There are two aspects to the analysis to be undertaken here. Firstly there are some basic accounting measures to see how suppliers are being treated in terms of payment. Therefore, in the next section, we measure the number of creditor days and the current ratio to see whether the privatized companies appear to have changed their policy in terms of how long suppliers need to wait for payment. Also of interest is how the different primary fuel industries that supply the electricity industry have fared since privatization. Therefore we later consider the mix of primary fuel.

Supplier Payment Terms

Firstly we shall consider the current ratio for each of the companies over the period. This measure simply divides the current assets by the current liabilities to consider how liquid the companies are, i.e. could they manage to pay their current creditors out of their current assets. The details of this analysis on a company by company basis are provided in table 8.16 below. In twelve of the fifteen companies the current ratio is lower in 1994/5 than it is in 1990/1. The real change is actually between 1993/4 and 1994/5, as there is little consistent pattern until this time. The difference between 1993/4 and 1994/5 is very apparent in twelve of the fifteen companies with the ratio falling by at least 0.3 and is caused by both falls in current assets and increases in current liabilities. Even in 1994/5 ten of the fifteen companies have current ratios more than or equal to 1.0 and this would suggest that they should not experience significant difficulties in paying their current liabilities.

In the years 1995/6 and 1996/7 the current ratios show some interesting developments. Four of the RECs have recorded significant decreases in current ratio and two now have current ratios as low as 0.5 and 0.4. In both cases this is primarily as a result of dramatic increases in current liabilities. Conversely

Manweb and Northern report much higher current ratios. In the case of Manweb this is caused by higher current assets, but for Northern it signifies a much lower level of current liabilities. For National Grid both the levels of current assets and current liabilities increase over the period, but the increase in current assets is much greater and these are more than three times higher in 1997 than in 1995.

Table 8.16 Current ratios

	1990/1	1991/2	1992/3	1993/4	1994/5	1995/6	1996/7
East Midlands	1.3	1.5	1.3	1.3	0.9	0.8	0.9
Eastern	1.4	1.4	1.3	1.0	1.4	2.1	1.0
London	1.1	1.4	1.1	1.7	1.0	0.9	1.0
Manweb	1.4	1.5	1.6	1.5	1.0	1.4	1.5
MEB	1.3	1.5	1.1	1.2	0.9	0.7	0.5
Northern	1.3	1.5	1.6	1.8	1.2	1.4	2.3
Norweb	1.5	1.7	1.6	1.6	1.1	0.9	1.0
Seeboard	1.4	1.3	1.4	1.5	1.1	1.6	0.8
Southern	1.6	1.5	1.3	1.4	1.6	1.1	0.8
Swalec	1.3	1.1	1.0	1.0	0.7	1.0	1.1
SWEB	1.2	1.2	1.2	1.5	1.0	0.5	0.4
Yorkshire	1.4	1.3	1.2	1.2	1.2	1.3	1.4
National Grid	0.7	0.5	0.7	0.8	0.4	0.5	0.9
National Power	1.1	1.2	1.2	1.9	1.2	1.0	1.1
Powergen	1.2	1.2	1.4	1.1	0.8	0.7	0.8

Source: Annual reports of the companies 1991-7

Given that it is unlikely that the electricity companies will fail to pay their debts, it is perhaps of greater importance to the suppliers as to how quickly they are paid. Creditor days can be calculated from accounting data, although this is based on the year-end trade creditor figure and this may not be a fair reflection of the level of trade creditors throughout the whole year. Such window dressing is not contrary to law or Accounting Standards, but can mislead people analyzing the data. Having said this, it is hoped that by looking at the fifteen companies over a period of time the analysis should not be seriously weakened. The following formula has been used to calculate creditor days:

$$\text{Creditor days} = \frac{\text{Trade creditors} * 365 \text{ days}}{\text{Purchases}}$$

NB: The purchases are as per value added calculations

The results of these calculations are provided in table 8.17 below. In every single company the creditor days calculated in 1994/5 is higher than that for

1990/1. In many of the RECs there is approximately a 50 per cent increase, although the increases in Northern, SWEB and Yorkshire are much smaller. The RECs have increased their purchases over the period and so the increase in trade creditors is higher even than 50 per cent. This would certainly suggest that over the period suppliers have lost out in terms of creditor days in the period. The results are similar in the National Grid with creditor days increasing by 66 per cent and an increase of 11 per cent in purchases the result of a very significant increase in trade creditors. Creditor days have increased in the Generators, but to a lesser extent. There was a large increase between 1990/1 and 1992/3, but then levels have fallen back between 1992/3 and 1994/5.

Table 8.17 Creditor days

	1990/1	1991/2	1992/3	1993/4	1994/5	1995/6	1996/7
East Midlands	25.2	26.3	28.7	42.0	41.9	48.7	37.3
Eastern	29.5	24.9	27.3	33.3	47.4	37.2	36.9
London	27.1	25.1	26.7	39.6	43.0	46.5	37.8
Manweb	22.9	34.5	33.2	36.0	37.1	51.1	36.1
MEB	21.9	16.0	27.2	34.2	33.0	47.2	41.4
Northern	29.0	28.1	29.2	35.6	30.6	51.1	42.0
Norweb	17.0	28.0	31.7	33.1	34.0	49.1	44.5
Seeboard	28.0	25.5	28.4	32.4	41.4	61.6	59.4
Southern	20.1	21.7	28.5	32.9	43.0	68.9	45.1
Swalec	24.8	25.5	33.5	37.2	38.1	50.3	31.0
SWEB	33.0	36.1	31.2	35.5	36.5	65.8	39.7
Yorkshire	20.4	22.0	23.6	22.6	23.7	34.1	25.8
National Grid	138.2	164.2	168.0	203.5	229.6	218.1	441.3
National Power	22.4	24.5	39.0	27.0	24.4	28.5	22.9
Powergen	37.8	38.7	54.3	43.5	48.9	54.8	50.3

Source: Annual reports of the companies 1991-7

In the final two years there is not a consistent picture. There are six RECs who appear to take longer to pay their suppliers in 1997 than in 1995, but there are also six RECs who appear to take less time. The RECS do appear to increase creditor days in 1996, but this falls back in 1997. The largest change is seen in National Grid in 1997. This is caused by the fall in purchases in the value added calculation as caused by the deconsolidation profits as discussed in the value added chapter earlier.

The Mix of Primary Fuel

As well as considering how companies have performed for suppliers as a whole it is also interesting to see how the different primary fuel supply industries have fared in relation to each other. We consider this here by considering the primary fuel used to generate electricity. The table below considers the changes in fuel input for electricity generation as reported in the Digest of UK Energy Statistics. This table shows a shift from coal and oil and into gas and nuclear, although coal remains the single largest primary fuel source for electricity generation in the UK. Therefore we could argue that the coal and oil industries have lost out over this period of time when compared to the gas and nuclear industries. The increase in other and decrease in hydro will be considered in more detail in the environmental section below.

Table 8.18 Fuel input for electricity generation

Type of fuel	1990 %	1991 %	1992 %	1993 %	1994 %	1995 %	1996 %	1997 %
Coal	67	64	60	51	49	47	42.0	36.5
Oil	9	10	10.5	8	5	5	4.5	2.5
Gas	0	1	2.0	10	13	16	21.0	27.0
Nuclear	18	22	23.5	28	28	28	28.5	29.5
Hydro	2	< 1	< 0.5	< 1	1	1	0.5	0.5
Other	0	1	1.5	2	2	1	1.5	2.0
Imports	4	2	2.0	2	2	2	2.0	2.0
Total	100	101.0	100.0	102	100	100	100.0	100.0

Source: Digest of UK Energy Statistics, DTI (1991-1997)

Concluding Thoughts on the Supplier Analysis

We have seen that in the first years after privatization there is a worsening in the average creditor payment period, although this does not continue to worsen throughout the whole period. We can say that the gas industry has definitely gained at the expense of the coal industry. The fall in coal usage is continuous throughout the period. This shortfall in fuel was met by remarkable increase in the amount of gas used over the period. It must be remembered that at the time of prizatization gas provided virtually none of the primary fuel used to generate electricity in the UK. As discussed earlier this should result in improved environmental emissions as gas and nuclear are cleaner than coal and oil, but some interviewees raised concerns as to the long-term availability of gas.

Environmental Analysis

The environmental impact of the electricity industry is significant in many ways, but most obviously in terms of greenhouse gas emissions and spent nuclear fuel management. We have already noted in the supplier section 6.6.2 above that there has been a shift in fuel used for electricity generation from coal and oil into gas and nuclear. The environmental effect of this, in terms of emissions, should be positive as gas and nuclear are cleaner than coal and oil. In order to consider the process of the electricity industry we are going to analyze data relating to primary fuel used through to electricity supplied. This process will attempt to take into account the efficiency of generation, transmission and distribution, and final use. This is achieved in the following sections:

- Fuel used in generation to electricity generated;
- Electricity generated to electricity supplied; and
- Electricity supplied as compared to changes in GDP.

In addition we shall also consider the absolute level of emissions caused by the generation of electricity and finally take a closer look at the developments in renewable energy through the period. The government reports on the UK energy industry and therefore throughout this analysis figures for the UK (not England and Wales) are used. The data considered here is taken from the Digest of United Kingdom Energy Statistics 1991-1997.

Fuel Used to Generate Electricity

The purpose here is to consider the actual efficiency of the process of generating electricity from primary fuels. Renewables are included within other, but are considered in more detail below.

**Table 8.19 Fuel used in generating electricity
(million tonnes of oil equivalent)**

Type of fuel	1990	1991	1992	1993	1994	1995	1996	1997
Coal	49.84	49.98	46.94	39.61	37.11	36.10	33.01	28.55
Oil	8.40	7.56	8.07	5.78	4.05	3.60	3.49	1.86
Gas	0.55	0.57	1.54	7.04	9.86	12.54	16.40	20.93
Nuclear	16.26	17.43	18.45	21.49	21.21	21.37	22.18	22.99
Other	1.28	1.33	1.55	1.39	1.50	1.59	1.52	1.75
Net imports	1.03	1.41	1.44	1.44	1.45	1.40	1.44	1.42
Total	77.36	78.28	78.00	76.75	75.18	76.60	78.04	77.50

Source: Digest of UK Energy Statistics, DTI (1991-1997)

This would suggest that the total fuel used to generate electricity in the UK over this period has remained relatively constant, fluctuating by 4 per cent over the period. The significant changes are the decrease in coal and oil and increase in gas and nuclear as suggested above. In terms of million tonnes of oil equivalent, coal used has dropped by 42.7 per cent between 1990 and 1997. Oil has dropped by 77.9 per cent using million tonnes of oil equivalent. By 1995 the amount of gas used has increased by nearly 23 times from 6,405GWh[3] to 145,835GWh. If we now consider the total electricity generated by this fuel, as depicted in table 8.20 below, we see that it has increased by 4.6 per cent, from 319.7TWh[4] to 345.3TWh) over the period, an increase that has not been matched in total by the increase in fuel input according to Table 8.19

Table 8.20 Total electricity generated

Type of fuel	1990 TWh	1991 TWh	1992 TWh	1993 TWh	1994 TWh	1995 TWh	1996 TWh	1997 TWh
Conventional steam	245.4	244.5	232.3	202.6	190.2	186.4	177.8	149.4
CCGT	0.3	0.6	3.4	23.4	37.9	49.7	67.1	88.5
Nuclear	65.7	70.5	76.8	89.4	88.3	89.0	94.7	98.1
Other	8.3	7.3	8.5	7.7	9.0	9.4	7.8	9.3
Total	319.7	322.9	321.0	323.1	325.4	334.5	347.4	345.3

Source: Digest of UK Energy Statistics, DTI (1991-1997)

The electricity generated by conventional steam stations (this primarily relates to coal and oil) has fallen by 39.1 per cent whilst we note larger falls in both coal and oil input. This would suggest that these fuels are being used more efficiently. Similarly, if we consider the levels of gas being used by the major power producers, we see the electricity generated per gas input (in terms of GWh/million tonnes of oil equivalent) rising from 3,326 to 3,960 between 1993 and 1995 (the period of time where CCGT makes a significant contribution to electricity generated) and there is a further improvement by the year ending in 1997 to 4,228 GWh / million tonnes of oil equivalent. Overall as the amount of gas used in generation has increased so the efficiency of the gas generation has increased by a total of more than 27 per cent in 1997 compared to 1990. If we consider the nuclear element we see the productivity change from 4,044 GWh / million tonnes of oil equivalent in 1990 to 4,267 GWh / Million tonnes of oil equivalent in 1997, a 5.5 per cent increase in efficiency over the period. Therefore each of the main fuels appears to improve in efficiency over the period. If we consider the total efficiency we see an improvement to 4,455 GWh / Million tonnes of oil equivalent in 1995 from 4,133 GWh / Million tonnes of oil equivalent in 1990; an increase of 7.8 per cent over the period. Therefore the efficiency gains in gas generation are far greater than those achieved by the more traditional primary fuels used for electricity generation.

Electricity Generated to Electricity Supplied

The data above suggests an improvement in the efficiency of electricity generation, but this generated electricity still has not reached the final users. The electricity is then transmitted and distributed to customers through the network. Electricity is also lost through this process. Table 8.21 below provides data on the amount of electricity lost in the network.

Table 8.21   Efficiency of the electricity network

	1990 TWh	1991 TWh	1992 TWh	1993 TWh	1994 TWh	1995 TWh	1996 TWh	1997 TWh
Electricity available	309.4	317.0	315.2	318.6	322.7	331.7	343.9	343.1
Losses in network	25.0	26.2	23.8	22.8	30.9	24.9	29.6	25.6
Total supplied	284.4	290.8	291.4	295.8	291.8	306.8	314.3	317.5
Efficiency (%)	91.9	91.7	92.5	92.8	90.4	92.5	91.4	92.5

Source: Digest of UK Energy Statistics, DTI (1991-1997)

The best year post-privatization is 1993, but there is no discernible trend in this data and it can not be claimed that the efficiency is definitely improving or worsening. This would suggest that the efficiency of the network has remained relatively constant over the period. There appears to be an improvement from 1991 to 1993, but then there are high losses in 1994. The figures quoted here are not equal to the total electricity supplied as it only considers the electricity that uses the network and hence excludes electricity used on the site where it is generated. This explains the different 'total electricity supplied' figures considered in the next section.

Electricity Supplied as Compared to Changes in GDP

This section considers how efficiently electricity is being used in the UK. This is done by considering how the total electricity supplied has changed as compared to changes in the GDP. This is done in Table 8.22 below. The table shows that the absolute level of energy usage in the UK has increased by nearly 10 per cent. This is against a 12.9 per cent increase in GDP over the same period. The actual efficiency worsens for the first two years post-privatization, 1991 and 1992, and then generally improves from this time onwards. The largest single increase in efficiency is in the final year where the total electricity supplied actually falls very marginally whilst GDP increases by more than 3 per cent. By the end of the period this would suggest an improvement in efficiency, but it must be remembered this is still an increase in the absolute level of electricity supplied.

Table 8.22 Efficiency of the electricity usage

	1990	1991	1992	1993	1994	1995	1996	1997
Total electricity supplied (TWh)	300.1	302.8	300.8	303.8	307.9	317.1	329.6	329.0
GDP at factor cost (£bn 1990 prices)	478.9	468.9	466.5	476.9	495.9	508.2	524.5	540.6
Efficiency of use (£bn / TWh)	1.60	1.55	1.55	1.57	1.61	1.60	1.59	1.64

Source: Digest of UK Energy Statistics, DTI (1991-1997)

Overall in terms of efficiency of the electricity industry we can see improvements in generation, but not in the networks and less so in the usage. The actual level of electricity generated and supplied has increased and this is disappointing as there is believed to be considerable scope for improved efficiency, especially at the point of consumption.

Levels of Emissions

The analysis to date has suggested that the total levels of electricity generated and supplied in the UK have increased, but that this has been generated marginally more efficiently and from cleaner fuels. Given this we would expect the levels of emissions to have decreased over the period. Table 8.23 provides data on emissions for the period 1990 to 1997.

Table 8.23 Levels of emissions (Million tonnes)

Emissions	1990	1991	1992	1993	1994	1995	1996	1997
Carbon Dioxide	54.00	53.00	51.00	46.00	44.00	44.00	43.00	40.00
Sulphur Dioxide	2.72	2.53	2.43	2.09	1.76	1.59	1.32	1.03
Nitrogen Oxides	0.78	0.72	0.69	0.57	0.53	0.50	0.45	0.37

Source: Digest of UK Energy Statistics, DTI (1991-1997)

These are the most significant, in terms of volume, environmentally damaging emissions made by the electricity industry. The table clearly shows a reduction in levels of emissions in the period. It has been suggested in earlier chapters that the most important emission is carbon dioxide, and this has fallen by 25.9 per cent over the period. Even larger decreases have been made in emissions of sulphur dioxide and Nitrogen oxides, 62.1 per cent and 52.6 per cent respectively. Friends of the Earth (1997) suggest that 1990 levels of carbon dioxide emissions in the UK need to be reduced by 22 per cent by 2010 and by 89 per cent by 2050. Therefore the reductions made to date appear to more than satisfy the earlier target by an earlier date. Obviously these reductions need to be maintained through to 2010 and there are some potential difficulties in doing this.

As mentioned above the level of electricity being generated continues to rise and therefore unless technology continues to find more and more ways to reduce emissions from this generation then emissions will begin to rise again.

There also remains a concern about the ability to achieve the more long-term goal of much greater reductions by 2050. Greater use of gas would reduce levels of emissions, but another problem is that UK gas reserves are not inexhaustible and may run out within 20 years. Also replacing coal and oil with gas will not be sufficient as gas generation still produces emissions. The question is how can this be achieved if levels of electricity used continue to increase and the 'easy' savings, by shifting to gas and nuclear, have already been made. Further, in the longer term there is the whole question of nuclear generation. Generating electricity with nuclear fuel is clean in terms of the emissions that we are discussing here, but leaves a significant problem in terms of spent fuel management as well as public health and safety concerns from nuclear plants. Public concerns about these problems appear, for the present, to make more nuclear power politically impossible. Therefore the levels of nuclear generation would appear in the present climate to be likely to fall between now and 2050. This appears increasingly likely with the planned decommissioning of the Magnox fleet of nuclear power stations and at present no plans for any replacements. This therefore leaves renewable sources, and we consider these in the next section.

Renewable Sources Used to Generate Electricity

The best way to reduce the environmental impact, including nuclear spent fuel management, of the electricity industry is to increase the amount generated from renewable sources. Therefore it is interesting to consider how the levels of electricity generated by renewable sources have changed over the period.

Table 8.24 Electricity generated from renewable sources (GWh)

Type of fuel	1990	1991	1992	1993	1994	1995	1996	1997
Onshore wind	9	11	33	218	342	352	486	665
Small scale hydro	127	142	149	159	159	212	86	159
Large scale hydro	5,080	4,482	5,282	4,143	4,935	5,072	3,275	3,969
Landfill gas	139	208	377	447	517	566	705	880
Sewage sludge digestion	316	328	328	378	361	367	400	400
Municipal solid waste combustion	223	239	281	399	717	747	778	934
Other biofuels	0	1	52	140	280	344	326	335
Total	5,894	5,411	6,502	5,883	7,311	7,649	6,056	7,341
% of total generated	1.8%	1.7%	2.0%	1.8%	2.2%	2.3%	1.7%	2.1%

Source: Digest of UK Energy Statistics, DTI (1991-1997)

There have been increases in the use of electricity generated from renewable sources in the period except in the case of large-scale hydro. The levels produced from large-scale hydro are relatively constant and such developments are not favoured by environmental groups.[5] If we therefore ignore large-scale hydro, we see that the electricity generated from other types of renewable sources has increased by more than 3 times. This sounds a lot but actually relates to an increase from 0.25 per cent to 0.77 per cent of the total electricity generated in the UK. These levels are far behind some other European countries and remain disappointing.

Concluding Thoughts on the Environmental Analysis

Some improvements appear to have been made in terms of the environmental performance of the electricity industry. Simply considering the emissions from the industry paints a hopeful picture, with significant reductions over the period, although the ability to take these reductions further is open to question. In terms of efficiency and the use of renewable sources of energy there have been marginal improvements over the period, but in neither case do these appear sufficient for optimism about larger increases in the future. Also the level of electricity that is generated from renewable sources remains very low and perhaps this is the most disappointing development, or lack of development, to be noted from this analysis. Having said this, the industry is very much in the hands of the Government in this respect. It is the Government that sets energy policy, as can be seen by the more recent introduction of targets for electricity generated from renewable sources. Therefore in terms of how the environment has fared from privatization, the answer appears to be that it has neither benefited nor lost. This is because the same policies could have been set by the government irrespective of whether the industry was publicly or privately owned. In fact it could be argued that environmental policies would be easier to implement and face less opposition if the city / shareholder were not directly involved.

Conclusions

Over the course of this chapter and the preceding three chapters we have explored the performance of the electricity industry in England and Wales in a number of different ways. In chapter 5 we analyzed the industry using the concept of value added and the findings from this analysis has been summarized in the two tables, 8.25 and 8.27. As with the analysis in chapter 7 it is thought necessary to separate the analysis into two sub periods in order to consider whether there is any discernable changes due to the changed circumstances in the industry from 31 March 1995.

Table 8.25 Major changes in the distribution of value added (1991-1995)

	Sales	Purchases	VA	Lab. costs	Int. + Tax	Net change
Generators	↓£191m	↓£1,031m	↑£840m	↓£241m	↑£270m	↑£811m
Nat. Grid	↑£284m	↑£46m	↑£238m	↑£4m	↑£5m	↑£229m
The RECs	↑£1,790m	↑£876m	↑£914m	↓£91m	↑£180m	↑£825m
Total	↑£1,883m	↓£109m	↑£1,992m	↓£328m	↑£455m	↑£1,865m

This table demonstrates the most significant changes identified from the value-added analysis. It demonstrates that there has been an increase in value added primarily caused by the squeezing of purchases and labour costs, which have not increased in line with sales. This would appear to suggest that approximately £1,865million of cash has been generated in the year ending 1995, as compared with the year ending in 1991. This extra cash could be used to pay dividends, buy capital equipment or be retained or used in other ways. The following table indicates how this extra cash has been used:

Table 8.26 Analysis of changes in spending (1991-1995)

	Extra cash	Increased Dividends	Increased Capital exp.	Retained or other
Generators	£811m	£187m	£69m	£555m
National Grid	£229m	£58m	£104m	£67m
The RECs	£825m	£731m	£215m	-£121m
Total	£1,865m	£976m	£388m	£501m

This clearly shows that the majority of the redistribution from suppliers and employees has gone to shareholders in the form of dividends. In addition there has been some increased level of capital expenditure. The more detailed stakeholder analysis performed in this chapter also shows that the shareholders are definite winners from privatization. Employees of the industry at the time of privatization have been rewarded in monetary terms either through 'generous' redundancy packages or levels of pay that have increased over the period. In terms of job security, however, there has been a significant worsening and given the changes in employee levels it can be said that employees as a whole have lost out. The sacrifice of employees for profit suggests a significant reduction in the influence of employees as a group. Over this initial period domestic consumers do not appear to benefited in terms of prices as compared to industrial consumers and the rate of inflation, but quality may marginally have improved. Overall industrial consumers may have benefited very marginally from privatization. Suppliers appear to have lost out as they now have to wait significantly longer for their money than was previously the case. Finally the environment is now experiencing lower emissions, but this is not as a result of privatization rather because of Government energy and environmental policies.

Table 8.27 Major changes in the distribution of value added (1995-1997)

	Sales	Purchases	VA	Lab costs	Int + Tax	Net change
Generators	↓ £540m	↓ £576m	↑ £36m	↓ £48m	↓ £34m	↑ £118m
Nat. Grid	↓ £20m	↓ £38m	↑ £18m	↓ £15m	↑ £30m	↑ £3m
The RECs	↓ £691m	↓ £161m	↓ £530m	↓ £359m	↑ £262m	↓ £433m
Total	↓ £1251m	↓ £775m	↓ £476m	↓ £422m	↑ £258m	↓ £312m

There is clearly a change here as the level of sales has been reduced over this period of time. As a result of this purchases have needed to be further squeezed, but in the case of the RECs this was insufficient to compensate fully. Therefore further reductions have been made to employee costs, but again these are insufficient to cover the reduced sales in the RECs. This would appear to suggest that the Generators have managed to produce additional cash over this period, but that the RECs have not. We now consider what effect this has had on the levels of dividends and capital expenditure undertaken by these companies. As for the earlier period we now consider the changes in spending over this period.

Table 8.28 Analysis of changes in spending (1995-1997)

	Change in cash available	Increased Dividends	Change in Capital exp.	Retained or other
Generators	£118m	£1382m	-£259m	-£1005m
National Grid	£3m	£29m	-£158m	£132m
The RECs	-£433m	£498m	£115m	-£1046m
Total	-£312m	£1909m	-£302m	-£1919m

This table demonstrates that the pressure on cash caused by reduced revenues appears to have decreased the levels of capital expenditure, which is a concerning development. One of the justifications for privatization was that the necessary levels of investment would not be made within the public sector. This evidence, however, does not suggest that increased investment is being made from within the private sector yet such investment is crucial to the future of the industry. If we examine how levels of capital expenditure have changed across the whole industry over the years 1991-1997 the CRI (1998) reports the figures in Table 8.29 below. This table shows a mixed story. In terms of the actual equipment required to ensure that consumers receive electricity the supply side of the industry is the least important, as it is the generating capacity and the wires that ensure that this happens. There has been a large fall in the capital expenditure in generation and this is primarily due to the fall in capital expenditure in the nuclear part of the industry. There are no nuclear plants being built and closure dates have been announced for the Magnox fleet. This will require a new level of investment into generating plant, not necessarily nuclear, in the future. Capital expenditure has also fallen in the other areas of generation as well.

Table 8.29 Levels of capital expenditure

	1990/1	1995/6	1996/7	Change 1996/7 on 1990/1
	£m	£m	£m	%
Generation	1,313	1,005	514	-61
Transmission	253	167	182	-28
Distribution	743	920	1085	+46
Supply	21	36	59	+180

Source: Adapted from CRI (1998)

The transmission element of the industry has also seen a decline in investment, although slightly less at 28 per cent in nominal terms over the period. In contrast the capital expenditure in the distribution network has increased at a faster rate than inflation and therefore suggests a real increase in investment. It is difficult to speculate whether these changes are results of more efficient programmes, changes in approach or the advent of new technology. We can suggest that investment in the infrastructure is crucial to the future supply of electricity and therefore should not be an area that is too readily cut.

The pressure on cash has not caused a similar decline in dividends, although part of the increased dividends in 1997 is a special dividend by National Power of £1,207m. The present trend for increased dividends from a lower level of revenue is not sustainable in the long term. It is this pressure that appears to provide a strong impetus to rationalize the industry through merger and take-over. Such rationalization provides greater opportunity for cost reduction, but also reduces the specific influence of the capital markets. As part of a larger group, these companies specific contribution to shareholders is hidden and therefore this provides greater flexibility. From the analysis in the previous chapter it would appear that the large gains were made by the shareholders up to the time of the take-overs. The groups that now include RECs do not appear to be providing any sort of abnormal return despite the RECs themselves still providing excellent accounting returns. The change may, to some extent, be related to the regulation of the industry. Professor Littlechild first set the new distribution price cap in August 1994 but then reconsidered his proposals in March 1995. It was reported (in the *Financial Times* 8th March 1995) that:

> Professor Littlechild cited recent share price rises as one of two main reasons why he was re-opening the price control review. The second is that the Trafalgar House bid for Northern Electric.... said Professor Littlechild "seems to indicate more financial strength (in the regional companies) than there seemed".

This resulted in a more stringent price-cap and sent a clear signal that regulation was being tightened. This was not the only issue that was raised by Professor Littlechild's change of heart. A cornerstone of the present regulatory system is that the regulators stick to their side of the bargain. It is therefore not surprising that the *Economist* (29th July 1995) reported that:

> on July 25th a committee of Members of Parliament complained that his change of mind over the electricity price controls damaged the credibility of the regulatory system - a biting criticism, given that Mr Littlechild himself devised Britain's hands-off style of regulation.

It is believed that such actions lead to an increased risk (a regulatory risk) for the privatized businesses and damage the incentive for efficiency on which the system is based. Again this may well influence the stock market performance of the companies in the industry. In contrast the consumers appear to fare better in this period. The real price of electricity has fallen and quality, as measured by customer minutes lost, the regulator's standards and number of complaints, has improved. The reliability of these quality measures can be questioned, but it seems reasonable to suggest that some improvements have been made. Also some improvements have been made in terms of emissions, although little headway appears to have been made in terms of efficiency and renewable sources. In contrast employee numbers continue to tumble and therefore workloads must be increasing. The information for suppliers is rather tenuous, but there is no evidence that they have benefited in this period.

Chapters 5 to 8 have analyzed the relative benefits and costs to the stakeholders groups since privatization. In summary the analysis has shown the following:

Table 8.30 Summary of winners and losers from privatization

Stakeholder group	Privatization to 31/3/1995	From 31/3/1995 to 31/3/1997
Shareholders	Significant gains	Gains for acquired shareholders Less clear for the acquirers
Employees	Significant losses	Losses
Domestic Consumers	Lose on price, gain on quality	Gains on price and quality
Industrial Consumers	Gains on price and quality	Gains on price and quality
Suppliers generally	Losses on payment terms	No clear message
Coal and oil industries	Losses in market share	Losses in market share
Gas and nuclear industries	Gains in market share	Gains in market share
The environment	Reductions in emissions	Reductions in emissions

This summary table reflects the corporate social performance of these privatized companies by using a stakeholder approach, as developed in earlier chapters. These results are interesting and the reasons for these changes need to be better understood. Therefore chapter 9 will consider how these changes came about and how they might be explained. In order to do this resource dependency theory and institutional theory will be used to analyze the events.

Notes

[1] Seeboard was the only company to be taken over by January 1996 that did not count as one of the companies with the highest reductions in employee numbers.

[2] This table is also shown as table 7.12 in chapter 7.

[3] GWh stands for Giga Watt hours. Giga denoted 10^9.

[4] TWh stands for Tera Watt hours. Tera denoted 10^{12}.

[5] Large-scale hydro developments 'are no longer considered desirable by anyone. It has been recognized that this type of generation is bad as it affects the local freshwater habitat of fish. In the US such hydro plants are being demolished.' (Quoted from Environmental interview.)

Chapter 9

Theorizing the Results

Introduction

Thus far we far used a value added analysis and stakeholder framework as tools to consider the corporate social performance of the of the privatized electricity industry between privatization and March 1997. The previous chapter concluded that certain stakeholder groups have benefited more than others since privatization. The value added analysis and stakeholder framework enabled us to see how the corporate social performance had changed over the period. As yet though no theoretical explanation for these relative changes in benefits has been offered. This chapter considers these findings in light of institutional and resource dependence theory. More specifically this analysis draws heavily on the work of Oliver (1991), which considers 'the convergent insights of institutional and resource dependence perspectives' (p.145). This chapter will next consider these theories and the framework developed by Oliver (1991) before applying it to the present case. Then the results of the previous chapters will be reviewed in light of this framework to discover whether it can more fully explain the developments over this period of time.

Institutional Theory

Institutional theory gives prominence to the cultural and social environment within which organizations and individuals exist and act. More specifically 'social knowledge and cultural rule systems' (Scott, 1995, p. xiv) are considered key to understanding behaviour. Scott (1995) charts the early history of institutional theory into three distinct strands of its role in economics, political science and sociology. Important within this early work was the concept that there were cultural and historical forces that resulted in a social framework within which actions are undertaken. Some of these theorists did analyze institutional structures, but it was only later that organizations became the main concern of the theory and analysis. Selznick (1957) suggests that:

> Institutionalization is a process. It is something that happens to an organization over time, reflecting the organization's own distinctive history, the people who have been in it, the groups it embodies and the vested interests they have created, and the way it has adapted to its environment.

In what is perhaps its most significant meaning, "to institutionalize" is to infuse with value beyond the technical requirements of the task at hand.' (pp.16-17)

Neo-institutional theory appeared in the 1970s and has spawned a significant amount of literature. The key concern of this literature are the causes of organizational stability or change and DiMaggio (1988) claims that drivers of change and stability have been identified on the basis of 'preconscious understandings' (p.3). Further, he suggests that central to institutional theory is an assumption, often implicit, that there is a universal desire for the reduction of uncertainty and for survival.

At an individual level behaviour is shaped by the rules and norms of the organization and in this way decisions can be made more easily as the process becomes routine with set processes to follow (March and Simon, 1958). Decisions can be made more easily as cultural forces restrict the options open to the decision-maker (North, 1986). This is to say that despite an unlimited range of possible choices and strategies only a very small percentage of these are considered as appropriate due to the institutional context. Thus in the words of DiMaggio and Powell (1991):

> Cultural frames thus establish approved means and define desired outcomes, leading business people to pursue profits, bureaucrats to seek budgetary growth, and scholars to strive for publication. (p.28)

These outcomes are institutionalized in our modern society and as such they refer to institutionalization as an outcome. It is important to distinguish between this and institutionalization as a process. As an outcome institutionalization is not political and relates to rules and 'taken-for-granted scripts' that influence individual's behaviour within organizations. These rules and scripts are useful as they help in reducing uncertainty, legitimating certain activities and hence assisting in the continuation of the organization. DiMaggio (1988) recognizes that there is a 'strong parallel' with these taken-for-granted scripts and the 'false consciousness' discussed by neo-Marxists such as Lukes (1974). Both literatures suggest that some actions are inconceivable to individuals, despite the fact that they would benefit. This is argued to be because there is a preconscious understanding that these actions are not acceptable in that society, but in reality this means that they would be obstructed by 'political or economic elites'. Bordieu (1979) and Giddens (1984) have also considered the role of the taken-for-granted in the dominance of certain interests in society more generally.

If an organization has become institutionalized, i.e. institutionalization is the outcome, then this is seen as a hindrance to change and innovation. The rules and scripts ensure that activities are performed in a common manner. This is to say that they become ritualistic and the actual purpose and appropriateness of the action is no longer questioned, but simply accepted. It is in this respect that institutions, or organizations that have been institutionalized, are considered difficult and slow to change. In fact DiMaggio and Powell (1991) suggest that organizational change will be 'episodic and dramatic' and will occur when the rules and taken-for-granted scripts are questioned and considered to be inappropriate. By the very nature, and definition, of institutionalization this can only happen infrequently. Burns and Flam (1987) argue that it is the setting and changing of rule systems that has resulted in the 'major power struggles in modern societies' (DiMaggio and Powell, 1991). This is an extremely interesting argument in relation to the case under consideration here. With the election of the Conservative government in 1979 there was a change in political and economic ideology that had a direct and material impact on the electricity industry. The shift towards the right and the free market meant that the institutional practices that were taken-for-granted in the industry since nationalization were no longer accepted without question. A new set of rules and culture were demanded. This appears to fit exactly the episodic and dramatic change identified by DiMaggio and Powell (1991). They further suggested that:

> Fundamental change occurs under conditions in which the social arrangements that have buttressed institutional regimes suddenly appear problematic. (p.11)

This will be returned to later in the chapter when a more detailed consideration of the case study will be undertaken in light of the theories discussed here. If we now turn to institutionalization as a process we can see that there are very different considerations. First and foremost, power, authority and interest are essential ingredients of institutionalization as a process, but institutionalization as an outcome is unaffected by them. Therefore the process of institutionalization is influenced by powerful actors. DiMaggio suggests that the form of an organization and the levels of institutionalization will be dependent upon the 'relative power of the actors who support, oppose, or otherwise strive to influence it' (p.13). Similarly Meyer and Rowan (1983) suggest that institutional rules are, and can be, manipulated and used creatively by actors to achieve their own ends. The process does not end here though, as the powerful actors will want to maintain these institutional rules and therefore they require 'strategies of control'. Two specific strategies are the indoctrination of newcomers such that they do not question the taken-for-granted scripts and also reliance on the support of government and legislation to reinforce the legitimacy of the rules.

In actual fact Scott (1995) suggests that there are three different processes that create and maintain institutions. These are referred to as the 'Three Pillars of Institutions' and he summarizes the key differences between these three pillars in a table, which is reproduced below (Table 9.1). Each of the three pillars affords an organization some level of legitimacy that, in institutional theory, is seen as a prerequisite for continued acceptance and activity. By being seen to be legitimate organizations achieve a level of support within the society where they operate. Obviously the regulative pillar can be easily recognized as relevant to this case as it is a regulated industry. The normative pillar reminds us of the discussion in chapter 2 concerning business ethics and the concern as to whether the business is managed ethically or to certain moral standards.[1] According to Scott the third pillar, the cognitive pillar, is given greater emphasis by neo-institutional theory. A cognitive conception of institutions emphasizes that organizations 'attempt to be isomorphic in their structures and activity pattern' (Scott, 1995, p.44) and this is most clearly portrayed through imitation. It is therefore suggested that both individuals and organizations attempt to combat uncertainty by copying the actions, processes or structures of others that face the same set of environmental conditions and hence uncertainties (Hawley, 1968). The degree of isomorphism and its causes has been one of the key areas of empirical institutional research. DiMaggio (1988) suggests that this research has provided convincing, i.e. that it has been frequently replicated, evidence that isomorphism does occur. It is suggested that early adopters of new innovations can be predicted by the fit of the innovation to the specific circumstances of the organization. These can be considered to be rational organizations and DiMaggio and Powell (1983) consider this to be 'competitive isomorphism'.[2] In contrast later adopters can not be so easily predicted and as such appear to be imitating the early adopters and in fact are not doing this on the grounds of efficiency. In these cases DiMaggio and Powell argue that institutional isomorphism is present.

Table 9.1 Varying emphases: three pillars of institutions

	Regulative	**Normative**	**Cognitive**
Basis of compliance	Expedience	Social obligation	Taken for granted
Mechanisms	Coercive	Normative	Mimetic
Logic	Instrumentality	Appropriateness	Orthodoxy
Indicators	Rules, laws, sanctions	Certification, accreditation	Prevalence, isomorphism
Basis of legitimacy	Legally sanctioned	Morally governed	Culturally supported, conceptually correct

Source: Scott (1995 p.35) Reprinted by permission of Sage Publications, Inc.

DiMaggio and Powell (1983) suggest that there are three drivers of institutional isomorphism. These are coercive isomorphism that is political in nature and aids organizational legitimacy, mimetic isomorphism that is used to counteract uncertainty, and normative isomorphism that is associated with professionalization. DiMaggio and Powell contrast this with the work of Weber, commenting that he correctly recognized the move towards bureaucracy, but that in fact organizations have gone further than this. They argue that this is because Weber was incorrect in emphasizing the importance of the rational, competitive pressures of capitalism that he likened to an iron cage imprisoning humanity 'perhaps until the last ton of fossilized coal is burnt' (Weber, 1952, pp.181-82). Instead, they argue it is the institutional drivers that lead organizations to 'become more and more homogeneous' beyond that which can be explained by competition. DiMaggio and Powell further argue that it is 'the state and the professions, which have become the great rationalizers of the twentieth century' (p.147).

Returning to the drivers of isomorphism, we see that this idea of the state and professions as powerful actors in institutional theory is reinforced. We see that the state is a prominent, although not the only source, of coercive isomorphism. The authority of the state, where authority is defined as legitimated power (Scott, 1987), to impose legislation upon organizations is prevalent in modern societies and was certainly the key instigating factor in the privatization programme in the UK. Meyer and Rowan (1977) and Meyer and Hannan (1979) suggest that it is primarily as a result of the power of the state that the homogeneity of organizations and their use of rituals has increased. Also the spread of the professions with normalized education, teaching accepted techniques and rules has led to the increase of normative isomorphism. Scott (1991) proposes that the professions are actually even more heavily associated with cognitive (or the mimetic) modes of influence than the normative. It is the proliferation of the professions throughout organizations that results in the mimicry apparent in mimetic isomorphism.

This is not the only instance where a distinction is drawn between competitive and institutional pressures. Meyer and Rowan (1991) suggest that organizations can be placed on a continuum that has organizations that are subject to competitive market forces at one extreme and institutional pressures at the other. Therefore organizations that operate within competitive markets are forced into looking for technical solutions to problems and the emphasis is very much on efficiency improvements. In contrast Scott and Meyer (1991) define institutional organizations as those where there are rules and requirements that must be adhered to if they are to be considered legitimate and given the necessary levels of support within their own environment. These institutional pressures will be in the ascendancy when the competitive pressures are restricted and this is the case where there are barriers to entry into an industry, or in non-profit organizations, or in state owned organizations. This may well explain the preponderance of institutional research into state owned or non-profit organizations as they are not under the same level of market forces. Hinings and Greenwood (1988) suggest that state owned and privately owned organizations operate under different 'institutionally legitimate definitions of efficiency and effectiveness' (p.56). Therefore there are differences in ownership, but also differences in performance expectations and measurement. Private sector companies are monitored almost completely against economic criteria and comparatively non-profit organizations have greater flexibility in defining performance. This is another reason why institutional theory is relevant to the transformation of the electricity industry from public to private ownership.

Not all institutional theorists see competitive and institutional pressures as mutually exclusive and therefore organizations can and are subject to both institutional and competitive pressures.[3] Scott and Meyer (1991) are actually very specific about the possibility of organizations being subject to both technical and institutional pressures, as the following quote demonstrates:

> Organizations such as utilities, airline companies, and banks are viewed as subject to highly developed technical *and* institutional pressures. They face both efficiency / effectiveness demands as well as pressures to conform to procedural requirements. As a result, we would expect their administrative structures to be larger and more complex than those of organizations facing less complex

environments. In general, organizations of this type carry out tasks that combine complex technical requirements with a strong "public good" component. (p.123)

Where technical and institutional pressures are both evident there is a conflict and the organization needs to manage this if it is to survive. Institutional theory suggests that one way in which this is possible is to de-couple, or loosely couple, the different components of their activities. It is argued that where organizations are not operating in competitive markets, but are facing institutional pressures, they can de-couple their activities by setting poorly defined broad goals and attempt to avoid evaluation on efficiency criteria. The lack of competition enables the organization to not optimize its performance on technical criteria and it is more important that they are seen to conform to the institutional pressures. If this is successfully achieved the organization can be seen to be legitimate. Obviously in the electricity industry the companies have been protected, to some extent, from competition through government regulation, but as mentioned above they are still facing technical pressures for efficiency. This, therefore, makes it more difficult to completely de-couple the operations, and measures of efficiency and effectiveness are certainly made in annual reports and in the measures considered by the regulator. There was, however, a clear example of a lack of integration between different constituents evidenced in chapter 6,[4], and this suggests that there is some degree of loose coupling being utilized. Such devices are used to provide a buffer around different operations to protect them from the technical and competitive forces.

In conclusion institutional and neo-institutional theorists are sceptical that organizations are truly efficient and further that all organizations are institutionalized to some degree. DiMaggio and Powell (1991) suggest that this must be the case given that the rate of 'environmental change frequently outpace the rates of organizational adaptation' (p.33). This implies that inefficient organizations survive and they argue can continue to do so over relatively long periods of time. The survival of such organizations is largely thanks to the institutionalization of organizations generally. We have also seen that institutionalization is believed to reduce uncertainty by restricting the strategic choices open to the institutional actors. Interestingly, this is an area of the theory for which there appears little empirical evidence. Instead the majority of empirical study has concentrated upon organizational form and the degree and causes of isomorphism. A significant exception is the study and framework designed by Oliver (1991). This framework incorporates resource dependency theory and therefore we shall very briefly outline the central tenets of this theory before discussing the framework in more detail.

Resource Dependency Theory

In resource dependency theory there is a focal organization with which other organizations interact and undertake transactions. From this alone there is already a strong resonance with the idea of stakeholders as defined and discussed in earlier chapters. This theory suggests that the focal organization is structured and managed in such a way so as to ensure that the resources essential to its activities are forthcoming (Pfeffer and Salancik, 1978). Further, the more important a resource is, or in other words the more dependent the focal organization is on a resource provided by another organization, the more the relationship will require careful management. As the resource becomes more important so the focal organization becomes more dependent on that provider. Obviously the scarcity of the resource and the lack of alternative supplies increases the dependence on an individual supplier. If alternative sources can be identified so the level of dependence falls and this was tested empirically and supporting evidence found by Pfeffer and Leong (1977). Crucial to this theory is the concept that the need for the resource results in a power relationship. According to Emerson (1962), the power of actor A over actor B was equal to the dependence of B upon A.

In resource dependency theory the focal organization will have its choice of actions restricted by the external pressures from organizations upon which it is dependent. Therefore the focal organization will need to take into account and respond to these external demands if it is to continue to operate and hence survive (Pfeffer and Salancik, 1978). The fact that the focal organization has multiple relationships with external organizations of varying dependence means that it needs to manage the conflicting interests (Pfeffer, 1982). As this is the case, central to resource dependency theory is the management of these conflicts and, more proactively, attempts are made to manipulate the external environment of critical resources (Thompson, 1967). Empirical research premised on resource dependency theory has considered the effect these power relations have on administrative structure (Tolbert, 1985) and is therefore interested in similar research questions to those considered by institutional theory. The ability to manipulate the external environment, however, is seen as a way to reduce uncertainty and provide stability and survival into the future. In effect this management of the external environment in resource dependency theory is a significant departure point from institutional theory (Pfeffer, 1982).

Combining the Theories

There are both similarities and differences between institutional and resource dependency theories. It is the emphasis that is different - instead of resource streams, information flows and influence relations, institutional theory proposes cultural and historical factors and their sources are crucial (Scott, 1987). These factors result in rules and practices that Scott suggests are 'important types of resources and that those who can shape them possess a valuable form of power' (p.508). This suggests that institutional theory could be added to resource dependency theory as it simply identifies another resource, which can be added to the more normal tangible resources already considered.

As these theories both consider organizational structure, but do so from different standpoints, it is perhaps not surprising that the two approaches have been combined in some instances. Tolbert (1985) argues that:

By combining resource dependence and institutionalization perspectives, a much fuller explanation of the process of administrative differentiation was provided than could have been by either perspective independently.

Organizational phenomena are much too complex to be described adequately by any single theoretical approach. (p.12)

This combination of the approaches is intuitively appealing to me as it combines the consideration of power with the acknowledgement of institutional pressures. The management of key resources[5] and attempts to manipulate their importance were apparent in the interviews undertaken in this research. At the same time the newly privatized companies clearly copied organizational structures from other private sector companies as they attempted to distinguish themselves from their public sector history. These issues are to be considered in more detail in the coming sections. Firstly, though, it is important to clarify that the purpose of this chapter is not to consider organizational structure per se, but to consider the 'strategic response' of the companies over the period from privatization to 31 March 1997. Oliver (1991) notes that the empirical research into institutional theory has concentrated upon institutional processes, organizational structures and organizational change and has relatively neglected strategic responses to its institutional environment. In order to address this omission Oliver developed a framework that draws on both institutional and resource dependency theories to consider 'Strategic Responses to Institutional Processes'. This framework has subsequently been used in the management accounting literature to consider the design of performance measurement systems (Modell, 2001). It is to this framework that we now turn.

Oliver's Typology

Firstly Oliver (1991) provides a comparison of resource dependency and institution theories. She summarizes this into Table 9.2 below. This provides a useful starting point and hopefully confirms much of the discussion from earlier in this chapter. The next development is to consider what strategic responses are open to the actors within organizations. If we consider the very first difference noted by Oliver, it is that there is a difference in the degree of choice of behaviour dependent upon which theory, or perspective as Oliver terms them, is adopted. In fact it is this difference that is a key distinction and seen from another perspective can suggest alternative responses. The response chosen will depend upon the exact pressures being exerted and as such will specifically be influenced by the degree of institutional pressures. On the occasions where institutional pressures are high the response is extremely limited to what habit and convention suggest are socially acceptable. In contrast where institutional pressures are low then the choices open to the organization are greater and will revolve around the specific management of the conflicting visible external pressures.

Table 9.2 Comparison of institutional and resource dependence perspectives

		Divergent foci	
Explanatory Factor	**Convergent Assumptions**	**Institutional Perspective**	**Resource Dependence Perspective**
Context of Organizational Behaviour	Organizational choice is constrained by multiple external pressures	Institutional environment Non-choice behaviour	Task environment Active choice behaviour
	Organizational environments are collective and interconnected	Conforming to collective norms and beliefs Invisible pressures	Coping with interdependencies Visible pressures
	Organizational survival depends on responsiveness to external demands and expectations	Isomorphism Adherence to rules and norms	Adaptation Management of scarce resources
Motives of Organizational Behaviour	Organizations seek stability and predictability	Organizational persistence Habit and convention	Reduction of uncertainty Power and influence
	Organizations seek legitimacy	Social worthiness Conformity to External criteria	Resource mobilization Control of external criteria
	Organizations are interest driven	Interests institutionally defined Compliance self-serving	Interests political and calculative Non-compliance self-serving

Source: Oliver (1991, p.147)

Oliver provided a more detailed breakdown of the different potential responses depending upon the environment faced by the organization. The more institutional pressures faced the more likely the organization is to respond to these pressures through the habitual adoption of techniques that have worked in the past, the copying of techniques that have worked for other organizations, or compliance with the rules and norms of the environment. This was termed acquiescence and is at the institutional extreme. As the institutional pressures are high so the response is very much an institutional theory one. So we see ritual, isomorphism and obedience to rules and norms that are straight from the realms of institutional theory. In this case the institutional pressures are dominant and so the appropriate strategic response is to reduce uncertainty by following and copying institutionalized routines. This strategy should, according to institutional theory, legitimate the organization's activities and hence ensure its survival.

The second possible strategic response was labelled compromise by Oliver. This begins to recognize the conflicts that are apparent in organizations. The different constituents, or stakeholders, have different needs and demands and these need some form of management or strategic response. At this level of strategic response the emphasis is on balancing, placating and negotiating with the different 'institutional stakeholders'. This response still encompasses and accepts a great deal of institutional pressure, but there is some degree to which the organization takes a more active role in attempting to promote their own interests.

Thirdly, the organization can attempt to avoid conforming and where this is done it must be concealed. Therefore to the external constituents it appears that the organization is conforming to the institutional pressures, whereas in reality it is not. The tactics employed here are akin to the loose coupling and de-coupling discussed earlier under institutional theory. Another tactic suggested by Oliver is escape and this actually entails leaving the arena where the institutional pressure is being exerted. Therefore organizations can relocate either geographically or in terms of the activities undertaken in order to escape stringent institutional pressures.

Defiance is the fourth strategic response. As with avoidance, the institutional pressures are resisted, but this is done openly. Therefore this would suggest institutional norms are simply ignored and this is not concealed. Going even further, or being even more active, the actual institutional rules can be contested or 'assaulted' such that their efficacy is questioned. Given the implication that institutional pressures and rules can lead to inefficiencies, this is one way in which the institution itself can be attacked.

Finally the most active strategic response is to actually manipulate the environment within which the organization operates. This can be done by co-opting the source of the pressure, influencing the shaping of the values and criteria, and controlling or dominating the actual institutional stakeholders and processes. This is the most extreme form of proactive management of the environment and institutions. Therefore it is still within the realm of institutional theory, but it is looking at institutionalization as a process and is attempting to influence this process. As noted earlier, this process, unlike institutionalization as an outcome, is seen to be extremely political and is therefore dependent on the interests and power of the organizations that attempt to influence the process.

The different strategic responses can also be contrasted in terms of resource dependency theory. To acquiesce suggests that there is only institutional pressure and further that the conflicts between the different resources is insignificant. All of the other responses are alike in that they recognize the conflict, but differ in the extent to which they are the more dependent or the more powerful in the given relationship. As we move towards defiance and manipulation it can be seen that the power of the focal organization is sufficient for it to be setting the agenda, and not being dictated to in the same way.

If we accept these strategic responses it is next important to consider what factors enable different organizations to enact different strategic responses.

Therefore, what particular environmental, historical, social or legal factors result in the adoption of a specific strategic response? To this end Oliver identified five institutional factors, each consisting of two predictive dimensions. It is hypothesized that depending on the influence of these predictive dimensions an organization will adopt a given strategic response, as is depicted in the two tables below. Within Table 9.3 for each institutional factor identified there is an associated research question and two predictive dimensions. Each of the predictive dimensions from Table 9.3 then is classified as a predictive in the left-hand column of Table 9.4. It is then suggested that the strategic response of the organizations will depend on these predictive factors. Clearly it could be possible within a single situation for the different predictive factors to give conflicting strategic responses. For example it could be the case that an organization could be faced with a situation where there is high multiplicity and also high uncertainty. These different predictive factors would suggest different strategic responses and the model does not suggest how such conflicts can be resolved. Nevertheless the predictive factors and their related strategic responses do provide a useful starting point.

Table 9.3 Oliver's antecedents of strategic responses

Institutional Factor	Research Question	Predictive Dimensions
Cause	Why is the organization being pressured to conform to institutional rules or expectations?	Legitimacy of social fitness Efficiency or economic fitness
Constituents	Who is exerting institutional pressures on the organization?	Multiplicity of constituent demands Dependence on institutional constituents
Content	To what norms or requirements is the organization being pressured to conform?	Consistency with organizational goals Discretionary constraints imposed on the organization
Control	How or by what means are the institutional pressures being exerted?	Legal coercion or enforcement Voluntary diffusion of norms
Context	What is the environmental context within which institutional pressures are being exerted?	Environmental uncertainty Environmental interconnectedness

Source: Oliver (1991, p.160)

Table 9.4 Oliver's institutional antecedents and predicted strategic responses

Predictive Factor	Strategic Responses				
	Acquiesce	Compromise	Avoid	Defy	Manipulate
Cause					
Legitimacy	High	Low	Low	Low	Low
Efficiency	High	Low	Low	Low	Low
Constituents					
Multiplicity	Low	High	High	High	High
Dependence	High	High	Moderate	Low	Low
Content					
Consistency	High	Moderate	Moderate	Low	Low
Constraint	Low	Moderate	High	High	High
Control					
Coercion	High	Moderate	Moderate	Low	Low
Diffusion	High	High	Moderate	Low	Low
Context					
Uncertainty	High	High	High	Low	Low
Interconnectedness	High	High	Moderate	Low	Low

Source: Oliver (1991, p.160)

In the next section we shall examine each of these five factors and responses in turn to see whether this adequately explains the performance of the electricity industry since privatization.

The Electricity Industry in England and Wales (Privatization – 1997)

The privatization of this industry saw a dramatic change in its institutional environment as it was transferred from the engineering driven public sector to the financially driven private sector. Therefore we see that the two 'great rationalizers of the twentieth century' that create a lot of institutional pressures have both gone through a dramatic change with reference to this industry. The Conservative governments from 1979 onwards were clearly following a privatization programme that was predicated on the efficiency of the private sector. The efficiency of the private, as opposed to the public, sector was the key argument for privatization and the regulatory regime was also selected for its emphasis on efficiency. As part of this process the old public sector industry was characterized as inefficient and over-manned and therefore not socially legitimate. Viewed from this more institutional perspective the changes in the performance of the industry start to become more transparent. In actuality it is the government that is the primary institutional factor and this has been recognized by the privatized companies. Despite the transfer of the organizations from the public sector it is still the government that has the greatest power over the future of these organizations. We shall now look at this in more detail by first considering each of the predictive factors in terms of the companies' relationship with the government and then with each of the stakeholders identified.

The Government and the Regulator

On privatization the companies were to act under conditions as set out in the Electricity Act and they were to be subject to price-cap regulation as initially set by the government, but to be the responsibility of the regulator (OFFER) from that time onwards. At the time of this privatization the government had already privatized the telecommunications, gas and water industries and the rationale in terms of economic efficiency was well tried and the government had been re-elected subsequent to the privatizations of these other utility industries. Therefore it appears quite clear through the selection of the regulatory regime and the rhetoric of the time that there was a great deal of pressure towards economic efficiency. In addition, due to the election of the government under its free market, relatively right wing, policies, it can be argued that this was also seen as the socially legitimate way to run the industry. This is not so clear cut and the debate of the time and subsequently has shown that there were many dissenting voices that felt that this was not socially legitimate. Given that this legislation was accepted through parliament and that the government was elected when its desire to privatize the industry was known it would appear that the privatization was considered to be legitimate by the electorate. Therefore the cause of the institutional pressures on the newly privatized companies was for both economic efficiency and for social legitimacy. As this is the case Oliver (1991) suggests that the strategic response of the companies should be to acquiesce (see Table 9.4).

These privatized companies are obviously operating in a complex environment and are faced therefore with conflicting demands. What was interesting to note, however, was that all of the privatized companies visited recognized the government and the regulator as key constituents in their activities (see chapter 6). The government both directly and indirectly through the regulator have resources upon which the companies are dependent. The government has the power and authority to enact new legislation that can have a significant impact on the companies' activities and the regulator can also redefine the environment within which the companies operate. For example the periodic price reviews, the climate change levy, the introduction of the New Electricity Trading Agreement to replace the Pool, the importance of fuel poverty, and the need to meet renewable energy targets by the year 2010. This is a clear demonstration of the dependence that the companies have on these institutions. Therefore given this high level of dependence we would again be led to believe that the companies must acquiesce to the pressures from the government and the regulator.

The key institutional pressure is for the companies to be economically efficient, although the other areas of interest noted above are also important. In terms of economic efficiency, there is great synergy between this and the desire to create value for shareholders. In recent times there has been a shift in institutional pressures on publicly listed companies to adopt explicitly shareholder value approaches to management.[6] Therefore, as publicly listed companies, the electricity companies are also under pressure to manage for shareholders. The management of the companies have accepted this goal readily as it is consistent with their own desires. Especially as their own remuneration has in many cases been linked to this goal of economic efficiency. Oliver suggests that where there is consistency between the aims of the institutional pressure and the aims of the organization then we expect the level of acquiescence to be high.

Moving on to consider control as a predictive factor we see that, as the government initiated this change and has enacted legislation and regulation, there is clearly a coercive nature to the institutional pressures. With a high degree of legal coercion there is unlikely to be resistance and again the companies would be expected to acquiesce.

Finally we come to context as a predictive factor. Arguably the biggest uncertainties facing the companies throughout this period were the outcomes of the periodic price reviews and the introduction of competition into the market. These uncertainties are specifically dependent upon the government and the regulator and again this would tend to suggest that acquiescence is the appropriate strategic response. Also the environment in which these companies operate is interrelated, as contrasted with highly fragmented or purely competitive environments and this again points toward acquiescence.

To conclude under each of the five predictive factors the companies are likely to acquiesce to the institutional pressures of the government and the regulator. This suggests that the government is the dominant force in this industry and that institutional pressures are still high despite privatization. This would tend to suggest that in this way the industry is still more like a public sector, highly institutionalized organization, than its private sector counterparts. Another distinction commonly made in the institutional literature is that between the competitive and institutional environments, and in the period considered there was minimal true competition between the companies. This again suggests that it is not surprising to find that institutional pressures are indeed in the ascendancy.

This section suggests that the institutional pressure of the government and the regulator was high and this forces the companies to acquiesce to their demands. This has been discussed in general, but we now turn our attention as to how this has affected the specific stakeholders. Therefore we shall now consider whether the institutional pressures, primarily through governmental and regulatory actions, can explain how the different stakeholders have fared over the period. Table 8.30, in the conclusions section of chapter 8, summarizes how each of the stakeholder groups has fared since privatization. The following sections look at the predictive factors most relevant to each stakeholder group in order to attempt to highlight whether these adequately explain this performance.

The Shareholders

Obviously a key feature of the privatization programme was to create a new stakeholder group in the form of shareholders. The legitimacy of this stakeholder group is high in modern capitalist societies such as the UK. They have a legitimate claim as they are the owners of the organization and they are taking a risk by investing in these organizations. Therefore legislation in the UK is such that the directors of these companies have a fiduciary duty to manage the company with regard to the requirements of the shareholders.[7] The legitimacy of this group would, therefore, suggest that the company must acquiesce to their needs. This is also consistent with the general aims of private sector companies. The Conservative government was very much attracted to the idea of popular capitalism. A key component of this was to encourage more individuals to hold investments in companies. The privatization of utilities was deliberately designed such that levels of shares available to individuals and institutions were restricted to ensure a high number of shareholders. This desire can be argued to lead to a governmental desire to see good returns to shareholders on two different levels. Firstly, if these individuals are to be encouraged to invest more in the stock market then it is essential that their first experience with such investment is a profitable one. This is to say that these individuals are less likely to invest again if they do not benefit from good returns from their investments. At a second level the success is important as popular capitalism was one of the cornerstones of the Conservative government's electoral success and so a failure, i.e. a great number of people losing money on a privatization, could have severely disadvantaged the Conservative party in future elections. This is to say that a great number of voters getting a large windfall in terms of capital gains in shares could only be positive at the time of the next election. McAllister and Studlar (1989) conclude that the selling of shares to the public increased the Conservative vote, in the 1987 election, by 1.6 per cent.

Each of the above arguments would appear to suggest that the companies are likely to acquiesce to the needs of shareholders. However they are only one of a multiplicity of constituents and the power of any single shareholder could be seen to be relatively low. More broadly speaking it is the capital market as a whole that is extremely powerful. It is argued that a failure to provide appropriate returns to shareholders will result in the sale of shares, a devaluing of the share price, and the company becoming a take-over target. Until the government sold its golden share in 1995 there was no such threat of take-over. This would appear to suggest that the actual dependence of the companies on shareholders was actually quite low up until 1995. After the government's sale of its golden share this all changed and in fact the ten of the twelve RECs were purchased before 31 March 1997. This was an important time in the history of the industry and there was much debate concerning the efficacy of these acquisitions many by non-UK companies. At this time the government, through legislation or the workings of the Monopolies and Mergers Commission, had the opportunity to prevent these acquisitions. Instead they were allowed to go ahead[8] and again there were great benefits to the shareholders at that time. As we saw in chapter 7, the returns to shareholders leading up to the take-overs were very high. This represented another windfall to the followers of popular capitalism, although it must be noted that many of them had sold their shares long before this point in time. The new owners, larger companies, many controlled outside the UK, can be argued to be less obviously important to the government. Certainly in terms of voting they have no direct say in elections and so it could be suggested that there would be less institutional pressures from the government to ensure returns to these companies.

Overall the key point appears to be that the shareholder is seen as a socially legitimate stakeholder entitled to benefit from the risk of their investment. Further, this is supported be the government who had a vested interest in good returns being provided to shareholders. In addition, Carter and Crowther (2000) provide evidence that there was also a change in institutional pressure from professionals. They argue that prior to privatization the engineering profession was dominant, but this changed to a financial / accounting dominance. As mentioned earlier, professionalization is a great source of institutional power. The success of the accounting / financial profession in gaining this position of ascendancy also favours shareholders. Certainly traditional finance and accounting clearly privilege the shareholder over all other stakeholders, so this further suggests that the appropriate strategic response is to acquiesce to the needs of shareholders.

Employees

The rights of employees and their collective associations, the unions, were very much in decline through the 1980s. When elected Margaret Thatcher had a clear goal to reduce the power of trade unions as is evidenced by the following passages from Margaret Thatcher's (Thatcher, 1993) memoirs:

> We also had to deal with the problem of trade union power, made worse by successive Labour governments and exploited by the communists and militants who had risen to key positions within the trade union movement – positions which they ruthlessly exploited in the callous strikes of the winter of 1978-9. (pp. 97-8)

The Conservative administration of that time made a clear statement of its opinion of Unions with the steel strike of 1980 and the coal miners' strike of 1984-85, which it resisted at all costs.

> Yet the coal strike was always about far more than uneconomic pits. It was a political strike. And so its outcome had a significance far beyond the economic sphere. From 1972 to 1985 the conventional wisdom was that Britain could only be governed with the consent of the trade unions. No government could really resist, still less defeat, a major strike; in particular a strike by the miners' union. Even as we were reforming trade union law and overcoming lesser disputes, such as the steel strike, many on the left and outside it continued to believe that the miners had the ultimate veto and would one day use it. That day had now come and gone. Our determination to resist a strike emboldened the ordinary trade unionist to defy the militants. What the strike's defeat established was that Britain could not be made ungovernable by the Fascist Left. Marxists wanted to defy the law of the land in order to defy the law of economics. They failed, and in doing so demonstrated just how mutually dependent the free economy and a free society really are. It is a lesson no one should forget. (pp.377-8)

There was a clear message that the labour market needed to be more efficient and that this would be the best support for employees generally. At the same time it was made abundantly clear that publicly owned utilities were inefficient and over-manned. This effectively sent out an extremely strong message to the organizations that they had a responsibility to reduce employment levels. It is also argued that another motive for privatization is the inability to reduce the power of trade unions from within the public sector. Therefore a transfer of ownership to a fragmented private sector also fragments the power of the Unions. Also, as discussed above, the primacy of the shareholder over the employee has been clear within the private sector, and this is as well institutionalized as any rule in modern societies. This is even made clear in the literature of the Nineteenth Century in France, where Zola (1885) writes:

> Is it right, whenever a crisis comes, to let the workers die of starvation so as to keep the shareholders' dividend intact? However you put it, sir, the new system is a disguised wage-cut, and that is what we are up against, for if the Company must economize, it is quite wrong for it to be doing so wholly at the workers' expense. (1954 ed., pp.215-6)

In terms of the predictive factors, we can see that the social legitimacy of trade unions and at a different level the rights of employees were being questioned. In addition it was the behaviour of employees that was blamed for economic inefficiency. The nature of the regulation was specifically to target efficiency, but the implied definition of efficiency is to reduce costs and as employee costs is one of the largest costs this also applies a significant institutional pressure to reduce employment. Individual employees had little power and as a combination their power was being reduced and undermined by the government. This shows that there was an inconsistency between the stated aims of the organizations and the needs of employees. Due to the governmental stance on Unions and the labour market there was certainly no coercion to defend employee rights, and overall it is clear that the appropriate strategic response is to defy or manipulate the employee group. There are limits to how far this could go because there is still employment law, in terms of health and safety and working conditions, and there is some protection from the labour market,[9] but overall the companies were in a position to defy employees on many matters. As some employees are still required it is necessary that these are appeased and so the remaining employees have been paid relatively well.

Consumers

If we consider the relationship between the consumer and the company it is clear that at this time the power was with the companies. Due to the lack of competition the consumers, with the exception of the largest customers towards the end of the period under review, had no choice as to who provided their electricity. Also, as argued earlier, there is no realistic alternative to or substitute for electricity in modern society and so they are heavily dependent on the Electricity Company.

This would suggest that the companies could defy or manipulate these customers, but this was recognized by the government at the time of privatization. Customers were supposed to win as part of the privatization deal and at the same time it was clear that they needed protection. Therefore within the duties of the regulator it is clearly stated that the consumer must be protected in terms of price charged and continuity of supply. The very nature of the regulation was also focused upon the price to consumers. The priority given to consumers, however, was made clear in the duties of the regulator, where they were specifically considered secondary as opposed to the primary duty to be able to finance activities (McGowan, 1993).

The needs of customers were certainly considered legitimate and the design of the regulatory regime was specifically to target prices to the customers and economic efficiency. The regulator is certainly a strong source of institutional pressure on behalf of the consumer. There is coercive pressure for the companies to appease the regulator, but no institutional or competitive reasons for them to go beyond this. Therefore the real gains or losses to the consumer in terms of prices over the period are clearly mandated by the regulator. Even more interesting is that the price-cap is negotiated and as such the companies have the opportunity to influence the level at which it is set. This is truly where the companies can try to manipulate the outcomes. The more stringent the price-cap the harder it will be to keep shareholders happy and also there is great uncertainty as to the exact scope for cost cutting that leaves the process open to manipulation. The leniency of the initial price-cap can be considered to be a success story for the organizations' ability to manipulate the process. The government had clearly stated its intention to privatize the industry and this placed it in a relatively weak position. It did not want to be seen to fail on one of its promises. Therefore the major obstacles to the privatization needed to be appeased and obviously the management of the organizations were one such obstacle. An easier price-cap was also consistent with a successful sale and the uncertainty surrounding future performance suggests that in this instance the government acquiesced to the organizations' demands. This I feel is a key instance where the organizations were able to use significant pressure to manipulate the environment in which it was to operate for the next five years. At the time of the regulator's price-cap reviews it had become apparent from the gains made by the companies that the price-cap had been too lenient. The organizations, however, again had an input into the review process and they strongly fought for a relatively lenient setting. Again, the uncertainty concerning the future actually makes the regulator's, as the decision-maker, task more difficult. They were faced with multiple pressures with employee groups, the organizations and shareholders wanting a lenient price-cap and the consumers requiring more stringent cuts. In addition the companies were the providers of the key financial information as to their performance over the previous period. Again at this point in the process there is a strong incentive for the companies to 'game' the system - to try and suggest that returns are not good and that future returns or efficiency gains will be hard to come by. An interesting case is the 1995 review of electricity distribution in England and Wales. It was considered necessary to introduce a one-off price reduction of 11 per cent, 14 per cent or 17 per cent for each of the RECs. This was as well as a tightening of X, which was in line with those seen in the earlier reviews (from X = -1.3 per cent on average to X = 2 per cent). However, this was not the end of the story as this review was reconsidered by OFFER one year later. Therefore, one year after being told to cut distribution charges by at least 11 per cent, the RECs were told to make a further 10 per cent, 11 per cent or 13 per cent reduction. This was deemed necessary as within this year the regulator had noted further evidence regarding the financial strength of the RECs. This suggests that in the original process the financial information provided to the regulator underestimated the financial strength of the companies. In fact it was the Trafalgar House bid for Northern Electric, a market mechanism, that warned the regulator as to the true strength of the companies. This would appear to suggest that the companies again successfully manipulated the regulatory process to provide a lenient price-cap. This would certainly appear to be an area where the companies themselves were able to follow a far from acquiescent approach and this was to the detriment of the consumers, who in total benefited very little from privatization.

The quality of supply and service is more difficult as there are standards in place to guarantee performance, but the penalties attached are certainly not at a level that makes any failure unthinkable. In fact companies have failed against standards throughout the period. A real quality of supply would involve employees and investment, and this is inconsistent with the shareholder aims discussed above. What is interesting here is that a strategic response actually stated by one of the companies interviewed was a desire to be 'average'. This strategy was based on the belief that exceptional behaviour, either good or bad, would simply result in more attention from the regulator, i.e. more institutional pressure, and therefore a strategy of avoidance has been adopted.

Overall the companies have acquiesced to the governmental / regulatory coercion to follow the price-cap formula, but have done little else. The defining moment for this group is the periodic review by the regulator. At this stage the companies have certainly attempted to manipulate the process. In addition the companies have attempted to avoid further interference from the regulator by following a strategy of mediocrity.

The Suppliers

If we start with suppliers generally we see a philosophy towards contracting out and cost cutting in the public sector.[10] Therefore suppliers generally were given little attention and their needs were left to the market for redress. The demands for economic efficiency are inconsistent with building trusting relations with suppliers, instead it is price that first and foremost is the decision criterion. In addition due to their size and purchasing power, the electricity companies are, in almost all cases, more powerful than the suppliers. The suppliers will tend to be more dependent upon the electricity companies than vice versa. There are also a large number of potential suppliers with whom the companies can choose to transact. All of these features point towards an ability to defy or manipulate their relationships with their suppliers. Therefore it is not surprising that suppliers in general have not fared well in the analysis performed.

If we consider the specific suppliers of the primary fuel to the industry we see another interesting institutional environment. The ability of a fuel to be used in generating electricity depends upon its generating capacity and the criteria by which the pool, as it was at this time, chooses which generators should be used. This decision is primarily of importance to the generators and the industries supplying the primary fuel as opposed to the National Grid or the distribution and supply companies. In this period of time the big change noted is the increased use of gas over coal and this was dependent upon a political decision to allow extra gas-fired generating capacity to be built. This decision has been justified on marginal cost grounds, but according to the coal industry if the full cost is considered then these facilities were actually more expensive than the idle coal generating capacity that they replaced. In addition gas fired generation can claim to be greener and cleaner than its coal counterpart and this consistency of objectives will be revisited below. The coal industry clearly feels that the process was manipulated by the gas industry that, it claims, had more resources at its disposal to manipulate the decision making process. In contrast the Conservative government had clearly shown its disapproval for the coal industry and its powerful trade union, through its resistance to the earlier coal miners' strike. This battle, eventually lost by the coal miners, really questioned the legitimacy of the coal industry on economic efficiency grounds and hence paved the way for its lack of influence later. The ability of the gas industry to influence the political decision to allow the 'dash for gas' demonstrates their greater power than that of the coal industry, who in contrast had to silently acquiesce to a smaller and smaller proportion of generation capacity.

The Environment

The environment has seen reductions in the emissions of harmful gases that suggest that it has gained over the period. As with consumers the key to understanding this performance lies with the political interventions in the industry. The government has identified the area of climate change as an area of concern and therefore it must be considered. It is the government's decision to enable the dash-for-gas, as discussed in the previous section, which has contributed most significantly to the reductions reported. Therefore it is again very much the political process that has resulted in that decision. It is not really the electricity companies that are the focus of this decision, rather it is environmentalists and the primary fuel industries. The setting of targets for reduction is a negotiated process and also very much involves International opinion. This point was clearly made by the representative of the government, who suggested that the influences of the EU and the Kyoto agreement are crucial to the government's stance on the environment. As discussed in the previous chapter, there is agreement that something needs to be done, but the disagreement is as to what level of action is required. In these terms the influence of the gas industry again appears to have had a great deal of success, rather more so than the environmental lobby. The targets set by Friends of the Earth are of a completely different magnitude to those presently targeted by the government. The Environmental groups are opposed to the use of gas as the primary source of electricity and would rather see renewable fuels being used, but again only very marginal advances have been made in this respect. Also the inclusion of a nuclear element is an interesting problem, as public opinion appears to be against any further reliance on or building of nuclear reactors. In this case the environmental cause appears to be more successful, although this may well be primarily due to events at Chernobyl.

From the companies' point of view there is a need to acquiesce to the government's legislation, but again little else has been done. The savings made have, to paraphrase one city analyst, been a happy by-product of the dash-for-gas, which was undertaken primarily for different reasons as discussed above.

Conclusions

This chapter introduced institutional and resource dependency theory and attempted to use them to explain the performance of the electricity industry. The insights are telling and appear to further illuminate the findings through consideration of the factors that can predict the strategic response of the organizations. This chapter has demonstrated that in many ways the electricity companies are simply acquiescent to the demands of the government and its regulator. It is important to reiterate the importance of the government, the regulator and the political, and negotiated, process that has significant impacts upon how the different stakeholders fare. During this period of time the companies were not subject to true competition, although the RECs were compared under yardstick competition, and therefore the institutional pressures were still dominant. The importance of the government to this supposedly private sector industry is overwhelming and is therefore the primary cause of companies' strategic responses. In many ways it is the government's view of the importance of a stakeholder group that defines how that group will fare under the treatment of the companies. The coercive pressure of legislation enforces the companies to behave in a certain way.

Finally, there are interesting examples of the companies attempting to manipulate, with some success, these political processes. There is also some evidence of avoidance as a strategic response, through attempts to be average and through a strategy of diversification, thus reducing the regulated element of the business. In terms of the environment, the electricity companies again appear happy to acquiesce to the demands of the government, and it is really the primary fuel sector, which should be the focus here. The comparative success of the gas industry certainly becomes clearer and relates to the fact that this industry has greater resources and was able to manipulate the political process.

One source of power, or one resource, is information and this is one reason why social accounting is important, as it provides information to different stakeholder groups within society. Therefore one way of empowering a stakeholder group is to provide them with information from which informed decisions can be made. A social account, or corporate social report, could provide such valuable information. Over the last ten years there has been a marked increase in environmental reporting, but the vast majority of organizations have resisted the call for social accounts on the grounds of cost and the lack of appropriate standards. The next chapter explores recent developments in Internet reporting and Social accounting standards to consider what impact these may have on the future viability of greater social reporting.

Notes

[1] The work in this area, such as that of Parsons, suggests that shared norms and values were regarded as the basis of a stable social order in much the same way as Adam Smith suggested certain moral standards were a necessity for business.

[2] DiMaggio and Powell suggest that the work of Hannan and Freeman (1977) is concerned with this competitive isomorphism.

[3] Meyer and Rowan also appear to recognize this later in their 1991 paper as they discuss the conflict between institutional and competitive pressures.

[4] We saw in chapter 6 that the companies were explicitly using different messages for the different stakeholder groups. This provides a good example of loose coupling.

[5] This was considered as stakeholder management in chapter 6.

[6] See Cooper, Crowther, Davies and Davis (2001) for research into reasons for adopting shareholder value approaches to management.

[7] These duties and the primacy given to shareholders remain the same despite a recent parliamentary review (see DTI 2000a).

[8] It was only the attempted take-overs by the generating companies that were not allowed to proceed.

[9] The exact level of protection afforded by the labour market is a moot point, but it is certainly not perfect.

[10] It was only later with the election of the Labour government that new public management and best value became the philosophy.

Chapter 10

Recent Developments and the Future of Social Accounting

Introduction

One source of power is information and it is interesting to note that the less powerful stakeholders also appear to receive less information. Therefore one step forward towards redressing the power imbalance is to make companies more formally accountable for their actions. This could be done through a modern day corporate report and could incorporate a specific stakeholder framework. There are two immediate problems with this suggestion. The first is that this would greatly increase the work required by organizations to report to these stakeholders. Certainly in the past the issue of costs of disseminating such information has been seen as a deterrent, although not for shareholders. It is therefore considered here that this would only be appropriate for the very largest of organizations, which are effectively those with the most power. Also there is now a new medium for reporting information, the Internet, which raises possibilities and reduces costs, both economically and environmentally that was inconceivable at the time The Corporate Report was produced by the ASSC (1975). Therefore the next section considers the Internet as a reporting tool with specific reference to the use already made of it by companies participating in the electricity industry in England and Wales. Finally, much non-financial reporting is voluntary and therefore at present there is great scope for different organizations to report different information and to use different definitions in so doing. This is not a new problem, as financial accountants have faced the same problem for a considerable time. The response of the financial accountants has been to issue more and more standards, which include more and more strict definitions of terms, in an attempt to reduce uncertainty and ambiguity as much as possible. Again the success or failure of this process is an appropriate subject for a book in its own right. What is interesting to note, however, is that there have been three social accounting standards, or initiatives, produced recently that UK companies could voluntarily adopt. We introduced these in chapter 3 and in this chapter we will focus more specifically on the specific measures proposed under the GRI. This chapter also considers the appropriateness and usefulness of the GRI by comparing them to the stakeholder information needs identified through this research. Finally this chapter looks back at this book as a whole and considers its contribution and its limitations. It hopefully raises more research questions than it answers, as the areas of corporate social performance and reporting still have much to learn.

The Internet as a Medium for Reporting Corporate Social Performance

This section firstly considers the actual use made of the Internet by the electricity companies operating in the UK. This analysis was performed at a later date than the period discussed earlier in the research. This analysis was initiated towards the end of 2000 when the actual industry had changed markedly from that at 31 March 1997. The following table details the number of companies operating in each part of the industry at this time.

Table 10.1 The electricity industry in the UK in the year 2000

Generators in England and Wales (DTI)	7 companies accounting for approximately 80% of total in Winter 1999/2000 plus approximately 25 smaller companies
Transmission in England and Wales	1 company, the National Grid
Distribution networks in England and Wales at 31 August 2000 (DTI)	8 now owned by non-UK companies 2 now owned by the Scottish Electricity companies 1 owned by a UK generator 1 has been merged to form a multi-utility
Suppliers in England and Wales (OFGEM)	29 Business Electricity Suppliers, 18 of whom also supply Domestic Electricity
Scotland (DTI)	2 vertically integrated companies 1 other generation company Some 'other suppliers' the majority of which also supply in England and Wales

As a result of the mergers and take-overs in the industry there are now many groups of companies that offer vertically integrated electricity companies, and some that own more than one supply company. The analysis here will be based on 33 groups of companies, and this covers all of the industry except some of the smallest generators. As a first step it is necessary to see which of these 33 companies have Internet sites. The websites visited are listed in Table 10.2 below. All of the companies contacted either had a website or one was 'under construction'. In the three cases where the website was under construction there was a web address and a holding page in place, and some contact details were provided. Two of these companies are small independent supply companies and the third a small generator. The lack of a website is probably a resource issue, either in terms of time or money, as it is certainly the case that all of the larger companies had websites. In addition there were three companies generating in the UK that are subsidiaries of larger US groups of companies. In each of these cases there were no separate websites specifically relating to the UK activities, although one did list the UK generating capacity, and therefore the information was subsumed within much larger group information. There appears a difference here with the supply and distribution companies owned by non-UK interests, as there were separate websites for these companies. This is an interesting difference and it may well be that the fact that the generators are further removed from the final consumer, and therefore not operating in the competitive market for end users, results in less of a need for UK stakeholder communications.

Table 10.2 List of websites visited

Group Name	Internet Address
Edison Mission Energy	www.edisonx.com
AES	www.aesc.com
BNFL / Magnox	www.bnfl.com
Barking Power	www.thamespower.com
Teesside Power Ltd	www.enron.com
National Grid	www.nationalgrid.com
Midlands Electricity	www.meb.co.uk/GPU-Power/
Norweb	www.unitedutilities.com
Swalec	www.hyder.co.uk
SWEB	www.westernpower.co.uk
Aquila Energy Supplies	www.aquilaenergy.com/uk/
Atlantic Electric and Gas	www.atlanticeg.com
BizzEnergy	www.bizzenergy.com
British and Scottish Gas	www.gas.co.uk
Economy Power Ltd	www.economy-power.co.uk
Ecotricity	www.ecotricity.co.uk
Electricity Direct	www.electricity-direct.com
Enron Direct	www.enron.com
Maverick Energy	www.lloydlewis.co.uk
Pentex Oil & Gas	www.sabirenergy.com
Shell Power	www.shellgasdirect.co.uk
UK Electric Power	www.ukelectric.com
Utility Link	www.basicpower.co.uk
Innogy	www.innogy.com
Nuclear Electric	www.british-energy.com
Powergen	www.powergenplc.com
Eastern Group	www.eastern.co.uk
London Electricity	www.london-electricity.com
Northern Electric	www.northern-electric.com
Seeboard	www.seeboard.com
Yorkshire Electricity	www.yorkshire-electricity.co.uk
Scottish Power	www.scottishpower.plc.uk
Scottish and Southern Energy	www.scottish-southern.co.uk

The next stage was to visit each of these sites with the express intention of considering what information was available and how this was targeted at the different stakeholder groups. Specifically of interest is the amount of information, but also whether there appeared to be any hyperlinks or interaction with stakeholder groups. Due to the potential for companies to update their websites at any time this research only provides a snapshot. The websites were visited over a two-week period at the end of February - beginning of March 2001 and will, no doubt, have subsequently changed. This limitation is acknowledged and an interesting area for further research would be to monitor the evolution of the websites over a period of time. Further it is noted that this is very much exploratory research, due to the limited history of the Internet and academic interest in the stakeholder concept. The next section considers each of the stakeholder groups in turn.

Shareholders

Given the earlier research we would expect that companies would give priority to this stakeholder group and that we could expect to see some shareholder communication through company websites. In actual fact for the purposes of shareholders the companies can be split into three categories. Those companies that are privately owned, that are a subsidiary of a larger group, and those companies that are listed on a stock exchange. The privately owned companies are all small supply companies, provide no financial information and may, in the case of a closely held company, report who the owners are, but may not. This lack of information is understandable as the shareholders are not as far removed from these businesses and probably have other more comprehensive communication channels. As such these shareholders are effectively internal to the business and will therefore receive internal communication. British Nuclear Fuels Limited (BNFL) is owned by the UK government and this is made clear on the website. Despite this the annual report is still made available, and in this instance the publication of the annual report must be aimed not at the shareholder, who will have other avenues of information, but a wider financial and stakeholder audience.

Subsidiaries of larger groups can be distinguished between generating companies and supply and distribution companies. As mentioned above, the generating companies owned by US companies do not have separate websites and there is very little UK-specific information. For supply and distribution companies there are separate websites and these are linked to the group companies. It is at the group level that shareholder communication is made as it is the group that is publicly owned. The US companies provide comprehensive 'Investor Relations' sites that encompass annual reports, SEC documents, company presentations, press releases, share price and dividend information. This is a relatively standard shareholder offering and is also provided by the companies that are listed on the UK stock exchanges, with the exception of the SEC documents. Two of the more innovative elements were the opportunity for investors to join email lists providing company information and the provision of contact details for brokers or analysts that are following the companies' activities. The contact details for analysts or brokers, although hyperlinks were not provided, are more prevalent in US companies and the one UK company, Innogy plc, that have a broker coverage section were updating this page at the time this research was performed. These services are provided by a minority of companies, but appear to offer valuable information for existing and potential shareholders. Scottish Power do provide a link to the Shareholders' Association in Scotland (UKBASCOT), but otherwise up-to-date share prices externally provided were the only explicitly shareholder links.

Employees and Managers

This is an example of a stakeholder group that is internal to the organization and therefore there is, presumably, less of a need to use the Internet to communicate with them. This is supported by mention of employee newsletters and the Intranet as communication tools with employees, and there are also meetings and contact with managers that make the Internet an unlikely source of employee or management communication. This is borne out by the research. For the vast majority of companies the Internet is not used to communicate with existing employees, but rather potential employees. Therefore job opportunities are frequently listed on Internet sites and for the larger companies on-line application is possible. Within the ambit of recruitment most, but not all companies, refer to and provide their equal opportunities policy. Only two companies go further and refer to their involvement in national schemes that are linked to equal opportunities, such as Race 2000. Also some, usually the larger companies, are attempting to sell themselves as good employers with the kitemark 'Investors in People' and more unsubstantiated statements of 'positive working environments' and as 'learning' organizations. Finally the larger companies cite benefits, in terms of remuneration packages.

Health and Safety is an issue that is important to employees and as such some companies have produced Health and Safety reports (sometimes these are combined with environmental reports) that detail the safety record of the company. Approximately half of the companies provide a health and safety policy and report performance, although the smaller supply companies did not. Most of the reports appear to be unverified, but TXU Europe appears to have taken health and safety reporting a stage further. They 'use the RoSPA [Royal Society for Prevention of Accidents] audit system' and provide a great number of links to safety bodies. This is in sharp contrast to the other companies, which might provide a link to the H&SE, but little else. Again it must be remembered that policy and performance may well be reported internally not externally, but it is interesting that some companies see it as necessary and others do not. In the case of BNFL and British Energy, the two companies involved in the nuclear industry in the UK, both companies provide Environment, Health and Safety reports, and this is not surprising considering the central importance of safety in this industry. Scottish Power includes within its library an 'Employee Relations Report', although this relates to 1997/8, which has sections on Employee Development, Employee Relations and Employee Support, and this appears to go further than the other companies. This is, however, still not of the same scope, nor does it include the range of employee measures that are common, in employee reports in the late 1970s. In fact the decline of such employee or employment reports is evidenced by their absence.

Scottish Power refers to having positive relations with Trade Unions, although this is completely unsubstantiated, and there is no opportunity given for the Trade Unions to comment on this, nor are we told which Trade Unions are recognized. Similarly BNFL comment that there is a 'high level of employee union membership', but this is not taken any further. In fact the only company to provide a hyperlink to unions was Northern Electric, no other company mentioned Trade Unions.

Customers

Purely generating companies did not mention customers at all on their websites. It is only those companies that deal with the end users that comment on consumers. For these companies, most make such claims as to be 'focusing on customers' and assert that customer care is 'a way of life'. Such similar declarations mean that companies do not distinguish themselves from their competitors by saying this. Another constant feature for the supply companies with operational websites is that most provide the consumer with a 'savings calculator'. This enables the user to enter their present supplier and energy use and their potential savings from swapping supplier are calculated. It is interesting that none of the supply companies provide a full list of suppliers and their respective prices. The calculation is simply made in comparison to the consumers' present supply and does not take into account alternative suppliers. This is not that surprising, as only one company will be able to claim to be the cheapest supplier for a specific user and this will not be the same for all users. Also the companies do not, at this point, offer links to OFGEM's site where more complete comparisons are made. This is despite many of the companies actually providing links to the OFGEM site in other parts of their website. This is a seemingly obvious case of the companies making use of the Internet to control the message given to the stakeholder, or in the language of institutional theory, appears to be a case of decoupling.

In addition to price there is the issue of quality. Many of the more established companies reproduced OFGEM's guaranteed and overall standards. The information provided tended to be the standard and the required payment if this was not attained. For the distribution sector, there is a quality issue in terms of security and availability of supply. Most, but not all, of the distribution companies reproduced their quality of supply reports on their websites.

Suppliers and Business Partners

This is a stakeholder group that receives very little information on company websites, irrespective of the size of the company. In fact there were only two companies that provided any real information for suppliers or prospective suppliers. Both National Grid and Centrica have procurement policies and both operate a Vendor Qualification system through Achilles (a company that provides a 'full range of procurement services' and 'EC legislation and Supplier Database software' www.achilles.co.uk). Centrica operate this vendor database for contracts covered by EU directives and both of these companies provide links to the Achilles database. It may be that the nature of these two companies and their history in monopoly operations are the reason for this additional information.

A few other companies may refer to business partners, but this tends to be infrequent or limited to a small number. The exception to this is East Midlands Electricity, who provide a policy and a list of present external service providers. Overall this stakeholder group is by far the least represented on the company websites.

The Environment

The environment became an extremely important issue in the 1990s and continues to be so in the new millennium. The increase in the use of environmental reports is widely reported (see for example the work of Rob Gray). It is therefore not surprising that the environment is seen as an important issue for the electricity companies, to address on their websites. Therefore most companies do provide an environmental policy and access to externally verified environmental reports on their websites. Some companies have not provided this service, but they are the exception rather than the rule. Environmental reports are now well established in the electricity companies and this is probably due to the environmental impact of the industry noted earlier. The reports produced are significant and provide performance to date and targets for the future. The voluntary nature of environmental reporting means that these reports do not follow a standard format and this does make comparison difficult. Having said this, the largest environmental issue for the generating companies is the emission of greenhouse gases from the generation process, and performance is reported for each of the greenhouse gases. The recognized importance of the environment and the increased use of the Internet have coincided over the last decade, and therefore the ability to provide environmental reports electronically, rather than having to print vast numbers of copies, does make for a powerful argument for Internet reporting.

The companies report their performance and set targets for future performance, but do they provide links or an opportunity for comment by environmental pressure groups? Approximately half of the companies that report on environmental performance also provided links to some external environmental interest group. The most commonly linked sites were the DETR, the Environment Agency, the Environment Council, and Business in the Community. Also specific interest groups, such as the RSPB and the Wildlife Trust, were linked by a small number of companies, and this was usually because of a specific project undertaken by the company in concert with the group. The companies were almost all silent in terms of the more aggressive or confrontational environmental groups, such as Friends of the Earth and Greenpeace. In fact the only company to provide links with these organizations was BNFL, and this may be due to the fact that nuclear energy does not produce greenhouse gas emissions. Having said this, these groups are concerned about nuclear energy and therefore this link is unusual as it takes the stakeholder to a site that provides adverse commentary on the business. Two other companies refer to Friends of the Earth with respect to their Green Energy League Tables. These companies both performed well, but not the best, in these tables and draw the stakeholder's attention to this fact, although they do not provide a link to this website. This failure to let the stakeholder easily link to the special interest site allows the company to select the information given and does not provide the whole story.

Finally, one exceptional case was that of Shell. They have a subsidiary that operates in the electricity market and this provides links to the group site. Shell are well known for their social reporting and there is one unusual aspect to their website as well. This is that there is a section for comments on the Shell Report, and these are published irrespective of whether the comments are positive or negative. This allows the stakeholder to see numerous perspectives on Shell's performance as opposed to that reported. For example, there are especially strong comments against Shell's involvement in Nigeria. Most of the companies ask for feedback / comments on their websites or environmental reports, but Shell are the only company that is willing to publish these. This is an exceptional case of a company allowing individual stakeholders the opportunity to voice their thoughts on the social performance of an organization.

The Government and the Regulator

The companies do not specifically refer to or appear to be communicating with the government or the regulator. Any information is included more for the primary stakeholders' information. Therefore some companies provide a historical background to their companies and the UK electricity industry, and hence the role of government, the regulator and competition, but this is for the benefit of shareholders and consumers. In fact these secondary stakeholders can be seen to be a further information point for the primary stakeholder. One way that companies can assist their stakeholders in finding out more about their 'rights' and the working of the industry is by providing links to the secondary stakeholder. This is done by approximately half of the companies, with the most popular links being to OFGEM, the DTI and the DETR.

From the earlier interviews it appeared that the most widely recognized social issue in the electricity industry is that of fuel poverty, and this has certainly received significant governmental and regulatory attention. Therefore the links to OFGEM and the DTI should help inform interested stakeholders about this issue. In addition there is a special interest group called National Energy Action (NEA) that are specifically concerned with fuel poverty and report statistics relating to this issue. Twelve of the larger electricity companies are listed as business partners of this organization, but only a minority of these companies mention or provide a link to the NEA. This seems to be contrary to the expectation that the companies would use such support as evidence of a social conscience.

Other Stakeholder Groups Represented

Local communities are a very popular section on the websites of large companies. All of the larger companies made some reference to being 'good neighbours'. In order to support these claims companies provide examples of the projects they are presently undertaking that constitute some form of community involvement. There is a great deal of similarity between the schemes used by the competing companies, and they tend to focus on special need groups, such as the disabled or elderly, the environment (as discussed above), the arts, sport and education. In this area the larger companies were actually more likely to reproduce a policy statement and also to provide links with their partnership organizations. Therefore several of the companies provided links to Age Concern and Help the Aged, and many provided 'learning zones' for school children with links to 'Channel 4 Schools' and other educational sites.

Perhaps the weakest element of the reporting to local communities was some form of measurement of performance. This is difficult to do and therefore this scattergun approach of detailing individual projects undertaken appears to have been universally accepted. A feature of the US companies is the different emphasis placed upon the monetary amount of assistance provided. In the UK this is not emphasized, although information on how to apply for sponsorship is given.

The trade body the Electricity Association was a popular link for the electricity companies. Similarly the nuclear companies also provide numerous links to nuclear associations, both nationally and internationally. These associations are funded and supported by the companies and are extremely positive about the activities of the companies. It is therefore to be expected that the Internet user will be directed to this other source of positive public relations.

Finally, one of the most popular aspects of the companies' websites was media relations. The major feature of this section is as an archive of company press releases. All large companies provided this service and some other summary fact sheet about the company. The companies do not provide a more complete service of news about the company. This is to say that it is only company press releases that are provided and not press comment generated from other sources. It can be argued that such a service would provide a more balanced view of the companies, but this has not been undertaken. The companies do not refer to their competitors except as part of their savings calculator, discussed above, and neither do they provide links to their websites. Due to the possible adverse affect of such links, where it might be possible for customers or potential customers to find a better deal, this is not surprising.

Concluding Thoughts on the Internet as a Social Communication Media

It must be remembered that this research is essentially exploratory, as there is little previous work in the area. It is possible that the websites contain more information than I accessed. In defence, a strict routine of trying to access all pages was followed in order to ensure that the coverage was as complete as possible. Similarly the site searches and site maps were used when possible, although not all sites offered these services. A further defence could be that, if the information could not be found through this process, then it is not easily accessible and therefore will not be found by most stakeholders.

As evidenced above, the Internet is already being widely used by the electricity companies, but the voluntary nature of this reporting leads to distinct differences in quantity and quality of information. Considering only the larger companies, the most consistent features are the shareholder information, and this includes an electronic copy of the annual report. Also all of the large generating companies provided environmental reports, although the actual content of these was not analyzed in great detail. This would seem to provide further evidence of the importance of these two groups for social legitimacy. In contrast the information for customers and employees was minimal and aimed, on the whole, at targeting potential customers and employees. Suppliers receive even less information and overall this may well reflect the free market attitude taken to these three stakeholder groups.

The companies are extremely selective in the links provided and it is very unusual to find any adverse commentary included in any way. It may well be that this can be changed in the future, but one wonders where pressure for such a change will come from. The companies themselves would clearly not benefit unless they were seen to be in some way superior to the other companies.

The selective reporting and lack of dialogue on the Internet raises significant doubts as to whether it has resulted in greater accountability. The lack of links to other stakeholder voices appears to be a form of decoupling where these sites are propaganda vehicles for the companies in which there is no room for dissenting voices. The majority of the information provided was previously available in other forms and so the actual use of the Internet does not necessarily mark a significant change in the competitive pressures for information. The widening access to the information, as it is now accessible from anywhere in the world (assuming you have a computer and a link to the Internet), may in the future improve accountability. At present this is still debatable as access to the Internet, although growing rapidly, is still in the hands of the minority. Also education, geography and wealth will limit certain stakeholders' ability to access information via the Internet. This could also be argued to be true of other media used by companies, but should not be ignored as a very real accountability issue in the future. At present it seems possible to conclude only that the Internet has the potential to improve accountability, but that this is by no means a forgone conclusion, as it will depend on both how organizations' use of the Internet develops and how truly accessible the Internet becomes.

The Global Reporting Initiative (GRI)

In chapter 3 we saw that:

> The Global Reporting Initiative (GRI) is a long-term, multi-stakeholder, international process whose mission is to develop and disseminate globally applicable *Sustainability Reporting Guidelines* (*"Guidelines"*). These *Guidelines* are for voluntary use by organisations for reporting on the economic,

environmental and social dimensions of their activities, products, and services. (GRI, 2002, p.1)

The GRI separates the performance indicators into three categories, economic, environmental and social. The environment is clearly considered under the environmental section that includes an energy 'aspect'. This aspect includes core indicators relating to 'energy use segmented by primary source'. Additional indicators also consider 'initiatives to use renewable energy sources and to increase energy efficiency'. In addition 'Greenhouse gas emissions' is a core indicator under the 'Emissions, Effluents and Waste' section of the guidelines. Therefore if the electricity organizations were to follow the GRI guidelines, and report both the core and the additional indicators, they would provide the information identified by the stakeholders interviewed here. It is important to remember here that the environmental stakeholders interviewed felt that this environmental issue was by far the most important one facing the industry and therefore this paper has concentrated on this issue. This is not to say that other environmental issues, whether identified by the GRI or not, are not important.

Interestingly in the GRI (2002), as opposed to GRI (2000), the economic indicators are split into five different aspects: customers, suppliers, employees, providers of capital and the public sector. This list is comparable to the list of stakeholders identified in this research. We shall now consider the indicators identified for each of the stakeholder groups considered here. Within the economic section the performance indicators identified for customers are:

EC1.   Net sales. (Core)
EC2.   Geographic breakdown of markets. (Core)

Under the social performance indicators there are also sections for customer health and safety, products and services, advertising and respect for privacy. These indicators tend to relate to descriptions of policy or numbers and type of non-compliance with regulations. Within the additional measures the number of complaints upheld by regulatory or similar official bodies and it is also suggested that 'results of surveys measuring customer satisfaction' be reported. Also within the additional social indicators there is a section on competition and pricing that requires companies to report on policy and 'court decisions regarding cases pertaining to anti-trust and monopoly regulations'.

For suppliers the following specific indicators are suggested:

EC3.   Cost of all goods, materials, and services purchased. (Core)
EC4.   Percentage of contracts that were paid in accordance with agreed terms, excluding agreed penalty arrangements. (Core)
EC11. Supplier breakdown by organisation and country. (Additional)
EN33. Performance of suppliers relative to environmental components of programmes and procedures described in response to Governance Structure and Management Systems section. (Additional)

Suppliers continue to receive relatively less attention, although EC4 and EC11 would appear to be valuable information. In contrast there is a considerable amount of information relating to employees. As well as the economic information relating to the total payroll and benefits there is a considerable amount of information within the social performance indicators, which provides sections on 'Labour Practices and Decent Work' and 'Human Rights'. Within these sections there are aspects concerned with employment, health and safety, and training and education that provides information relating to the non-financial aspects of the employee information needs identified in this research.

Finally, the information for the providers of capital includes distributions made and 'increase/decrease in retained earnings at end of period'. Within the organizational profile section there is also a section on the 'scale of the reporting organisation' and also suggests that 'significant changes in size, structure, ownership, or products/services that have occurred since the previous report' should be reported. In addition:

> Reporting organisations should choose the set of measures best suited to the nature of their operations and stakeholders' needs. Measures should include those that can be used specifically to create ratios using the absolute figures provided in other sections of the report (See Annex 5 for information on ratios). (GRI, 2002, p.40)

Within the Annex 5 productivity and efficiency ratios are suggested and these include 'financial efficiency ratios (e.g., profit per share)' and 'financial performance ratios (e.g., return on equity, return on operating assets)' (p.84). The measures suggested here are organization specific and therefore do not include the wider market measures identified in the shareholder interviews.

Overall, including the details noted in chapter 3, the GRI appears to cover stakeholder dialogue, stakeholder information needs, as identified here, and recognizes the need for external verification. Most of the information not included in the GRI is either too commercially sensitive or more relevant to an industry or the economy rather than the individual organization. Certainly the employee and environmental measures appear to be well covered. There is, however, relatively less information for consumers and suppliers and this may be due to the market nature of these transactions. At present the measures included are insufficiently defined and lacking in detail to be considered a standard in the same way as financial reporting standards. Financial reporting standards have been becoming longer, as the standard setters attempt to prescribe accounting rules that are as precise as possible and cover as many eventualities as possible. The GRI guidelines have a long way to go if they are to match this and therefore it must be true that there is scope for subjectivity and 'creative accounting' within the measures suggested.

It must be remembered that the GRI is voluntary and many of the indicators identified here are considered to be additional, as opposed to core. There remain research questions as to how many organizations, in the UK, Europe and globally, will adopt the GRI and to what extent those adopting it will report on all of the indicators. If only a minority of companies adopt the guidelines, and those that do adopt do so incompletely, then there is a case to make the guidelines mandatory for the largest companies. Such a step would improve the general level of information available to stakeholders, but appears to be unlikely in the future. At present those interested in the 'business case' social accounting appear to be content that it remains voluntary.

The GRI does provide guidance for organizations who want to go further than is presently common, but this should be seen as a starting point for the future development of social accounting – an area that will continue to evolve, as the business context changes to societal and environmental pressures. Owen, Swift and Hunt (2001), however, express concern as to the appropriateness of the social accounting standards. They believe that these are based too heavily on the 'business case' for social and environmental accounting and fear that the 'radical edge' of the early movement of Social Audit Ltd has been lost. In fact they suggest that, due to the high level of corporate representation in the bodies responsible for these standards, it may well be the case that these standards have been 'captured' by corporate interests. The 'business case' may result in companies only ever being socially or environmentally concerned for instrumental, as opposed to ethical, reasons. They further fear that this results in stakeholder management, as witnessed in this research, instead of stakeholder accountability.

Conclusions

This research started with a consideration of the role of businesses in modern capitalist societies. It argued that the traditional shareholder view of that role was originally reached within a moral and ethical context, which suggested some restrictions were necessary on the activities of businesses. It is through a form of contract with society that these businesses are incorporated into modern societies and therefore, it was argued, the responsibility such organizations have to society should not be forgotten. Given this social contract it was suggested that there is a need to understand and appraise how these organizations perform for the societies within which they operate, and a stakeholder perspective was adopted to do this. This was argued to be appropriate, as it enabled the different interests within a society affected by an organization's activities to be considered. Stakeholder theory takes a pluralistic view of society, in that there are multiple factions and interests that make a single society. In order to provide a contextual setting for this consideration of societal performance the electricity industry in England and Wales was considered. Utility industries are especially interesting as they include a natural monopoly component that was owned and operated by the UK government for several decades until the privatization programme of the 1980s and early 1990s. In addition to the natural monopoly, the other elements of the industries had benefited from a monopoly status over the nationalized period. Therefore these industries were sold to the private sector without the normal free market mechanisms to protect consumers, and more widely society, from possible monopolistic behaviour from the companies. This general feature of the privatized utilities and their necessity to modern societies makes them a productive area for research. In addition the structure of the electricity industry, in terms of the vertical and horizontal separation into fifteen companies on privatization, was a new development that suggested that this was a more advanced privatization than the earlier ones.

Given this foundation a framework of measures was provided by which to consider the stakeholder performance of this industry, which was grounded in both performance measurement literature and industry specific interviews with both stakeholders and organizations. This framework was then used to appraise the stakeholder, and hence social, performance of the industry. The results of this analysis were then interpreted with the assistance of institutional and resource dependency theory as developed into considerations of strategic response by Oliver (1991). In addition this chapter has considered some relatively recent developments that, in my opinion, have relevance to how this type of research can move forward in the future. These were firstly, the Internet as a medium for providing information, and secondly, the development of social accounting standards specifically the GRI. As a result of these developments the potential for standardized social accounting is now greater than ever before, but there is a concern amongst some academics that this will not result in true stakeholder accountability.

Contributions and Limitations

In many ways this research is inspired and refers back to past work that to some extent has been forgotten in much of the present day accounting literature. As such three inspirations for this work were: firstly the work of Charles Medawar (1976, 1978) and Social Audit Ltd (1973a, b), which in many ways did similar analyses, although with much greater access and resources, to the one attempted here. In some ways Tony Tinker's (1985) 'Paper Prophets' is similar and this was also a great stimulation. Finally, 'The Corporate Report' published by ASSC in 1975, was a more institutional attempt to consider a wider stakeholder form of accounting, which unfortunately eventually failed. It would be an interesting case for further research to see exactly which pressures were responsible for its eventual failure, although it would seem clear that they are likely to be institutional pressures either from the actual accounting practitioners or the government. Therefore this research reconsiders ideas and techniques that to some extent have been discarded in the context of a societal development, privatization. This research provides an in-depth consideration of a unique case that is both political and economic in nature. The documenting of such cases in detail is a valid and important form of research and can be likened to documenting the history of the present. It is important that multiple perspectives and understandings of this case, and more generally the operations of businesses, are provided so that future research can be informed and that the theories and frameworks developed can be progressed.

The detailed stakeholder analysis of the electricity industry for the period 1991 to 1997 uses publicly available information (primarily the companies' annual reports, the regulator's reports and government statistics) to demonstrate that certain stakeholder groups have benefited more than other groups in the post-privatization period. Most clearly this can be seen in the redistribution of wealth that has occurred over this period of time. The analysis in chapter 6 clearly demonstrated that in 1997 shareholders received dividends that were £2,885m higher than in 1991, although £1,207m of this related to a special dividend paid by National Power for the purposes of 'major capital restructuring'. Nevertheless the ordinary level of dividends has increased by £1,678m. Over the same period purchases fell by £884m and labour costs fell by £750m. Therefore there has been an incredible redistribution of wealth from suppliers and employees to shareholders. This should be considered in the light of the fact that at the time of privatization the government White Paper suggested that:

> a modern, competitive (electricity) industry will be created, widely owned by the public, and more responsive to the needs of customers and employees… There are real benefits in prospect for the customer, employee and the economy (Cm 322, 1988, p.16).

This analysis shows that for the majority of consumers any gains have been minimal and that the employee group as a whole has not benefited. A further contribution of this research is that it considers a broader range of stakeholders than done in previous research (for example the research of Shaoul, 1997; and Froud *et al.*, 1998). This is most clearly demonstrated by the consideration of the environmental effects of the industry. The most significant contribution in this respect is the finding that the role and power of the regulator and even more so the government is still very strong. Therefore despite privatization the industry is heavily influenced by the need to acquiesce to the needs of government. This research provides evidence of how the privatized companies attempt to align themselves with the government and the regulator. In this context Oliver's framework, which draws upon institutional and resource dependency theories, was useful to explain how the strategic responses of the companies is constrained. This finding has importance for the future of public policy and therefore this is discussed in below. A further contribution of this research is that it uses Oliver's framework from an external perspective at a macro level to consider strategic responses.

Another contribution is the use of an interview based case study approach to consider social accounting and corporate social performance. This is still a relatively under used research method in this context and more such fieldwork has been called for (see Gray, 2000). The benefit of using this approach, as opposed to say a survey-based study, was the ability to discuss the issues in more depth and clarify points to a much greater extent than is possible using surveys. Also my own personal experience of using surveys (Cooper *et al.*, 2001) resulted in an extremely disappointing response rate that can question the validity of the results. This case research method can also be seen as a limitation. Due to practical time considerations and the availability of appropriate stakeholder representatives, only two of each kind were interviewed. Further, this was restricted, on the whole, to one interview with one representative from each organization. It was considered imperative that two different organizations were approached for each stakeholder group so that any organization or interviewee bias could be cross checked with an independent source, but ideally future research will go into greater depth with stakeholder groups. Again, referring back to the work of Social Audit Ltd, it is clear that the number of interviews performed for these reports were far more extensive, but so were their resources. It is hoped that these interviews are of considerable value due to the wide-ranging perspectives and backgrounds of the interviewees, organizations and stakeholders that they represented. The interview data provides some unique and telling insights into the workings of stakeholder management in these electricity companies. The findings suggest that this is being managed in an instrumental way that is certainly not consistent with the more normative aspirations of stakeholder theorists.

A further contribution was the combination of the literature and the interview data to produce a stakeholder performance measurement framework. This grounding in the literature and interview data enabled the framework to be focused on the particular industry and also to draw on what is of practical use at the moment. In some cases this focusing may have gone too far, as in the case of the Environment where the issue of climate change came through so forcefully that it was the only issue considered. It is not the opinion of the author that this is the only important environmental issue being raised by the operations of these electricity companies and multi-national organizations more generally. In practical terms this focussing on a single environmental issue again helped restrict the research, and if this had not been the case the environmental aspect to the research may have ended up dominating the social. It is certainly true that environmental management, performance and accounting are topics for complete books in their own right and have already been so. This research was specifically interested in the social implications of this industry and as such the environment was considered to be only part of the issues to be considered. A further limitation is that in some ways the framework developed is a compromise, as the information available to be analyzed was also a consideration. This was most clearly a problem for the employee and supplier stakeholders, and this would appear to be yet further evidence of their relative lack of power as stakeholder groups. The employment reports advocated and actually used by some organizations after the Corporate Report was published contained a relative plethora of segmented information that is simply no longer available. Government and company information is aggregated and allows little true analysis other than at industry and company levels. This lack of information is another resource that is withheld from the public that allows these companies to operate within society. In my opinion it would definitely be in the public interest for this information to be made available such that these companies can be made more fully accountable. A further concern is the accuracy of the information actually provided. This was specifically highlighted by an important figure in a consumer organization, who suggested that the reliability of consumer information could as a minimum be questioned, but at worst is actually worthless or misleading. This is a limitation of relying upon publicly available data as a source. This information is secondary and as such has not been gathered personally from the source directly by the researcher. In contrast, many would argue that such publicly available data is more reliable as it has been audited or submitted to the regulator, where there are penalties if the information were to be discovered to be inaccurate.

At no time in this research was it considered appropriate to use statistical techniques to analyze the data, as much of the interview data was qualitative and the actual analysis was based on the whole population of the industry. These contributions, with their acknowledged limitations, are seen by the author as being firmly in the realm of social accounting and corporate social performance. There is, in my opinion, a definite need for more social accounting, as the power of large multinational organizations appears to inexorably grow and globalize. The increased size, power and influence these organizations have should be a cause for concern for societies and their governments. It appears that the real power lies with the organizations, who can choose where to operate and hence put intense pressure on countries to accede to tax breaks or special concessions to ensure their continued operations in a specific country. This appears to be a reversal of the power relations that would be expected if the social contract approach to companies were accepted. Given the importance of power within modern society and specifically the considerable power of the government, the final section of this book will consider the public policy implications of this research.

Public Policy Implications and Recommendations

This research has demonstrated that following privatization of the electricity industry in England and Wales there has been a redistribution of wealth to shareholders from other stakeholders, most notably suppliers and employees. Therefore the claims that the privatization of utility industries would result in benefits to all does not appear to be substantiated with the benefit of hindsight. Therefore the first public policy implication is that, where there is a constrained future revenue stream, as there is in the regulated utility industries, increased returns to private shareholders can only be achieved through redistribution. Therefore claims that such privatization will benefit all can not be made for any future privatizations. Further, perhaps even more damning evidence has recently been provided by the Rail industry and the collapse of the privatized Rail network company Railtrack.

The privatization programme appears to have been completed and the government now has a policy of Public-Private Partnerships (PPP), which includes the Private Finance Initiative (PFI). Shaoul (2002) states that PPP is justified on the grounds that it is a way to generate funding, which would not be available from the public sector, and that such initiatives provide 'greater value for money'. This is similar to privatization in that it is looking to the private sector to solve the investment problems of the public sector. Froud and Shaoul (2001) provide analysis of the PFI for NHS hospitals and they conclude that the PFI process does not necessarily provide better solutions. Shaoul (2002) undertakes 'A Financial Appraisal of the London Underground Public-Private Partnership' and concludes:

Finally, this analysis demonstrates why the capital-intensive public infrastructure industries, and other public sector activities that provide vital public services on a universal and comprehensive basis, have been in public ownership not just in Britain but all over the world. They are simply too risky and/or not cash generative enough for the private sector. If the project goes ahead, the private sector partners and their financial backers, far from assuming risk under the PPP, are set to get income streams guaranteed in one form or another by the public sector, while the Government, Transport *for* London, London Underground, the workforce and the public as individuals carry the risk. (p.59)

This has an incredibly strong resonance with some of the findings from this research. When the private sector requires its return, a return that is not required within publicly funded projects, then this could well be at the expense of some other stakeholder group. Similarly, it was noted here that the 'real risks' associated with the electricity industry remained with government and were not transferred to the private sector, in exactly the same way as is suggested in this PPP initiative. To date the lessons of privatization do not appear to have appreciated by the Government and therefore we are in danger of repeating the same mistakes over and over again.

Finally, there has also been the UK Company Law Review and the Turnbull committee report that appear relevant to government policy towards corporate governance, which is at the very heart of the stakeholder – shareholder debate. The UK Company Law Review Steering Group decided to reject a wider, more pluralist approach to directors' duties. Instead they preferred 'an inclusive approach', which suggests that directors need to consider both the long and the short term with 'a view to achieving company success for the benefit of shareholders as a whole' (DTI, 2000a). This appears to reinforce the primacy given to shareholders that was discussed in chapter 2, and the importance of the wider society, as suggested by a social contract, is again left either implicit or non-existent. Therefore the present New Labour government appears to have moved away from the concept of stakeholder capitalism, with which they were associated prior to the 1997 election, and towards an enlightened shareholder approach.

In contrast, Friedman and Miles (2001) suggest that the Turnbull committee report may hold some hope of increased accountability for social, ethical and environmental issues. This is because it suggests that there is a need for directors to manage risk (Lake, 1999), and part of this risk is reputational risk. There is some hope that the need to consider risks to reputation may put social and environmental behaviour 'onto their corporate governance agenda' (Friedman and Miles, 2001). It would appear to me that this is unjustifiably optimistic, as once again the link is left unclear or implicit and is unlikely to have any realistic effects on corporate governance and corporate ethics. Until government explicitly recognize the importance of the social and the environmental it seems to me that the present inequalities will continue to worsen.

Given the failure of the privatization and the PFI policies to actually produce the promised benefits for all the justification for such policies needs to be revisited. Further, the government's social and environmental role needs to be made more explicit. Three ways in which this could be done are through legislation, regulation and mandatory reporting.

This thesis argues that there is a need for companies to consider a broader range of stakeholders and to engage with their needs, as recommended under AA1000, if there is to be an increased level of accountability. Unfortunately the recent company law review did not support this view, but it is the author's opinion that this is a missed opportunity. Secondly, in a regulated industry the role of the regulator should be expanded to incorporate the social and environmental aspects of the industry. Some very minimal steps have already been taken in this direction, but much more could be done. This book has highlighted a redistribution of wealth between stakeholders in a regulated utility and therefore would strongly recommend that the regulator should be appraising these companies' performance using an explicitly stakeholder approach. Therefore the use of value added analysis and a stakeholder performance measurement model, as designed in this thesis, should be an important analytical tool for the regulator and for others when considering corporate social performance. Alternatively, the regulator could require the companies to produce a social report along the lines of the GRI. This provides a comprehensive measurement of performance under social, economic and environmental performance and would greatly increase stakeholder awareness of the issues in an industry. This would also address the lack of information presently available to certain stakeholder groups identified in this book. A requirement to produce such detailed social reports should be mandated to all companies above a certain size, possibly based on market capitalization such as the FTSE 100. This would certainly mean going further than requiring companies to discuss social, environmental and reputational issues, as suggested in the company law white paper discussed above. Finally, it is the author's belief that the introduction of these three recommendations would be beneficial to society, as some of the endemic power asymmetries would, to some extent, be highlighted and could therefore provide a first step towards them being redresses. The reduction of such power asymmetries should be a priority for government within a pluralistic understanding of modern society in the 21st Century.

Bibliography

Adams, C and Harte, G. (2000), 'Making discrimination visible: the potential for social accounting', *Accounting Forum*, Vol. 24(1), pp.56-79.

Adams, C. A., Hill, W. Y., and Roberts, C. B. (1995), 'Environmental, Employee and Ethical Reporting in Europe', *Research Report 41*, Certified Accountants Educational Trust, London.

Agle, B. R.,Mitchell, R. K. and Sonnenfeld, J. A. (1999), 'Who matters to CEOs? An investigation of stakeholder attributes and salience, corporate performance and CEO values', *Academy of Management Journal*, Vol. 42(5), pp.507-25.

Allan, D., Day, R., Hirst, I. And Kwiatowski, J. (1986), 'Equity, gilts, treasury bills and inflation', *Investment Analyst*, Vol. 83, pp.11-18.

Altman, E. I. (1971), *Corporate bankruptcy in America*, Heath Lexington Books, Lexington, MA.

Argandona, A. (1998), 'The stakeholder theory and the common good', *Journal of Business Ethics*, Vol. 17(9/10), pp.1093-1102.

Argenti, J. (1976), *Corporate Collapse: The Causes and Symptoms*, John Wiley, New York.

Argenti, J. (1993), *Your organization: What is it for?*, McGraw-Hill, London.

Arnold, G. (2002), *Corporate Financial Management*, Second Edition, Financial Times, London.

ASSC, (Accounting Standards Steering Committee) (1975), *The Corporate Report*, ASSC, London.

Atkinson, A. B. (1996), 'Seeking to explain the distribution of income', in J. Hills (ed.) *New inequalities: The changing distribution of income and wealth in the United Kingdom*, Cambridge University Press, Cambridge.

Atkinson, A. A., Waterhouse, J. H., and Wells, R. B. (1997), 'A stakeholder approach to strategic performance management', *Sloan Management Review*, Spring.

Atkinson, G. (2000), 'Measuring Corporate Sustainability', *Journal of Environmental Planning and Management*, Vol. 43(2), pp.235-252, published by Taylor & Francis Ltd, http://www.tandf.co.uk/journals.

Aupperle, K. E (1984), 'An empirical measure of corporate social orientation', *Research in Corporate Social Performance and Policy*, Vol. 6, pp.27-54.

Aupperle, K. E., Carroll, A. B. and Hatfield, J. D. (1985), 'An empirical examination of the relationship between corporate social responsibility and profitability', *Academy of Management Journal*, Vol. 28(2), pp. 446-463.

Ball, R. J. (1968), 'The Use of Value Added in Measuring Managerial Efficiency', *Business Ratios*, Summer, pp.5-11.

Barclays Capital (2001), *Equity-Gilt Study*, Barclays Capital, London.

Becker, L. C. (1992), 'Placed for pluralism', *Ethics*, Vol. 102, pp.707-719.

Beesley, M. and Littlechild, S. (1983), 'Privatisation: principles, problems and priorities', in C. Johnson (ed.) (1988) *Privatisation & ownership – Lloyds Bank Annual Review*, Pinter, London.

Belkaoui, A. (1984), *Socio-economic Accounting*, Quorum Books, Connecticut.

Bendheim, C. L., Waddock, S. A. and Graves, S. B. (1998), 'Determining best practice in corporate-stakeholder relations using Data Envelopment Analysis: An industry-level study', *Business and Society*, Vol. 37(3), pp.306-338.

Bennett, M. and James, P. (1998), *Environment under the spotlight – Current Practice and Future Trends in Environment-Related Performance Measurement for Business*, Chartered Accountants Educational Trust, London.

Bennett, M. and James, P. (1999), 'ISO 14031 and the future of Environmental Performance Evaluation' in M. Bennett, P. James and L. Klinkers (eds.) *Sustainable Measures: Evaluation and Reporting of Environmental and Social Performance*, pp.76-97, Greenleaf, Sheffield.

Bentham, J. (1789), *Introduction to the Principles of Morals and Legislation*, many editions.

Berle, A. and Means, G. (1933), *The modern corporation and private property*, Commerce Clearing House, New York.

Bishop, M. and Kay, J. (1988), *Does Privatisation work? – Lessons from the UK*, Centre for Business Strategy, London Business School, London.

BNFL, (2000), *Annual Report and Accounts*, BNFL.

Bordieu, P. (1979), *Outline of a theory of practice*, Cambridge University Press, New York.

Bowey, A. M. (1974), *A guide to manpower planning*, Macmillan, London.

Bowie, N. E. and Freeman, R. E. (1992), 'Ethics and agency theory: An introduction', in N. E. Bowie and R. E. Freeman (eds), *Ethics and agency theory*, Oxford University Press, New York.

Boyce, G. (2000), 'Public Discourse and decision making: Exploring possibilities for financial, social and environmental accounting', *Accounting Auditing and Accountability Journal*, Vol. 13(1), pp.27-64.

Brealey, R. A. and Myers, S. C. (1996) *Principles of Corporate Finance: International Edition*, 5th Ed., McGraw-Hill, London.

Brennan, M. (1994), 'Incentives, Rationality and Society', *Journal of Applied Corporate Finance*, Vol. 7(2), pp.31-39.

Brenner, S. N., and Cochran, P. (1991), 'The stakeholder theory of the firm: Implications for business and society theory and research', Paper presented at the annual meeting of the International Association for Business and Society, Sundance, UT.

Brignall, S. and Ballantine, J. A. (1996), 'Interactions and trade-offs in multi-dimensional performance management', Warwick Business School Research Bureau, No. 247.

Bryman, A. (1989), *Research Methods and Organisational Studies*, Routledge, London.

Buchanan, D. A., Boddy, D. and McCalman (1988), 'Getting in, Getting on, Getting out, Getting back: the Art of the Possible', in A. Bryman (ed.) *Doing Research in Organisations*, Routledge, London.

Bucholz, R. A. and Rosenthal, S. B. (1997), 'Business and society: What's in a name', *International Journal of Organizational Analysis*, April.

Burchell, S., Clubb, C., and Hopwood, A. G. (1985), 'Accounting in its social context: Towards a history of value added in the United Kingdom', *Accounting, Organizations and Society*, Vol. 10(4), pp. 381-413.

Burns, T. and Flam, H. (1987), *The Shaping of Social Organization*, Sage, Newbury Park, California.

Caeldries, F. (1993), 'On the sustainability of the capitalist order: Schumpeter's capitalism, socialism and democracy revisited', *Journal of Socio-Economics*, Vol. 22(3), pp.163-185.

Carr, E. H. (1981), *What is History?* Penguin, Harmondsworth.

Carroll, A. B. (1993), *Business and Society: Ethics and Stakeholder Management*, 2nd edn, South Western Publishing, Cincinnati, Ohio.

Carter, C. and Crowther, D. (2000), 'Unravelling a profession: The case of engineers in a British regional electricity company', *Critical Perspectives on Accounting*, Vol. 11(1), pp.23-49.

Chakravarthy, B. S. (1982), 'Adaptation: a promising metaphor for strategic management', *Academy of Management Review*, Vol. 7, pp.35-44.

Chakravarthy, B, S. (1986), 'Measuring Strategic Performance', *Strategic Management Journal*, Vol. 7, pp.437-458.

Child, J. W. and Marcoux, A, M. (1999), 'Freeman and Evan: Stakeholder theory in the original position', *Business Ethics Quarterly*, Vol. 9(2), pp.207-223.

Churchman, C. W. (1967), 'Why measure?', in C. W. Churchman and P. Ratoosh (eds) *Measurement Definition and Theories*, Wiley, London, pp.83-94.

Clarkson, M. B. E. (1994), 'A risk based model of stakeholder theory', Proceedings of the Second Toronto Conference on Stakeholder theory, Toronto Centre for Social Performance and Ethics, University of Toronto.

Clarkson, M. B. E. (1995), 'A Stakeholder Framework for analysing and evaluating Corporate Social Performance', *Academy of Management Review*, Vol. 20(1), pp.92-117.

Cm322 (1988), *Privatising electricity: the governments proposals for the privatisation of the electricity supply industry in England and Wales*, Department of Energy, HMSO, London.

Competition Commission (2000), *Sutton and East Surrey Water plc. A report on the references under sections 12 and 14 of the Water Industry Act 1991*, The Stationery Office, London.

Cooper, S., Crowther, D., Davies, M. and Davis, E.W. (2001), *Shareholder or Stakeholder Value: The Development of Indicators for the Control and Measurement of Performance*, CIMA, London.

Cooper, S., Crowther, D. and Carter, C. (2001a), 'Towards a semiology of the Periodic Review of UK Regulated Utilities', *Financial Accountability & Management*, Vol. 17(3), pp.291- 297.

Cooper, S., Crowther, D. and Carter, C. (2001b), 'Regulation – the movie: a semiotic study of the periodic review of UK regulated industry', *Journal of Organizational Change Management*, Vol. 14(3), pp.225-238.

Cooper, D J. and Scherer, M. J. (1984), 'The value of corporate accounting reports: arguments for a political economy of accounting', *Accounting, Organizations and Society*, Vol. 9(3/4), pp.207-232.

Copeland, T., Koller, T. and Murrin, J. (1996), *Valuation: Measuring and managing the value of companies*, 2nd Edn, John Wiley & Sons, New York.

Corbett, D. (1992), *Australian Public Sector Management* Allen and Unwin, St Leonards.

Cornelius, I. G. and Davies, M. L. (1997), *Shareholder Value*, Financial Times Publishing, London.

CRI (1998), *The UK Electricity Industry Financial and Operating Review 1996/97*, CIPFA, London.

Crowther, D., Davies, M. and Cooper, S. (1998), 'Evaluating corporate performance: a critique of Economic Value Added', *Journal of Applied Accounting Research*, Vol. 4(II), pp.3-34.

Cyert, R. M. and March, J. G. (1963), *A Behavioural Theory of the Firm*, Prentice-Hall, Englewood Cliffs, NJ.

Day, J. F. S. (1986), 'The Use Of Annual Reports By UK Investment Analysts', *Accounting and Business Research*, Vol. 16(64), pp.295-308.

De Tocqueville, A. (1835), *Democracy in America*, many editions

DiMaggio, P. (1988), 'Interest and Agency in Institutional Theory', in L.G. Zucker (ed.) *Institutional Patterns and Organizations*, pp.3-22, Ballinger, Cambridge, Massachusetts.

DiMaggio. P. and Powell, W.W. (1983), 'The Iron Cage Revisited: Institutional Isomorphism and Collective Rationality in Organizational Fields' *American Sociological Review*, Vol. 48(April), pp. 147-160.

DiMaggio, P. J. and Powell, W.W. (1991), 'Introduction' in W.W. Powell and P.J. DiMaggio (eds.) *The New Institutionalism in Organizational Analysis*, pp. 1-40, University of Chicago Press, London.

Dimson, E. and Brealey, R. (1978), 'The risk premium on UK equities', *Investment Analyst*, Vol. 52, pp.14-18.

Dimson, E., Marsh, P. and Staunton, M. (2001), *The Millennium Book II: 101 years of Investment Returns,* London Business School and ABN Amro, London.

Donaldson, T. (1982), *Corporations and morality,* Prentice Hall, Englewood Cliffs, NJ.

Donaldson, T. (1989), *The ethics of international business*, Oxford University Press, New York.

Donaldson, T. and Preston, L. E. (1995), 'The stakeholder theory of the corporations: Concepts, Evidence and Implications', *The Academy of Management Review*, Vol. 20(1).

Doyle, P. (1994), 'Setting Business Objectives and Measuring Performance', *European Management Journal*, Vol. 12(2), pp.123-132.

Drucker, P. (1984), 'The new meaning of corporate social responsibility', *California Management Review*, 26, pp.53-63.

Drury, C. (2003), *Cost & Management Accounting*, 5th Edition, Thomson, London.

DTI (1991), *Digest of United Kingdom Energy Statistics*, DTI, London.

DTI (1992), *Digest of United Kingdom Energy Statistics*, DTI, London.

DTI (1993), *Digest of United Kingdom Energy Statistics*, DTI, London.

DTI (1994), *Digest of United Kingdom Energy Statistics*, DTI, London.

DTI (1995), *Digest of United Kingdom Energy Statistics*, DTI, London.

DTI (1996), *Digest of United Kingdom Energy Statistics*, DTI, London.

DTI (1997), *Digest of United Kingdom Energy Statistics*, DTI, London.

DTI (2000a), *Modern Company Law for a Competitive Economy: Developing the framework*, A consultation document from the Company Law Steering Group, DTI, London.

DTI (2000b), *Digest of United Kingdom Energy Statistics*, DTI, London.

Easterby-Smith, M., Thorpe, R. and Lowe, A. (1991), *Management Research: An Introduction*, Sage, London.

The Economist (1996), 'Stakeholder Capitalism: Unhappy families', Vol. 338(7952), 10 February 1996.

Edwards, J., Kay, J. and Mayer, C. (1987), *The Economic Analysis of Accounting Profitability*, Clarendon, Oxford.

Eisenhardt, K. M. (1989), 'Agency theory: An assessment and review', *Academy of Management Review*, Vol. 14, pp. 57-74.

Electricity Association (1997), *Electricity Industry Review*, Electricity Association, London.

Electricity Association (1999), *International Electricity Prices: A summary of Results: 1990-1998*, Electricity Association, London.

Electricity Association (2001), *Electricity Industry Review 5*, Electricity Association, London.

Emerson, R. M. (1962), Power-Dependence Relations, *American Sociological Review*, Vol. 27, pp. 31-41.

Enderle, G. and Tavis, L. A. (1998), 'A balanced concept of the firm and the measurement of its long-term planning and performance', *Journal of Business Ethics*, Vol. 17(11), pp1129-1144.

Etzioni, A. (1964), *Modern Organizations*, Prentice-Hall, Englewood Cliffs, NJ.

Etzioni, A. (1998), 'A communitarian note on stakeholder theory', *Business Ethics Quarterly*, Vol. 8(4), pp.679-691.

European Commission (1995), *Externalities of the fuel cycles: ExternE project*, Directorate-General XII, Brussels.

Evan, W. M. and Freeman, R. E. (1988), 'A stakeholder theory of the modern corporation: Kantian capitalism', in T. Beauchamp and N. Bowie (eds), *Ethical theory and business*, pp.75-93, Prentice Hall, Englewood Cliffs, NJ.

Fankhauser, S. (1994), 'Evaluating the social costs of greenhouse gas emissions', *The Energy Journal*, Vol. 15(2), pp.157-184.

Ferner, A. and Colling, T. (1991), 'Privatization, regulation and industrial relations', *British Journal of Industrial Relations*, Vol. 29(3).

Ferner, A. and Colling, T. (1993), 'Privatization of the British Utilities – regulation, decentralization, and industrial relations', in T. Clarke and C. Pitelis (eds), *The Political Economy of Privatization*, Routledge, London.

Fisher, I. (1930), *The theory of interest*, Macmillan, New York.

Fitzgerald, L., Johnston, R., Brignall, T. J., Silvestro, R. and Voss, C. (1991), *Performance Measurement in Service Businesses*, CIMA, London.

Foley, B. and Maunders, K. (1977), *Accounting Information Disclosure and Collective Bargaining*, Macmillan, London.

Foster, C. (1994), 'Rival explanations of public ownership, its failure and privatization', *Public Administration*, Vol. 72, Winter, pp.489-503.

Franks, J. and Harris, R. (1989), 'Shareholder wealth effects of corporate takeovers: the UK experience 1955-1985', *Journal of Financial Economics*, Vol. 23, pp.225-249.

Freeman, R. E. (1984), *Strategic management: A stakeholder approach*, Pittman, Boston.

Freeman, R. E. and Evan, W. M. (1990), 'Corporate Governance: A stakeholder interpretation', *The Journal of Behavioral Economics*, Vol. 19(4), pp. 337-359.

Friedman, A. L. and Miles, S. (2001), 'Socially Responsible Investment and Corporate Social and Environmental Reporting in the UK: An Exploratory Study', *British Accounting Review*, Vol. 33, pp.523-548.

Friedman, M. (1962), *Capitalism and Freedom*, University of Chicago Press, Chicago.

Friends of the Earth (1997), 'Power in Balance: Energy Challenges for the 21st Century', Discussion Paper 3, Friend of the Earth, London.

Froud, J., Haslam, C., Johal, S., Shaoul, J. and Williams, K. (1998), 'Persuasion without numbers? Public policy and the justification of capital charging in NHS trust hospitals', *Accounting Auditing & Accountability Journal*, Vol. 11(1), pp. 99-125.

Froud, J. and Shaoul, J., (2001), 'Appraising and Evaluating PFI for NHS Hospitals', *Financial Accountability & Management*, Vol. 17(3), pp.247-270.

Froud, J., Williams, K., Haslam, C., Johal, S., and Williams, J. (1998), 'Caterpillar: Two Stories and an Argument', *Accounting, Organizations and Society*, Vol. 23(7), pp.685-708.

George, G. (1983), 'Financial Reporting to Employees', *Accounting Forum*, September, pp.17-25.

Giddens, A. (1984), *The Constitution of Society*, University of California Press, Berkeley.

Gioia, D. A. (1999), 'Practicability, paradigms, and problems in stakeholder theorizing', *The Academy of Management Review*, Vol. 24 (2), pp.228-232.

Goodpaster, K. E. (1991), 'Business ethics and stakeholder analysis', *Business Ethics Quarterly*, Vol. 1(1), pp.53-73.

Gray, R. (1992), 'Accounting and environmentalism: an exploration of the challenge of gently accounting for accountability, transparency and sustainability', *Accounting, Organizations and Society*, Vol. 17(5), pp.399-425.

Gray, R. (1998) 'Imagination, a bowl of petunias and Social Accounting', *Critical Perspectives on Accounting*, Vol. 9, pp.205-216.

Gray, R. (2000), 'Current developments and trends in social and environmental auditing, reporting and attestation: a review and comment', *International Journal of Auditing*, Vol. 4(3), pp.247-268.

Gray, R. (2002), 'The social accounting project and accounting organizations and society: privileging engagement, imaginings, new accountings and pragmatism over critique?', *Accounting, Organizations and Society*, Vol. 27(7), pp.687-708.

Gray, R., Bebbington, J. and McPhail, K. (1994), 'Teaching ethics and the ethics of accounting teaching: Educating for immorality and a case for social and environmental accounting education', *Accounting Education*, Vol. 3(1), pp.51-75.

Gray, R., Bebbington, J. and Walters, D. (1993), *Accounting for the Environment*, Paul Chapman, London.

Gray, R., Dey, C., Owen, D., Evans, R. and Zadek, S. (1997), 'Struggling with the praxis of social accounting: Stakeholders accountability, audits and procedures', *Accounting, Auditing & Accountability Journal*, Vol. 10(3), pp.325-364.

Gray, R., Kouhy, R., and Lavers, S. (1995), 'Corporate social and environmental reporting: A review of the literature and a longitudinal study of UK disclosure', *Accounting Auditing & Accountability Journal*, Vol. 8(2).

Gray, R., Owen, D. and Adams, C. (1996), *Accounting and Accountability: Changes and Challenges in corporate social and environmental reporting*, Pearson, London.

Greenley, G. E. and Foxall, G. R. (1997), 'Multiple Stakeholder Orientation in UK companies and the implications for company performance', *Journal of Management Studies*, Vol. 34(2).

GRI (2000), *Sustainability Reporting Guidelines on Economic, Environmental and Social Performance,* see www.globalreporting.org.

GRI (2002), *Sustainability Reporting Guidelines,* see www.globalreporting.org.

Hand, J. R. M. (1990), 'A Test Of The Extended Functional Fixation Hypothesis', Accounting Review, Vol. 65(4), pp.739-763.

Hand, J. R. M. (1991), 'Extended Functional Fixation and Security Returns Around Earnings Announcements: A Reply To Ball And Kothari', Accounting Review, Vol. 66(4), pp.739-746.

Hannan, M. T. and Freeman, J. H. (1977), 'The population ecology of organizations', *American Journal of Sociology*, Vol. 82, pp.1420-1443.

Harrington, L. K. (1996), 'Ethics and public policy analysis: Stakeholders' interests and regulatory policy', *Journal of Business Ethics*, Dordrecht, April.

Hasnas, J. (1998), 'The normative theories of business ethics: A guide for the perplexed', *Business Ethics Quarterly*, January, pp.19-42.

Hawley, A. H. (1968), 'Human Ecology' in D.L. Sills (ed.) *International Encyclopaedia of the Social Sciences*, pp.328-337, Macmillan, New York.

Heidegger, M. (1967), *Being and Time*, translated by J. Macquarrie and E. Robinson, Blackwell, Oxford.

Held, D. (1987), *Models of Democracy*, Polity Press, Oxford.

Heskett, J., Jones, T., Loveman, G., Sasser, E. and Schlesinger, L. (1994), 'Putting the Service Profit Chain to Work', *Harvard Business Review*, March-April, pp.164-174.

Hilton, A. (1978), *Employee Reports: How to communicate financial information to employees*, Woodhead-Faulkner, Cambridge.

Hinings, B. and Greenwood, R. (1988), 'The Normative Prescription of Organizations', in L.G. Zucker (ed.) *Institutional Patterns and Organizations*, pp.53-70, Ballinger, Cambridge, Massachusetts.

Hirsch, F., (1978), *Social Limits to Growth*, Routledge and Kegan Paul, London and Henley.

Hirshleifer, J. (1958), 'On the theory of optimal investment decisions', *Journal of Political Economy*, pp.329-372.

Hobbes, T. (1651), *Leviathan*, many editions.

Hodges, R. (1997), 'Competition and Efficiency after privatization: the role of the NAO', *Public Money and Management*, January-March, pp.35-42.

Hodges, R. and Wright, M. (1995), 'Audit and Accountability in the privatisation process. The role of the national audit office', *Financial Accountability & Management*, Vol. 11(2), pp153-170.

Holtham, G. and Kay, J. (1994), 'The assessment: institutions of policy', *Oxford Review of Economic Policy*, Vol. 10(3), pp.1-16.

Honore, A. M. (1961), 'Ownership', in A. G. Guest (ed.), *Oxford essays in jurisprudence*, pp.107-147, Oxford, Clarendon Press.

HSE, (1997), *Health and Safety Statistics*, Health and Safety Executive, London.

Hummels, H. (1998), 'Organizing ethics: A stakeholder debate', *Journal of Business Ethics*, October, Vol. 17(13), pp.1403-1419.

Hussey, R. (1981), 'Getting the Financial Message across to Employees', *Accountancy*, May, pp.109-112.

Hussey, R. and Marsh, A. (1983), *Disclosure of Information and Employee Reporting*, Gower, Aldershot.

Husted, B. W. (1998), 'Organizational justice and the management of stakeholder relations', *Journal of Business Ethics*, April, pp.643-651.

Ibbotson Associates (1990), *Stocks, bonds, bills and inflation*, Ibbotson Associates 1990 Yearbook.

IDS (Income Data Service), (1995) *Report 697: Pay and Bargaining Prospects 1995/6*, September 1995.

Ingram, P., Wadsworth, J. and Brown, D. (1999), 'Free to Choose? Dimensions of Private-Sector Wage Determination, 1979-1994', *British Journal of Industrial Relations*, Vol. 37(1), pp.33-49.

Institute of Social and Ethical Accountability (ISEA), *AccountAbility 1000 – The foundation standard*, see www.AccountAbility.org.uk.

ISO (International Standards Organisation), (1997), *Environmental Performance Evaluation – Guidelines (ISO 14031)*, obtainable from national standards bodies.

Jackson, P.M (1982), *The Political Economy of Bureaucracy*, Philip Allan, Oxford.

Jenkinson, T. (1994), *The equity risk premium and the cost of capital debate in the UK regulated utilities*, University of Oxford, Mimeo.

Jenkinson, T, and Mayer, C. (1996), 'The assessment: contracts and competition', *Oxford Review of Economic Policy*, Vol. 12(4), pp.1-10.

Jensen, M. (1991), 'Corporate control and the politics of finance', *Journal of applied corporate finance*, Vol. 4(2), pp.13-33.

Jones, S. (1985), 'The Analysis of Depth Interviews', in R. Walker *Applied Qualitative Research*, Gower, Aldershot.

Jones, T. M. (1995), 'Instrumental stakeholder theory: A synthesis of ethics and economics', *The Academy of Management Review*, Vol. 20(2).

Jones, T. M. and Wicks, A. C. (1999), 'Convergent stakeholder theory', *The Academy of Management Review*, Vol. 24(2), pp.206-221.

Kant, I. (1804/1981), *Grounding for the metaphysics of morals*, trans. by J. W. Ellington, Hackett publishing, Indianapolis, In.

Kaplan, R. S. and Norton, D. P. (1992), 'The Balanced Scorecard - Measures That Drive Performance', *Harvard Business Review*, January / February 1992, pp.71-79.

Kaplan, R. S. and Norton, D. P., (1993), 'Putting the Balanced Scorecard to Work', *Harvard Business Review*, September / October, pp.134-147.

Kaplan, R. S. and Norton, D. P. (1996a), 'Using The Balanced Scorecard As a Strategic Management System', *Harvard Business Review*, January / February, pp.75-85.

Kaplan, R. S. and Norton, D. P. (1996b), *The Balanced Scorecard: Translating Strategy into Action*, Harvard Business School Press, Harvard.

Kaplan, R.S. and Norton, D.P. (2000), 'Having trouble with your strategy? Then map it', *Harvard Business Review*, September-October, pp.167-176.

Kuhn J. W. and Shriver, D. W. (1991), *Beyond success: Corporations and their critics in the 1990s*, Oxford University Press, New York.

Kultgen, J. (1987), 'Donaldson's Social Contract for Business', *Business and Professional Ethics Journal*, Vol. 5, pp.28-39.

Lake, R. (1999), 'The Turnbull Committee recommendations: an important step for accountability, but not big enough', *AccountAbility Quarterly*, 3rd Quarter, p.7.

Laughlin, R. C. (1990), 'A Model of Financial Accountability and the Church of England', *Financial Accountability & Management*, Vol. 6(2), pp.93-114.

Lee, T. A. and Tweedie, D. P. (1977), *The Private Shareholder & The Corporate Report*, ICAEW, London.

Lee, T. A. and Tweedie, D. P. (1981), *The Institutional Investor and Financial Information*, ICAEW, London.

L'Etang, J. (1995), 'Ethical Corporate Social Responsibility: A Framework for Managers', *Journal of Business Ethics*, Vol. 14, pp.125-132.

Lindblom, C. K. (1994), 'The implications of organizational legitimacy for corporate social performance and disclosure', paper presented at the Critical Perspectives on Accounting Conference, New York.

Littlechild, S. (1993), 'Foreword from the Director General of Electricity Supply', in *Electricity Distribution: Price control, reliability and customer service (consultation paper)*, OFFER, Birmingham.

Litz, R. A. (1996), 'A Resource-based-view of the Socially Responsible Firm: Stakeholder Interdependence, Ethical Awareness, and Issue Responsiveness as Strategic Assets', *Journal of Business Ethics*, Vol. 15, pp.1355-63.

London Electricity (1995), *Annual report and Accounts*, London Electricity.

Lukes, S. (1974), *Power: A radical view*, Macmillan, London.

Lyall, D. (1982), 'Disclosure Practices in Employee Reports', *The Accountant's Magazine*, July, pp.246-248.

Lynch, R. L. and Cross, K. F. (1991), *Measure Up! Yardsticks for Continuous Improvement*, Basil Blackwell.

Madden, B.J. (1999), *CFROI valuation: A total systems approach to valuing the firm*, Butterworth-Heinemann, London.

Maddison, D., Pearce, D.W., Johansson, P-O., Calthrop, E., Litman, T. and Verhoef, E. (1995), *Blueprint 5: The True Costs of Road Transport*, Earthscan, London.

March, J.G. and Simon, H.A. (1958), *Organizations*, Wiley, New York.

Marens, R. and Wicks, A. (1999), 'Getting real: Stakeholder theory, managerial practice, and the general irrelevance of fiduciary duties owed to shareholders', *Business Ethics Quarterly*, Vol. 9(2), pp.273-293.

Marsh, D. (1991), 'Privatization under Mrs Thatcher: a review of the literature', *Public Administration*, Vol. 69, Winter, pp.459-80.

Mathews, M. R. (1993), *Socially Responsible Accounting*, Chapman and Hall, London.

Mathews, M. R. (1995), 'Social and Environmental accounting: A practical demonstration of ethical concern?', *Journal of Business Ethics*, Vol. 14(8), pp.663-670.

Mathews, M. R. (1997), 'Twenty-five years of social and environmental accounting research: is there a silver jubilee to celebrate?', *Accounting, Auditing and Accountability Journal*, Vol. 10(4), pp. 481-531.

Maunders, K. T. (1984), *Employee Reporting: An Investigation of User Needs, Measurement and Reporting Issues and Practice*, Institute of Chartered Accountants in England and Wales, London.

McAllister, I. and Studlar, D.T. (1989), 'Popular versus elite views of privatization: the case of Britain', *Journal of Public Policy*, Vol. 9(2), pp.157-178.

McGowan, F. (1993), 'Electricity: The experience of OFFER', in T. Gilland and P. Vass (eds.), *Regulatory Review 1993*, London: Centre for the Study of Regulated Industries.

McSweeney, B. and Duncan, S. (1998), 'Structure or Agency? Discourse or Meta-narrative? Explaining the emergence of the financial management initiative', *Accounting, Auditing and Accountability Journal*, Vol. 11(3), pp.332-361.

Medawar, C. (1976), 'The social audit: a political view', *Accounting, Organizations and Society*, Vol. 1(4), pp.389-394.

Medawar, C. (1978), *The Social Audit Consumer Handbook*, Macmillan, London.

Meyer, J. W. and Hannan, M. T. (1979), *National Development and the World System: Educational, Economic and Political Change*, University of Chicago Press, Chicago.

Meyer, J. W. and Rowan, B. (1983), 'The structure of educational organizations' in J.W. Meyer & W.R. Scott (eds.) *Organizational Environments: Ritual and Rationality*, pp.68-84, Sage, Beverley Hills, CA.

Meyer, J.W. and Rowan, B. (1991), 'Institutionalized Organizations: Formal structure as Myth and Ceremony', in W.W. Powell and P.J. DiMaggio (eds.) *The New Institutionalism in Organizational Analysis*, pp.41-62, Unviersity of Chicago Press, London.

Meyer, J.W. and Scott, B. (1977), 'Institutionalized Organizations: formal structure as myth and ceremony', *American Journal of Sociology*, Vol. 83, pp.340-63.

Mill, J. S. (1863), *Utilitarianism*, many editions.

Miller, R. A. (1998), 'Lifesizing in an era of downsizing: An ethical quandary', *Journal of Business Ethics*, Vol. 17(15), pp.1693-1700.

Mintzberg, H. (1983), 'The case for corporate social responsibility', *The Journal of Business Strategy*, Vol. 4(2), pp.3-15.

Mitchell, R. K., Agle, B. R. and Wood, D. J. (1997), 'Toward a theory of stakeholder identification and salience: Defining the principle of who really counts', *The Academy of Management Review*, Vol. 22(4), pp.853-886.

MMC (1997), *Northern Ireland Electricity plc: A report on a reference under article 15 of the Electricity (Northern Ireland) Order 1992*, The Stationery Office, London.

Modell, S. (2001), 'Performance Measurement and Institutional Processes: A Study of Managerial Responses to Public Sector Reform', *Management Accounting Research*, Vol. 12(4), pp.437-464.

Monks, R. A. G. and Minow, N. (1991), *Power and Accountability*, Harper Collins Publishers, Glasgow.

Moore, G. B. (1999), 'Rawls, John', in E. Cashmore and C. Rojek *Dictionary of Cultural Theorists*, Arnold, London.

Morley, M. F. (1978), 'The Value Added Statement', Gee and Co. for the Institute of Chartered Accountants of Scotland.

Nagel, T. (1986), *The View from Nowhere*, Oxford University Press, New York.

National Consumer Council (NCC) (1997), *Electricity Takeovers: The Implications for Consumers*, NCC, London.

National Grid plc (1997), *Annual Report and Accounts*, National Grid.

National Power plc (1995), *Report and Accounts*, National Power.

National Power plc (1997), *Report and Accounts*, National Power.

North, D.C. (1986), 'The New Institutional Economics', *Journal of Institutional and Theoretical Economics*, Vol. 142, pp.230-237.

Northern Electric (1996), Annual Report and Accounts, Northern Electric.

OFFER (1992), *Report on customer services: 1991/92*, OFFER, Birmingham.

OFFER (1993), *Report on customer services: 1992/93*, OFFER, Birmingham.

OFFER (1994), *Report on customer services: 1993/94*, OFFER, Birmingham.

OFFER (1995), *Report on customer services: 1994/95*, OFFER, Birmingham.

OFFER (1996), *Report on customer services: 1995/96*, OFFER, Birmingham.

OFFER (1997), *Report on customer services: 1996/97*, OFFER, Birmingham.

Office for National Statistics (1998), *UK Environmental Accounts 1998*, HMSO, London.

OFGEM (1999), *Review of Public Electricity Suppliers 1998 to 2000: Distribution price control review draft proposals*, August 1999, www.ofgem.gov.uk/public/adownloads.htm

OFGEM (2000), *The Transmission Price Control Review of the National Grid Company from 2001 – Draft proposals*, June 2000, www.ofgem.gov.uk/public/pub01.htm

OFGEM (2001), *Review of Transco's price control from 2002 – Final proposals*, September 2001, www.ofgem.gov.uk/public/pub2001.htm

Ogden, S. (1995), 'Transforming frameworks of accountability: the case of water privatisation', *Accounting, Organizations & Society*, Vol. 20(2/3), pp.193-218.

Ogden, S. and Anderson, F. (1995), 'Representing consumers' interests: the case of the privatized water industry in England and Wales', *Public Administration*, Vol. 73, Winter, pp.535-59.

Ogden, S. and Watson, R. (1999), 'Corporate Performance and Stakeholder Management: Balancing shareholder and customer interests in the U.K. privatized water industry', *Academy of Management Journal*, Vol. 42(5) pp.526-538.

Oliver, C. (1991), 'Strategic Responses to Institutional Processes', *Academy of Management Review*, Vol. 16(1), pp.145-179.

Owen, D. L., Gray, R. H. and Bebbington, J. (1997), 'Green accounting: cosmetic irrelevance or radical agenda for change?', *Asia Pacific Journal of Accounting*, Vol. 4(2), pp.175-192.

Owen, D., Swift, T., Humphrey, C. and Bowerman, M. (2000), 'The new social audits: accountability, managerial capture or the agenda of social champions?' *The European Accounting Review*, Vol. 9(1), pp.81-98.

Owen, D., Swift, T. and Hunt, K. (2001), 'Questioning the role of stakeholder engagement in social and ethical accounting, auditing and reporting', *Accounting Forum*, Vol. 25(3), pp. 264-282.

Parker, D. and Martin, S. (1995), 'The impact of UK privatisation on labour and total factor productivity', *Scottish Journal of Political Economy*, Vol. 42(2), pp. 201-220.

Parker, L. D., Ferris, K. D. and Otley, D. T. (1989), *Accounting for the Human Factor*, Prentice Hall, Sydney.

Pearce, D. W. and Newcombe, J. (1998), *Corporate sustainability: concepts and measures*, mimeo (University College London/University of East Anglia, Centre for Social and Economic Research on the Global Environment (CSERGE)).

Pejovich, S. (1990), *The economics of property rights: Towards a theory of comparative systems*, Kluwer Academic Publishers, Dordrecht, The Netherlands.

Peters, T. J. and Waterman, R. H. (1982), *In search of excellence: Lessons from America's best run companies*, Harper & Row, New York.

Pfeffer, J. (1982), *Organizations and Organization Theory*, Pitman, Boston.

Pfeffer. J. and Leong, A. (1977), 'Resource Allocations in United Funds: Examination of Power and Dependence', *Social Forces*, Vol. 55, pp.775-790.

Pfeffer, J. and Salancik, G. R. (1978), *The External Control of Organizations: A Resource Dependence Perspective*, Harper & Row, New York.

Powergen plc (1997), *Annual Report and Accounts*, Powergen.

Preston, L. E. and Sapienza, H. J. (1990), 'Stakeholder management and corporate performance', *Journal of Behavioral Economics*, Vol. 19, pp.361-375.

Puxty, A. G. and Laughlin, R. C. (1983), 'Accounting Regulation: An alternative perspective', *Journal of Business Finance & Accounting*, Vol. 10(3).

Quinn, D. and Jones, T. (1995), 'An agent morality view of business policy', *Academy of Management Review*, Vol. 20(1), pp.22-42.

Rappaport, A. (1981), 'Selecting strategies that create shareholder value', *Harvard Business Review*, Vol. 59(3), pp.139-149.

Rappaport, A. (1986), *Creating shareholder value: The new standard for business performance*, The Free Press, New York.

Ravenscroft, D. and Scherer, F. (1987), *Mergers, Sell-Offs and Economic Efficiency*, Brookings Institution, Washington DC.

Rawls, J. (1973), *A Theory of Justice*, Oxford University Press, Oxford.

Real World Coalition (1996), *The Politics of the Real World*, Earthscan, London.

Roberts, R. W., (1992), 'Determinants of Corporate Social Responsibility Disclosure: An Application of Stakeholder Theory', *Accounting Organizations and Society*, Vol. 17(6), pp.595-612.

Rousseau, J. (1762), 'Du Contrat Social' translated as "The Social Contract" many editions.

Rowley, T. J. (1997), 'Moving beyond dyadic ties: A network theory of stakeholder influences', *The Academy of Management Review*, October, pp.887-910.

Ruf, B., K. Muralidhar, and K. Paul. (1993), 'Eight Dimensions of Corporate Social Performance: Determination of Relative Importance Using the Analytic Hierarchy Process', pp.326-30 in Dorothy P. Moore (ed.). Academy of Management Best Paper Proceedings. Atlanta, GA: Academy of Management.

Ryan, B., Scapens, R.W., and Theobald, M. (1992), *Research Method and Methodology in Finance and Accounting*, Academic Press, London.

SAI (Social Accountability International) (1997), *Social Accountability 8000*, see www.cepaa.org.

Salancik, G. R. and Pfeffer, J. (1974), 'The bases and uses of power in organizational decision making: The case of universities', *Administrative Science Quarterly*, Vol. 19, pp.453-473.

Samuels, R. (1981), *People's History and Socialist Theory*, London.

Scott, W. R. (1987), 'The Adolescence of Institutional Theory', *Administrative Science Quarterly*, Vol. 32, pp. 493-511.

Scott, W. R. (1991), 'Unpacking Institutional Arguments', in W.W. Powell and P.J. DiMaggio (eds.) *The New Institutionalism in Organizational Analysis*, pp.164-82, Unviersity of Chicago Press, London.

Scott, W. R. (1995), *Institutions and Organizations*, Sage, California.

Scott, W. R. and Meyer, J. W. (1991), 'The Organization of Societal Sectors: Propositions and Early Evidence', in W.W. Powell and P.J. DiMaggio (eds.) *The New Institutionalism in Organizational Analysis*, pp.108-142, University of Chicago Press, London.

Selznick, P. (1957), *Leadership in Administration*, Harper & Row, New York.

Sen, A. (1987), *On ethics & economics*, Blackwell, Oxford.

Shankman, N. A. (1999), 'Reframing the debate between agency and stakeholder theories of the firm', *Journal of Business Ethics*, Vol. 19(4), pp.319-334.

Shaoul, J. (1997), 'The power of accounting: reflecting on water privatization?', *Accounting, Auditing & Accountability Journal*, Vol. 10(3), pp.382-405.

Shaoul, J. (2002), 'A Financial Appraisal of the London Underground Public-Private Partnership', *Public Money & Management*, April-June, pp.53-60.

Sharfman, M. (1993), 'A Construct Validity Study of the KLD Social Performance Data', pp. 551-56 in Dennis Collins (ed.), Proceedings of the International Association of Business and Society. Hilton Head, SC: IABS.

Sharpe, W. F. (1964), 'Capital asset prices: A theory of market equilibrium under conditions of risk', *Journal of finance*, Vol. 19, pp.425-442.

Shocker, A. D. and Sethi, S. P. (1974), 'An Approach to Incorporating Social Preferences in Developing Corporate Action Strategies', in S. P. Sethi (ed.), *The Unstable Ground: Corporate Social Policy in a Dynamic Society*, Melville, California.

Smith, A. (1776), *The Wealth of Nations*, many editions

Smith, H. J. and Hasnas, J. (1999), 'Ethics and information systems: The corporate domain', *MIS Quarterly*, Vol. 23(1), pp.109-127.

Smith, T. (1992), *Accounting for growth, stripping the camouflage from company accounts*, Century Business, London.

Smith, H. W. (1975), *Strategies of Social Research: The Methodological Imagination*, Prentice-Hall, London.

Smith, C., Whipp, R. and Willmott, H. (1988), 'Case-Study Research in Accounting: Methodological Breakthrough or ideological Weapon?', *Advances in Public Interest Accounting*, Vol. 2, pp.95-120.

Social Audit Ltd (1973a), 'The case for social audit', *Social Audit Quarterly*, Vol. 1(1), pp.5-26.

Social Audit Ltd (1973b), 'Tube investments', *Social Audit Quarterly*, 1(3), pp4-66.

Sternberg, E. (1994), *Just Business: Business ethics in action*, Little, Brown and Company, London.

Sternberg, E. (1997), 'The Defects of Stakeholder Theory', *Corporate Governance: An International Review*, Vol. 5(1), pp. 3-10.

Sternberg, E. (1998), *Corporate Governance: Accountability in the Marketplace*, The Institute of Economic Affairs, London.

Stewart, G. B. III (1991), *The quest for value*, Harper Collins, New York.

Stewart, J. D. (1984), 'The Role of Information in Public Accountability', in: A. Hopwood and C. Tomkins (eds) *Issues in Public Sector Accounting*, pp.13-34, Philip Allan, Oxford.

Stoney, C. and Winstanley, D. (2001), 'Stakeholding: Confusion or Utopia? Mapping the Conceptual Terrain', *Journal of Management Studies*, Vol. 38(5), pp.603-626.

Suchman, M. C. (1995), 'Managing Legitimacy: Strategic and Institutional Approaches', *Academy of Management Review*, Vol. 20(3), pp.571-610.

Thatcher, M. (1993), *Margaret Thatcher: The Downing Street years*, HarperCollins, London.

Thompson, J. D. (1967), *Organizations in Action*, McGraw-Hill, New York.

Thompson, L. (1993), 'Reporting Changes in the Electricity Supply Industry and Privatisation', *Financial Accountability & Management*, Vol. 9(2), pp.131-157.

Tinker, A.M., Lehman, C. and Neimark, M. (1991), 'Corporate social reporting: Falling down the hole in the middle of the road', *Accounting, Auditing & Accountability Journal*, Vol. 4(1) pp.28-54.

Tinker, T. (1985), *Paper Prophets: A Social Critique of Accounting*, Holt, Eastbourne.

Tolbert, P.S. (1985), 'Institutional Environments and Resource Dependence: Sources of Administrative Structure in Institutions of Higher Education', *Administrative Science Quarterly*, Vol. 30, pp.1-13.

Toms, J. S., (2000), *Environmental Management Environmental Accounting and Financial Performance*, Chartered Institute of Management Accountants, London.

Trevino, L. K. and Weaver, G. R. (1999), 'The stakeholder research tradition: Converging theorists-non convergent theory', *The Academy of Management Review*, Vol. 24(2), pp.222-227.

Vickers, J. and Yarrow, G. (1988), *Privatisation: An Economic Analysis*, MIT Press, Cambridge, MA.

Vidaver-Cohen, D. (1999), 'Taking a risk: Max Clarkson's impact on stakeholder theory', *Business and Society*, Vol. 38(1), pp.39-43.

Waddock, S. A. and Graves, S. B. (1997a), 'Quality of management and quality of stakeholder relations', *Business and Society*, Vol. 36(3), pp.250-279.

Waddock, S. A. and Graves, S. B. (1997b), 'The corporate social performance-financial performance link', *Strategic Management Journal*, Vol. 18 (4), pp.303-319.

Watson, D and Head, A. (2001), *Corporate Finance: Principles and Practice*, 2nd Edition, Pearson, London.

Weber, M. (1952), *The Protestant Ethic and the Spirit of Capitalism*, Scribner, New York.

Wheeler, D. and Sillanpaa, M. (1997), *The Stakeholder Corporation: The Body Shop Blueprint for Maximising Stakeholder Value*, Pitman, London.

Williamson, O. E. (1985), *The economic institutions of capitalism*, Free Press, New York.

Woo, C. Y. and Willard, G. (1983), 'Performance representation in business policy research: discussion and recommendation', paper presented at 23rd Annual National Meetings of the Academy of Management, Dallas.

Wood, D. J. (1994), Essay in 'The Toronto Conference: Reflections on stakeholder theory', *Business and Society*, Vol. 33(1).

Woodward, D. G., Edwards, P. and Birkin, F. (1996), 'Organizational Legitimacy and Stakeholder Information Provision', *British Journal of Management*, Vol. 7, pp.329-347.

Woodward, J. (1970), *Industrial Organization: Theory and Practice*, Oxford University Press, Oxford.

Yin, R.K. (1994), *Case Study Research: Design and Methods*, 2nd Edition, Applied Social Research Methods Volume 5, Sage, London.

Zadek, S. (1998), 'Balancing performance, ethics, and accountability', *Journal of Business Ethics*, Vol. 17(13), pp.1421-1441.

Zald, M. N. (1970), *Power in Organizations*, Vanderbilt University Press.

Zola, E. (1885), *Germinal*, 1954 ed., Penguin, London.

Index